THE DRAGON FROM
CHICAGO

THE DRAGON FROM CHICAGO

THE UNTOLD STORY OF AN AMERICAN REPORTER IN NAZI GERMANY

PAMELA D. TOLER

BEACON PRESS
BOSTON

BEACON PRESS
Boston, Massachusetts
www.beacon.org

Beacon Press books
are published under the auspices of
the Unitarian Universalist Association of Congregations.

28 27 26 25   8 7 6 5 4 3 2 1

This book is printed on acid-free paper that meets the uncoated paper
ANSI/NISO specifications for permanence as revised in 1992.

Text design and composition by Kim Arney

All images courtesy of the Wisconsin Historical Society except image of Hotel Adlon:
George Grantham Bain Collection, Prints and Photographs Collection, LC-B2-404-2,
Library of Congress, Washington, DC. Quote: Gregor Ziemer, "Let Us Now Sing
the Praises of Sigrid Schultz," *Lost Generation Journal* (Winter 1976).

Library of Congress Cataloging-in-Publication Data

Names: Toler, Pamela D., author.
Title: The dragon from Chicago : the untold story of an American
reporter in Nazi Germany / Pamela D. Toler.
Other titles: Untold story of an American reporter in Nazi Germany
Description: Boston : Beacon Press, [2024] | Includes bibliographical
references and index. | Summary: "A captivating look at Sigrid
Schultz-one of the earliest reporters to warn Americans of the rising
threat of the Nazi regime"—Provided by publisher.
Identifiers: LCCN 2024001843 (print) | LCCN 2024001844 (ebook) |
ISBN 9780807019603 (paperback) | ISBN 9780807063125 (ebook)
Subjects: LCSH: World War, 1939–1945—Press coverage—United States. |
Schultz, Sigrid Lillian. | World War, 1939–1945—Journalists. |
Americans—Germany—History—20th century. | National socialism—Public
opinion. | War correspondents—United States—Biography. | Women war
correspondents—United States—Biography. | Germany—Foreign public
opinion, American. | Germany—Social conditions—1933–1945. |
Americans—Germany—Biography.
Classification: LCC D799.U6 S348 2024 (print) | LCC D799.U6 (ebook) |
DDC 940.54/8173—dc21
LC record available at https://lccn.loc.gov/2024001843
LC ebook record available at https://lccn.loc.gov/2024001844

The greatest service we could render our country was to try to marshal the facts as they were and not as propagandists tried to make them appear.

—SIGRID SCHULTZ

CONTENTS

"THAT DRAGON FROM CHICAGO"

One afternoon in April 1935, Sigrid Schultz, chief correspondent of the *Chicago Tribune*'s Berlin bureau, received a disturbing phone call from her mother.

A strange man had just delivered a sealed package to their apartment in Berlin. He told her mother the package contained important information for Schultz, but there was no need to bother her. It could wait until she got home.

After sixteen years of watching her daughter's career as a reporter in Berlin, Hedwig Schultz knew time was everything in the news business. Sigrid would not be home until late that night. Meeting deadlines for a newspaper published seven time zones away meant that working until midnight was an everyday occurrence, no matter how much it worried her mother. Hedwig decided not to wait. If the package was important, Sigrid could have someone pick it up.

It was important, though not in the way Hedwig thought. Sigrid Schultz suspected a Nazi trap.

Ever since Adolf Hitler had become chancellor of Germany in January 1933, the Nazis had alternately courted and punished foreign correspondents. They gave exclusive interviews to some and withheld access to press conferences from others. For their part, correspondents did their best to discover and report the truth without endangering themselves or their sources. It was hard to know where the lines lay. A correspondent for the London *Daily Telegraph* had been arrested for treason and held for several weeks because he described Nazi storm troopers goose-stepping through a small Bavarian city, rifles over their shoulders, a clear breach of the Treaty of Versailles. Many, Schultz included, were summoned by the Gestapo for questioning when they published articles that were not to the Nazis' liking. Occasionally the Nazis made an example of correspondents who crossed a Nazi-defined line by kicking them out of the country. But expulsion was a costly strategy. Once freed from the constraints of Nazi censorship and the threat of Gestapo retribution, expelled correspondents often became media heroes and wrote stories they would never have dared publish while in Germany.

Frustrated by the Nazis' inability to control foreign correspondents the way they controlled the German press, General Hermann Göring, Hitler's second-in-command, minister of the interior, and head of the Gestapo, came up with another way of dealing with members of the foreign press corps. Under Göring's direction, agents provocateurs masqueraded as anti-Nazi tipsters, offering reporters what they claimed was the inside scoop on military secrets—information that would have led to the arrest of any reporter foolish enough to use it in a story. The idea was that it would take only one spectacular espionage trial of an unwary correspondent, whether it resulted in expulsion or imprisonment, to bring the rest of the correspondents under control.

When one of her best sources warned her to be extra cautious about news tips from people she did not know well, Schultz spread the word to her colleagues. Throughout the fall of 1934 and winter of 1935, Schultz and her fellow correspondents noticed a rise in the number of anti-Nazi strangers who approached them with information that would be of more interest to a spy than a reporter.

The man who delivered Hedwig's mystery package sounded a great deal like someone who had recently visited Schultz trying to peddle dangerous "news." She had thrown him out of her office. Now she suspected this man was playing a variation on the same game.

Schultz rushed home and ripped open the package. It contained what looked like plans for an aircraft engine. Even if they were worthless, she knew she would be arrested as a spy if caught with them in her possession.

Afraid she didn't have much time before the Gestapo raided the apartment, Schultz tore the plans to shreds and burned them in the fireplace until the plans and envelope they came in were reduced to ash.

As she walked back to the office, Schultz ran into the man she had suspected of delivering the envelope. He was headed toward the apartment, accompanied by two large men whose demeanor—half thug, half military—screamed "secret police."

Small, blonde, and surprisingly formidable, Schultz stepped into their path. "Don't waste your time," she told them. "I already destroyed the envelope you left and all its contents."

Before they could react, Schultz hailed a passing cab. "Take me to the American embassy," she told the driver, in a voice that could be heard clearly from the sidewalk. (Her early training as an operatic soprano had its uses.) She was going to report the incident, and she wanted to be sure anyone listening knew it.

Enough was enough. It was time to let Göring know that she and the rest of the foreign press corps were onto his game.

⁃⁓⁃

Sigrid Schultz was the *Chicago Tribune*'s Berlin bureau chief and primary foreign correspondent for Central Europe from 1925 to January 1941. She was one of the first reporters—male or female—to warn American readers of the growing dangers of Nazism. She published at least 166 articles about Hitler and the rise of the Nazi Party before he became Germany's chancellor, including a rare 1931 interview with Hitler in which she warned *Tribune* readers that he was a serious threat.

Schultz was an American—more specifically, an American from Chicago—by birth, self-definition, and loyalty, but she was raised in France and Germany and educated in European schools. With a European's understanding of Europe, connections at many levels of Berlin society, and a colloquial command of several European languages, she had an advantage over other American journalists when it came to reporting on Germany. At a time when women reporters rarely wrote front-page stories, Schultz's byline was a regular feature in the *Tribune*. She often scooped her male counterparts on major news events, including the death of Weimar Germany's first president in 1925 and Hitler's nonaggression pact with Russia in 1939.[1] William L. Shirer, author of *The Rise and Fall of the Third Reich*, worked for the *Chicago Tribune* from 1925 to 1932, was a correspondent in Berlin for William Randolph Hearst's Universal News Service from 1935 to 1937, and broadcast from Berlin for the Columbia Broadcasting System (CBS) in the first days of the Second World War. He later admitted, "No other American correspondent in Berlin knew so much of what was going on behind the scenes as did Sigrid Schultz."[2]

After Hitler's rise to power, Schultz found creative ways around the Nazis' tightening control over the press. Described by fellow foreign correspondent Quentin Reynolds as "Hitler's greatest enemy,"[3] she reported on the passage of antisemitic laws, the opening of concentration camps, the closing of churches, and the reign of terror against Jews, Communists, and anyone who opposed Hitler's government. She accurately predicted Hitler's military intentions and shared details of Germany's rearmament. She demonstrated how the Nazis manipulated and misreported the news to their own people and attempted to control the foreign press through a combination of bribery and threats.

Her fearless reporting brought danger to both Schultz and her informants. But that danger was part of the job as she understood it. She took pride in the difference between true foreign correspondents and the lesser beings she dismissed as "junketeers," reporters who "never, never ask embarrassing questions at press conferences and tactfully fail to report stories that might annoy the powers-that-be." While she recognized that telling the truth without getting kicked out of the country required a constant balancing act, she believed it was a foreign correspondent's job to "pay scant attention to the efforts of governments to foist their pet views and propaganda on us by means of flattery, preferential treatment, boycott, and even threats."[4] Schultz was equally determined not to allow her stories to be shaped by the pet views of the *Chicago Tribune*'s owner, publisher, and isolationist in chief Colonel Robert McCormick—a balancing act that was at times just as difficult though not as dangerous.

<hr/>

Schultz decided to complain directly to Göring about the recent attempt to entrap her as well as attempts against other members of Berlin's foreign press corps.

She was considering how best to approach Göring—on her own or accompanied by an official from the American embassy—when the perfect opportunity arrived in the mail. Göring's aides had been pressuring the Foreign Press Club to host a gala luncheon to celebrate his recent marriage, his second, to the actress Emmy Sonnemann. The club had agreed, recognizing the need to maintain connections with the Nazi officials who were their sources. The event was to be held on May 2, a few days away, at the luxurious Hotel Adlon.

Because Schultz was the only woman on the club's board, she frequently served as the hostess of events in tandem with the board president. Diplomatic protocol dictated that Göring, as guest of honor, would be seated next to her. Perfect!

The general was clearly in a bad mood when he and his bride arrived at the luncheon. He stood in the middle of the hall and glared at the foreign correspondents seated at three long banquet tables: a massive scowling presence, his military uniform bespangled with decorations and his fingers laden with rings.

Göring was still scowling when he took his seat. Almost six feet tall, overweight, and getting fatter every year, he loomed over Schultz, who stood a scant five foot two[5] and had never regained the weight she lost during her hungry days as an enemy alien in Berlin during the Great War. But she did not let herself be intimidated by anyone.

After Göring had settled into his place, he pulled a card out of his pocket and had Schultz point out the reporters listed on it—British, French, and Swiss, as well as American. It was time for foreign correspondents to pay respect to the new Germany, he grumbled as he studied their faces. He was tired of reporters writing about clergymen being arrested and spreading sentimental nonsense about concentration camps. "We need those camps to teach discipline to elements that have forgotten all about it in the days of the weak Weimar Republic," he said.

Schultz had argued with Göring about concentration camps before. Instead of allowing herself to be distracted by the familiar debate, she took him to task about the agents provocateurs who had besieged the press corps in recent months. None of them were stupid enough to file a story with information that was clearly meant for spies, she told him, her voice quiet but firm.

Göring was so surprised he stopped eating. "You're imagining things," he snapped.

Schultz gave him details about specific attempts. When she told him she had informed the embassy about her experience, and that of others, he lost his temper. "Schultz, I've always suspected it: you'll never learn to show the proper respect for state authorities. I suppose that is one of the characteristics of people from that crime-ridden city of Chicago."

At the end of the meal, after toasting the newlyweds, the correspondents gathered around Göring, assuming he had strong-armed the club for the invitation as an opportunity to spin the news. He did not disappoint. Speaking from his borrowed soapbox, he claimed that

Germany's recent repudiation of the Versailles treaty and open rebuilding of its military were acts of peace, not war..As part of that peace plan, Germany intended to rebuild its air force as quickly as possible, in part by purchasing airplane plans and parts from American companies.

When he opened the floor to questions, Schultz couldn't resist needling him. "Given that your bankers and financial experts are telling Germany's creditors that you cannot pay your loans, how does Germany plan to pay for its purchases from the United States?" she asked.

Göring stepped forward, shook his fist in her face, and repeated himself: "Schultz, you'll never learn to show the proper respect toward state authorities."

A few correspondents laughed nervously. Then the room went silent. The correspondents from *The Times* (London) and *Le Journal* (Paris) moved forward, flanking Schultz in a show of support, their faces grim.

Göring got the message. The flow of Nazi provocateurs stopped for several months. Schultz took the credit, in her heart if not in public, as proud as if she had landed a front-page scoop, with the headline in "scare caps" across all eight columns of the *Tribune*.

Thereafter, Göring and his staff called her "that dragon from Chicago." Schultz embraced the title with pride.[6]

THE DRAGON FROM
CHICAGO

CHAPTER ONE

A TRILINGUAL CHILD

I think I chose my parents and my
hometown with remarkable wisdom.

—SIGRID SCHULTZ[1]

Sigrid Schultz lived in Chicago for only eight years, but she always considered it her hometown.

The daughter of a Norwegian portrait painter, Hermann Schultz, and his multiethnic wife, Hedwig, Sigrid always identified herself as Norwegian, but her ethnic background was more complicated than she acknowledged.

Her father was Norwegian, despite the name. (Sigrid would later become indignant when someone assumed she was German because of her "darn last name.") Her mother, who was born and raised in Wiesbaden, Germany, had what Sigrid described as a "cosmopolitan" background—an interesting word choice given its use as a code word for Jews by the Nazis and later the Soviets. Hedwig's paternal grandfather, Josef Jaskewitz, was a half-Russian, half-Polish opera singer, born in Vienna, who married a French woman. According to family lore, Hedwig's maternal grandfather was a Spanish soldier who followed Napoleon to Moscow. On the long cold march back from Russia, he decided he was done with walking and settled in Westphalia, where he married a German farmer's daughter. Or perhaps not. Sigrid, and her grandmother before her, weren't above family myth-building.

Sigrid was born in Chicago in January 1893, shortly before the world's fair known as the World's Columbian Exposition. Hermann

Schultz was always eager to travel in pursuit of a commission and it is probable that work related to the exposition drew the young couple to Chicago in the spring of 1892, shortly after their marriage. (It is also possible they wanted to leave Hedwig's hometown of Wiesbaden. Frau Jaskewitz was not pleased with her daughter's marriage to an artist with a case of wanderlust.)

Sigrid spent her early childhood in an area with the evocative name of Summerdale, now part of the Edgewater neighborhood on Chicago's North Side. The neighborhood, located within the Chicago city limits, was largely undeveloped. There were four houses on the block where the Schultz home stood. Native prairie, rich with prairie hens, pheasants, quail, and a riot of bright wildflowers, ran alongside the fenced-in gardens, creating a wild playground where Sigrid roamed in the company of three boys from the house closest to the Schultz home, protected by the family's St. Bernard, Barry, who had served as her "nanny" since she was a baby.

Hermann was a charismatic figure who formed rapid friendships with almost everyone he met, including a brief but important relationship with Chicago's five-time mayor, Carter Henry Harrison Sr. Hedwig was beautiful and charming. The Schultz home was a multilingual meeting place for artists, politicians, musicians, and what Sigrid later described as "a number of pretty wild Scandinavians."[2] Her parents hosted large gatherings of Chicago's Norwegian immigrant community, small dances, and dinner parties at which guests passionately discussed books, art, and politics. Hermann threw wilder parties in his downtown studio—gentlemen only—for his wealthy and powerful clientele.

Sigrid provided some of the entertainment at those parties, demonstrating her trilingual talents, just as other children of the period might be asked to play on the piano or recite a poem. Her parents were determined she would learn to speak English, German, and French, as they did, and insisted she answer questions in the language in which they were asked. Her first trick for the amusement of their guests was to trot out the corkscrew whenever Hermann told her, "*Apporte-moi le tire-bouchon.*"[3]

Sigrid's performances at her parents' parties led directly to her first introduction to antisemitism.

When Sigrid was seven, a French girl named Germaine moved to Summerdale with her parents. The two teamed up to put on multilingual skits for their parents' guests. Urged on by adult applause, the girls were always looking for new material. Sigrid thought she had found a new number for their repertoire after three older boys from outside the neighborhood invaded her prairie Eden. They sang a funny song, in a strange accent, which included the line, the only one she remembered later, "Ve sellim de socks for twenty-fife cents a box." Normally Sigrid and her "gang" would have let Barry chase the older boys away. This time she held Barry back because she wanted to learn the song.

One of her favorite adults was visiting the house when she got home. George Siegmund was a frequent guest in the Schultz house—a not-too-successful businessman who regularly came by to borrow books and discuss them with Sigrid's parents. Sigrid was excited about her new song, and Siegmund urged her to share it. She had not yet finished the first verse when, to Sigrid's shock, her normally gentle mother slapped her.

The violence of Hedwig's response to the antisemitic ditty was out of character. It was also unusual in a time when casual antisemitic statements were common among gentiles in the United States. That unprecedented and never-repeated slap makes more sense if Hedwig, and therefore Sigrid, were Jewish.

Morley Boyd, Wendy Crowther, and John F. Suggs, local historians in Westport, Connecticut, where Sigrid spent the last decades of her life, have made a plausible if not definitive argument that this was the case.[4]

Sigrid's own testimony on the subject is inconclusive. In an interview for the American Jewish Committee's William E. Wiener Oral History Library in 1971, Sigrid made it clear that her mother's family had business and personal connections with the Jewish community in Wiesbaden—Sigrid herself had extensive connections in Berlin's Jewish communities throughout her life there—but she did not claim to be Jewish then or in any other interview. In fact, on several occasions, she clearly stated that she was *not* Jewish.

There are plenty of reasons why Sigrid might have chosen to hide a Jewish heritage over the years, from protecting her job at the *Chicago Tribune*, given Colonel McCormick's deeply rooted antisemitism, to protecting her life in Nazi Germany.

Regardless of the facts of Hedwig's religious background, religion had never been a topic of discussion in the Schultz household. In fact, Sigrid did not remember ever hearing the word "Jewish" before that day. Siegmund, who was himself Jewish, held her on his lap and tried to explain religious differences and antisemitism in terms the distressed little girl could understand.

Later that day, Hermann went to talk to a friend at the Summerdale police station where he learned that young German immigrants often harassed Jewish street peddlers and stole from Jewish shop owners in their neighborhoods. Hermann was outraged that such things existed in the United States. He had witnessed similar incidents during his travels through Germany as an art student and, as he told Sigrid years later, considered them "a remnant of the darkest middle ages."[5]

Antisemitism had been a feature of American life from the beginning, but it had become more aggressive in recent years, tied to the country's financial problems of the 1890s and nativist concerns over immigration from Eastern and Southern Europe. Prosperous and well-assimilated Jewish families were subjected to new levels of social discrimination. Newly arrived, less powerful Jewish immigrants suffered from direct, sometimes physical, attacks. In the South, rioters sacked Jewish merchants' stores and marauding horsemen burned farmhouses belonging to Jews—actions uncomfortably similar to those forty years later in Germany. In the North, attacks were, for the most part, personal in scale. (Though not always. In 1891, five hundred employees of a New Jersey glass factory rioted for three days when the owner hired fourteen young Russian Jews to work alongside them. Most of the area's Jewish residents moved away as a result.)

Chicago had a well-established Jewish community prior to 1880, most of them immigrants from the German-speaking regions of Europe. In the 1880s, that population tripled with the rapid increase in new immigrants from Eastern Europe. New Jewish immigrants from Russia and Poland, with their distinctive dress and visible presence as street peddlers, were obvious targets for the violent antisemitism of the 1890s. Most often their tormenters resorted to stone-throwing and beard-pulling as well as verbal abuse. Occasionally such attacks escalated in violence, resulting in the death of a peddler or a rabbi.

Hermann couldn't solve the larger problem, but he could deal with the incident that had occurred in his own backyard. With the help of some older Summerdale boys, he identified the young bullies and arranged for them to be brought to the Schultz home several days later. Standing on the front porch with the protective Barry at his side, he questioned them about their actions and then bawled them out—first in English and then in German. Finally, Hermann warned them he and his friends would thrash them if they continued persecuting the

Jewish merchants in the neighborhood. Sigrid and her "gang" heard everything from a hiding place under the porch. She never forgot it.

———∞∞∞———

The idyllic Chicago childhood of Sigrid's memory, with its deep sense of security and community and its lessons in the importance of language, the power of hospitality, and the necessity of standing up against bullies and prejudice, came to an end in 1901, when Sigrid was eight.

Life in the Schultz household was not as easy as Sigrid's memories would suggest. The economic depressions of the 1890s, particularly the Panic of 1893, hit Chicago hard, despite the positive economic impact of the Columbian Exposition, which fueled a construction boom in the city before it opened and then brought twenty-seven million visitors, and their dollars, from around the world. The Schultz family was better off than many, but Hermann's friendships with Chicago's wealthy and artistically inclined elite could not entirely protect them from the effects of the economic downturn. Hermann took the train downtown to his studio every day, but commissions for portraits inevitably slowed.

Financial concerns were multiplied by health problems. The year Sigrid turned seven, sickness hit the household again and again. Sigrid caught "all the catching diseases that were around." Hermann came down with pneumonia twice.[6]

Hermann and Hedwig had made what they thought would be a permanent home in Chicago. But Hermann was once again feeling the urge to travel, which had driven him from Norway to France and Germany as a young man and would continue to shape the Schultz family's life for decades. Haunted by the fear of going stale artistically, he was eager to return to Paris, where he had studied at the Académie Julian, then the most prestigious art school in the world. He wanted to see old friends and, more importantly, find new artistic inspiration.

Travel might have remained a dream if Hermann hadn't received a lucrative commission for portraits of the king and queen of Württemberg from the Schwaben Verein, a Chicago social organization for German immigrants. When news about the commission spread, prosperous German Americans in Chicago, such as Hermann's friend and Sigrid's "play uncle" Oscar Mayer, of weiner fame, commissioned portraits of relatives in Germany. With several commissions in hand, and the prospect of more, Hermann Schultz became an American citizen on March 23, 1901—and immediately applied for a passport, stating his intention to go abroad with his family for the next two years. (Until the mid-1930s, a woman's citizenship in the United States was defined first by that of her father and then by that of a husband. That meant Hedwig automatically became a citizen when Hermann did.)

———&oo&———

After a brief stop in Paris, the Schultz family went to Wiesbaden, where Sigrid met her German relatives for the first time. Sigrid did not want to leave Summerdale and she found it hard to adjust. She was accustomed to running wild in the prairie near her Chicago home. Now strange adults expected her to conform to strict and unfamiliar standards of behavior. She was supposed to walk sedately, curtsy when greeted by adults, and keep quiet.

Unhappy with the change in circumstances, Sigrid rebelled against what she felt were unreasonable restrictions. (Fifty years later, she told a friend that she remembered with pleasure "the annoyance I used to cause nice old Wiesbaden ladies who used to try to teach obedience to the 'horrible, wild, American brat.'"[7]) Unkind pranks played against adults whom Sigrid felt had wronged her and her generally "fresh" behavior led to further restrictions. Sigrid and her grandmother were probably both glad when the Schultz family left Wiesbaden for Munich.

After several weeks in Munich, the family moved on to Stuttgart, the capital of Baden-Württemberg, where Hermann began work on the commissioned portraits of the king and queen. Now Sigrid found another reason to be unhappy with her life in Germany: school. She had loved school in Summerdale—so much so that she remained in contact with one of her teachers there for fifty years. But the German schools were a different experience. In both Munich and Stuttgart, her parents enrolled her in what she described as "fancy" schools for "little princesses" (literal and figurative) and daughters of the very wealthy—a benefit of Hermann's connections with the rich and powerful, though Sigrid did not feel it was a benefit at the time. In fact, she resisted the strictures of her new schools just as strenuously as she had those in Wiesbaden.

Sigrid quickly learned being a trilingual child in Summerdale did not mean she spoke colloquial German. In Stuttgart, she was placed in a class with younger children because her German was not fluent enough to allow her to keep up with those her own age. Worse, her teacher imitated her American accent and encouraged the other students to laugh at her. While it may not have been appropriate behavior for a teacher, there was some karmic justice in it. A few weeks earlier in Munich, Sigrid had pointed out to fellow students that their French teacher did not speak French and tried to lead a strike against learning from her.

The teasing ended when the local paper reported Hermann had been a dinner guest of the royal family. Suddenly teachers and students alike were eager to be Sigrid's friends.[8]

Sigrid and her mother were delighted when Hermann finished his German commissions and the family moved to Paris, which became their home base for the next eleven years while Hermann traveled in pursuit of commissions, following the social circuit of the wealthy across Europe.

Life in Paris had one thing in common with life in Summerdale: the Schultz home was a gathering place for artists, musicians, and intellectuals as well as members of Europe's gilded set. Friends from Hermann's days as an art student, musicians and artists from around the world, military men, diplomats, and socialites all flocked to his studio to attend small musical parties and hear the latest political gossip from his travels.

The Schultz family's life in Paris was both privileged and precarious. Hermann made a great deal of money when portraits were selling well, but Sigrid's parents spent it as fast as it came in. Hermann could not resist rare books and beautiful antiques. Hedwig was a soft touch for anyone with a sad story, giving as much as she could—and often more than they could afford.

Sigrid learned how fragile the family's finances were after they had been in Paris for two years. The family was preparing to return to Chicago when Hermann became seriously ill. He spent several months in a Paris hospital, where Hedwig visited him every day. When he began to recover, Hedwig suffered a serious attack of rheumatism that left her unable to walk. Their back-to-back illnesses used up whatever reserves they had managed to accumulate, and they were forced to sell their home in Summerdale and all the treasured possessions they had stored there for their return, a devastating loss from ten-year-old Sigrid's perspective.

Without a home to return to, the elder Schultzes put off going back to Chicago. It would be forty years before Sigrid would once again call the United States home.

⟨≈⟩

Once the family was settled in Paris, Sigrid was determined not to repeat the humiliation she had suffered in Stuttgart. At her own insistence, she spent a few months in a private school for students academically behind their age group. By the time she was eleven, her French was good enough—and the family's finances stable enough—for her to attend the Lycée Racine, the second-oldest girl's high school in Paris.

The school was founded in 1886 as part of the Third Republic's program of secularizing education. At the secondary school level, girls were segregated in separate schools taught by women instructors, where they studied a curriculum similar but not identical to that offered to boys in the public lycée system. The phrase used by French lawmakers to describe the two systems was *l'égalité dans la différence* (different but equal). As with "separate but equal," there was more difference than equality.

The boys' schools offered a seven-year program centered on Latin and modern languages, designed to prepare students for the baccalaureate exams, which in turn led to further education and opportunities. The girls' curriculum, a three-year program with an extra two years available for the intellectually ambitious, among whom Sigrid must be counted, did not award the prestigious baccalaureate degree. The curriculum included modern languages, French literature, history, *la morale* (a loosely defined ethics course), and introductory classes in mathematics and the natural sciences. Even the most demanding girls' lycées offered required classes in needlework and domestic economy instead of the Latin classics that were the heart of the curriculum for their male counterparts. (Sigrid did not mention the "girly" classes in her memories of her school years.)

The Lycée Racine and its sister schools were designed to produce educated wives and mothers for the new urban elite, not to promote female equality. Nonetheless, the presence of secular female instructors educated in competitive state-run *écoles normales*, as opposed to the nuns who had previously dominated women's education, was revolutionary. The women who taught at the Lycée Racine were members of the only significant body of professional career women in France in the first decades of the twentieth century. As such, they both inspired their students academically and embodied the possibility of respectable, and respected, alternatives to marriage for middle-class young women.

Women who taught in the secondary schools enjoyed not only financial independence but a social standing based on their own achievements.

The possibility of a career instead of marriage may well have been a new and welcome idea for Sigrid. Certainly, her own adult life would look more like those of the instructors she admired than that of her mother, who resembled the ideal wife the schools aimed to produce.

Sigrid received a different kind of education at home. Hermann Schultz believed a properly educated woman needed to know how to eat, drink, and entertain. He complained that too few women had cultivated tastes for food and wine, fewer still knew how much alcohol they could handle. He took it on himself to teach Sigrid both. When he was in Paris, he would take her to lunch each Thursday, when there were no classes at the lycée, to a restaurant chosen with an eye both to the quality of the food and to the state of what Sigrid always referred to as the family exchequer.

Hermann liked to think he was an educational pioneer, giving his daughter skills she would need as an independent woman earning her way in the world. He proved to be right: she would put those skills to good effect in her career, when entertaining sources was an important professional tool and holding her own with "the boys" in the bar at the Hotel Adlon was a survival tactic.

During school vacations, Sigrid and her mother traveled, some-times with her father and sometimes on family visits. Her mother insisted she spend time with her grandmother in Wiesbaden, both to improve her German and to maintain ties with that side of the family. (Sigrid succeeded at the first, not at the second.) The hated visits to Wiesbaden were balanced by vacations in Switzerland and several summers spent in Norway with her beloved Norwegian relatives, where she added Norwegian to her repertoire of languages. On one of these visits to Norway, Sigrid met a young Norwegian sailor to whom she became engaged at the age of fifteen.

<hr />

When Sigrid graduated from the Lycée Racine in 1911 at eighteen, she received a stack of prize books and a collection of wreaths made of gold-and-green paper laurel leaves that indicated first- or second-place honors in various classes, including first-place honors in Italian, her fifth language. She planned to attend the Sorbonne after graduation, but what the doctors initially diagnosed as a mild case of tuberculosis stopped her from enrolling.[9]

Despite the limitations imposed by her illness, Sigrid flung herself into French student life. Determined to be able to earn her own living, if necessary, she took a business course, which was something between secretarial school and a modern business degree. The quality of her typing over the years in letters and reports suggests Sigrid was not as successful a student in the business course as she had been at the lycée.

Sigrid also studied voice and was successful enough performing soprano parts to be offered a scholarship at the Conservatoire de Paris, regarded as the gateway to a serious musical career in France. She turned the scholarship down after learning she would be required to become a French citizen when she reached the age of twenty-one. Nothing, not even the possibility of becoming an opera star, would induce her to give up her American citizenship. She had lived in Paris longer than she lived in Chicago, but as far as she was concerned, that was the result of bad luck. She was an American, through and through.

Her most engrossing studies occurred at the Sorbonne. Even though she never enrolled, Sigrid unofficially attended classes in history and international law. She learned as a child that her family's financial fortunes varied with Europe's political climate. Whenever the kaiser indulged in a bit of sword-rattling, the possibility of war discouraged the wealthy—European aristocrats and American tourists alike—from ordering portraits. As a result, Sigrid read the newspaper headlines wherever they traveled, improving her language skills as she tried to understand the political events of the day. At the Lycée Racine and on family visits to Germany, she learned about what both sides believed was the inevitability of war between France and Germany, though she undoubtedly heard different versions of how and why war was coming. At the Sorbonne she plunged into the study of politics in general and war in particular with the same competitive spirit she had brought to her classes at the lycée.

※

For two years, Sigrid studied both music and politics with "fierce intensity."[10] But her health was getting worse. She was small to begin with—five feet two and slender. By the spring of 1913, she was dwindling away. Her father's prescription was a bottle of champagne a day. Not surprisingly, that course of treatment did nothing to help what her doctors still believed to be a mild case of tuberculosis.

The standard treatment for tuberculosis at the time was rest, healthful activity, and clean mountain air, so Sigrid's parents sent her to a *Kurhaus* in the Swiss mountains near Lucerne—more of a health resort than a sanatorium. The doctors there determined that she did not have tuberculosis. She was exhausted. She had overworked herself for several years, beginning at the Lycée Racine, where she had been determined to hold her own with the French girls around her. Fresh air, good food, and a chance to rest was exactly what she needed.

It would not be the last time she worked herself to the point of exhaustion.

<hr />

Sigrid's trip to Switzerland had unexpected consequences for the Schultz family.

Soon after she left Paris, her father went to Berlin in pursuit of possible commissions. Once there, he decided to stay for several months. He rented a studio with an adjacent apartment and quickly established a clientele of German industrialists and aristocrats. One of his most important subjects, both in financial terms and in social consequence, was the retired German general, Graf Ferdinand von Zeppelin, who was a hero of the Franco-Prussian War and the inventor of an eponymous airship—the zeppelin. Hermann sold copies of his portrait of Graf Zeppelin to many of the numerous organizations where German military men congregated. In the process, he made acquaintances with Germany's aristocratic military officers, some of whom would prove to be useful contacts for Sigrid in the future.

With Sigrid in Switzerland and Hermann in Berlin, Hedwig Schultz was alone in Paris. She had never lived alone, and apparently, didn't like it. Perhaps foreseeing that the ever-gregarious Hermann might be reluctant to break away from the interesting new circle of art lovers he had met in Berlin, she made the unilateral, and unprecedented, decision to move to Berlin. Despite a long-standing family belief that she was unable to handle practical matters, Hedwig made arrangements for their belongings to be shipped to Hermann's new studio. Only then did she inform her husband that she was coming to Berlin and would arrive a few days before the furniture.

The Schultz family had a new home base.

CHAPTER TWO

STRANDED

Fate ruled that I would have to spend many years
away from my native land, but that previous feeling of
knowing where my roots were saved me from ever becoming a real expatriate. The Schultzes would have a
number of attractive homes in Europe, but none could
ever compete in our hearts with the wide, hip-roofed
house on the edge of the prairie.

—SIGRID SCHULTZ[1]

For the second time in her life, the family's move to Germany marked
a turning point for Sigrid Schultz.

Sigrid was twenty years old. Her trip to the *Kurhaus* in Switzerland
was the first time she had traveled alone. And, like Hedwig, she made
an unexpected decision about what she would do next.

It would have been easy for Sigrid to return to student life in
Paris. It might have been even easier to follow her parents to Berlin,
where Hermann's studio was once again a multinational social center
for his colleagues, friends, and clients. Instead, perhaps inspired by her
teachers at the Lycée Racine, she decided to interrupt her studies and
find a job away from home.

Sigrid took a position teaching English and French at a privately
owned school whose proprietors described it as "a finishing school
for upper-class young ladies." It was located in Bad Sachsa, a spa and
resort in the Harz mountains, a few hours west of Berlin. The primary
draw for Sigrid was the nearby winter sports facilities at Ravensberg
Mountain. In the winter of 1913, she set out for the mountains with

her skis slung over her shoulder, ready to pay for her fun by teaching girls who were more interested in winter sports, singing clubs, and the local social life than their studies.

Living in Germany as an adult was a new experience for Sigrid. After her first unhappy months in Munich and Stuttgart as a child, the only time she had spent in Germany was on short visits to her mother's family in Wiesbaden. However much she disliked her maternal relatives, they were well-connected in the city's social and artistic circles. Similarly, the Germans who visited the Schultz studios in Paris and Berlin were drawn from the artistic and privileged classes: musicians, artists, scholars, military officers, barons, and industrialists.

By contrast, the "upper-class young ladies" at the school in Bad Sachsa were the daughters of what Sigrid dismissed as "wealthy grocers and such," middle-class people who could afford to send their daughters to a finishing school, where they hoped the girls would receive polish and make connections that would enable them to advance socially.[2] At twenty, Sigrid was only a few years older than her students, but she had little in common with them. The stories she told about them later sound like mash-ups of an F. Scott Fitzgerald short story and a Jane Austen novel. Much like wealthy American socialites of the time who traveled to England hoping to attract titled husbands, these students were primarily interested in the aristocratic but impoverished young lieutenants garrisoned in nearby towns who might be lured into marriage by their dowries. When they weren't trolling for spouses or climbing out their dorm windows after curfew to meet their beaus, they were speculating on the probability of imminent war, in which Germany would crush and subjugate the enemy. They were uncertain whether that enemy would be England, France, and/or Russia—and they didn't much care.

Her students' interest in what seemed like an inevitable war and their understanding of the politics involved were naive versions of two beliefs prevalent in Germany at the time. One was the conviction that the new German Empire, forged in the Franco-Prussian War, was a powerful state with a mandate to spread its *Kultur*—scientific, intellectual, and musical superiority—throughout the world, by military conquest if necessary. The other, equally influential, belief was that Germany was surrounded by hostile and envious powers in an increasingly unstable world. As a result of this second belief, Germany was constantly engaged in developing and refining military plans and making diplomatic alliances in preparation for the next European war, as were the other major powers to a lesser extent. Everyone expected war; no one expected the war they got.

While Sigrid was vaguely amused (or perhaps bemused) by her students' romantic preoccupations, social aspirations, and political opinions, she was disgusted by their open antisemitism, which was as much a part of the social environment as the belief in Germany's military and cultural superiority. In fact, it was an increasingly important element of that belief.

For that matter, a reinvigorated antisemitism was part of the social environment for Europe as a whole, not just Germany. The expansion of opportunities and rights for Jews in most European nations between the late eighteenth and mid-nineteenth centuries was met with more virulent forms of antisemitism, a word coined by journalist Wilhelm Marr in 1879 in a pamphlet titled *The Victory of Judaism over Germandom*. The "new" antisemitism combined long-standing religion-based myths and hatreds with modern "scientific" racism, linguistic and cultural nationalism, and a growing belief in an international Jewish conspiracy for world domination.

Sigrid might have been willing to ignore her students' casual antisemitism as the talk of girls who didn't understand the implications of what they were saying. But her ability to ignore its presence at the school ended when the school's owners rejected the application of a girl from a Jewish family. The girl seemed to be exactly the kind of student they wanted. Her family was wealthier and more socially prominent than that of most of their students. It was clear the proprietors rejected her only because she was Jewish. When Sigrid confronted them, they told her that while they themselves found such prejudices "deplorable and un-Christian," they had to consider the opinions held by their students and, more importantly, by their students' parents. Accepting Jewish students would damage the school's "all-Protestant" reputation and make it impossible for them to stay in business. They may well have been right. After all, professed Jews were not recognized at the kaiser's court even though they had legally enjoyed full rights as citizens of the German Empire since its formation in 1871.

Sigrid wasn't willing to accept antisemitism as a pragmatic business philosophy. When the school's owners offered her another semester of teaching, she turned them down and returned to Berlin, with a recommendation in her suitcase certifying her excellence as an instructor of English and French.[3]

Sigrid Schultz later said she could not have learned at the most expensive university half as much about the way of life, thinking, or aspirations of middle-class Germans as she did in her months teaching at Bad Sachsa in the winter of 1913–1914.

———

When the long-anticipated and yet totally unexpected war began in August 1914, Hedwig was bedridden with a rheumatic attack and too ill to travel. The Schultz family was stranded in Berlin.

As Germany went to war, Sigrid roamed Berlin with a young Norwegian cousin, watching excited crowds, mostly young, middle-class, and male, gather in public spaces—at the kaiser's palace, the chancellery, the Hapsburg Embassy, and Bismarck's statue at the Brandenburg Gate—singing and shouting patriotic slogans. They stood next to Berliners who threw bouquets to the troops as they marched through the city to the sound of regimental bands. More than once, Germans pushed the two foreigners to the front of the crowd so they could see.

Hard realities soon intruded. Hermann's income had always been a political barometer. With Germany actively at war, Berliners considered it unpatriotic to commission portraits from an artist who wasn't German. Since Sigrid was in Berlin taking care of Hedwig, Hermann resorted to his usual tactic in hard times and left the city in search of work. He rented a studio in Hamburg, hoping, unrealistically, that merchants there, who specialized in international shipping, would be less chauvinistic than war-mad Berliners.

Hedwig and Sigrid had always traveled on Hermann's passport as his dependents, as was typical at the time. Now that Sigrid was effectively in charge of the family's household in Berlin, she went to the American embassy and applied for a passport in her own name—the first step in finding work to keep the household afloat.

Several months later, Hedwig, too, filed for a passport in her own name, for purposes of "protection and identification." This was an enormous, and radical, step. Prior to the war, the State Department issued married couples joint passports in the husband's name, with the phrase "accompanied by his wife" or simply "and wife." Neither the wife's name nor her description appeared on the document. A note on Hedwig's passport application states, "Mrs. Schultz desires a separate passport for herself, her husband being abroad for a large part of the time." His absence was nothing new. Hermann had, one way or another, been "abroad for a large part of the time" for much of their marriage.

It was difficult for an American to find work in wartime Berlin, but Sigrid managed. With her language skills and Hermann's contacts in German society—not to mention that positive recommendation from the school in Bad Sachsa—she patched together an income as an English and French tutor for wealthy German families. Some of her students were children of Jewish businessmen who felt it was more important than ever for their sons and daughters to have a working knowledge of English and French. Others were from old-fashioned aristocratic families who considered French the international language of diplomacy and were appalled by the accents of the French instructors in the schools their children attended.

Sigrid quickly learned that many German aristocrats shared the social prejudices of her former finishing-school pupils. She lost one of her first students, the twelve-year-old son of a countess, when she refused to give up her Jewish pupils, even after the countess promised to get her all the pupils she wanted from the right (i.e., not Jewish) social circles. Sigrid once again chose principle over paycheck. She couldn't afford to lose the job, but she walked away from it. Nobody was going to tell her who was, or was not, socially acceptable.

Hermann wasn't the only one who experienced unemployment as a result of the war. Small businesses closed their doors when the owners were called to military service. Large firms downsized their workforces in expectation of reduced demand. As a result, the unemployment rate escalated in the first month of the war, from 2.7 percent in July to 22.7 percent in August.

As the war went on, even those members of the middle and working classes who still had money to spend suffered from the serious food and fuel shortages caused by Britain's blockade of German ports, the German military's failure to understand the domestic economy, and the German government's subsequent mismanagement of the same. Grain and bread shortages led desperate hausfraus to fill the gap in the family diet with potatoes, until potatoes became scarce too. Rising prices and inadequate supplies of meat, butter, and even jam—which poorer Germans turned to when they could no longer obtain drippings or butter to spread on their adulterated "war bread"—made putting food on the table a struggle.

Women lined up outside stores soon after midnight, bringing blankets and lightweight chairs to make themselves comfortable during the hours of waiting. Over time, lines became longer and food became less available. By October 1915, the absence of food in the markets led to "potato battles" and "butter riots" in Berlin's working-class neighborhoods, predecessors of the street violence that would become a regular feature of German politics a few years later.

As food became increasingly scarce and expensive, it also declined in quality. Bakers used a wide range of substances to stretch the flour in bread. Some were perfectly edible, if not what the German palate was accustomed to: ground corn, lentils and other legumes, chestnuts, soybeans, and bran. Other additions, such as sand and sawdust, were not. As staple foods became harder, if not impossible, to purchase, manufacturers began to offer substitutes. By the end of the war, more than eleven thousand substitute food products were on sale in Germany, including 33 kinds of fake eggs and 837 different forms of ersatz sausage.

Like other residents of Berlin, Sigrid and her mother endured the scarcities brought on by the war, and the exhaustion, weakness, and weight loss that accompanied them. They learned to make potato pancakes without fat, bake cakes with synthetic honey, and cook a raven so that it tasted like partridge—if the raven was young. Sigrid later claimed cornbread saved them. Because Germans did not like cornmeal and didn't know what to do with it, they could get cornmeal when nothing else was available.

Conditions went from bad to disastrous in the "rutabaga winter" of 1916–1917, when the failure of the potato crop meant most Germans were reduced to a diet of rutabagas. The government attempted to overcome the popular perception that rutabagas were fit only for animal fodder by dubbing them the Prussian Pineapple and providing recipes for soups, casseroles, cakes, breads, coffee, and even beer. A few months later, in the spring and summer of 1917, rutabagas, too, disappeared from the shops.

To add to the general misery, the winter of 1916 was unusually cold and wet. Homes and workplaces were unheated because the military had commandeered the petroleum and coal that Berliners used in their stoves and furnaces. The same fuel shortages forced the city to reduce service on Berlin's formerly robust public transportation system and to turn off many of the streetlights, leaving working Berliners to trudge through dark wintry streets without hope of warming up when they arrived home.

At first Sigrid and her mother were able to bribe the coal delivery boy with Hermann's private stash of expensive Havana cigars—an exchange that gave them an extra hundred pounds of coal now and then. Later, as fuel shortages grew worse, they considered themselves lucky when Sigrid brought home four or five briquets of compressed brown coal to feed the old-fashioned iron stove in Hermann's studio. During the worst of the winter, she used their Turkish rugs to build an adult version of a blanket fort around the stove where they could huddle.

With her mother bedridden and her father in Hamburg, Sigrid was not only the sole breadwinner for the household; she was also the one who stood in food lines and bartered with the neighbors. She tramped between teaching jobs and food queues through the cold dark streets. Like many Berliners during the war and the lean years that followed, she raised rabbits (she called them "bunnies") for food and trade on a narrow interior balcony above the studio's kitchen. "The hard part naturally, was to eat them," she wrote later. "But when you have been on a war diet for a longish time you get over false sentimentality."[4]

⸺∞⸺

As the cold winter turned to a hungry spring, a tough situation was about to get worse.

CHAPTER THREE

ENEMY ALIEN

A government can do anything it wants
as long as it gives enough potatoes and
enough beer to the German people.

—SIGRID SCHULTZ[1]

On April 6, 1917, the United States declared war against Germany. Aware that war was coming, the American embassy in Berlin contacted Hedwig and urged her to get the family out of the country as quickly as possible. But Hermann was hospitalized in Hamburg and would remain too fragile to travel throughout the war. Leaving the country without him was unthinkable. Staying meant the family became enemy aliens.

Unlike the American government, which held 2,300 German and Austrian nationals in internment camps during the war and arrested more than 10,000 others on various pretexts, the German government did not intern the small number of American citizens who were residents in the country when the United States entered the war. Instead, Germany limited their movements, forbidding them to leave the neighborhoods in which they lived. Schultz and her mother were required to have a special control card stamped at the local police station twice a day, presumably to enforce those travel limitations. These restrictions made Schultz's already difficult task of collecting enough food to feed her mother and herself even harder—or would have if Schultz had honored them. In fact, she violated the German orders every time she went to the homes of her pupils. Her ability to move around outside their neighborhood was no doubt helped by the fact that the policeman who stamped their control cards was a recipient of cigars from Hermann's dwindling stash.

As if her life weren't difficult enough, Schultz, like many women of her generation, suffered a serious personal loss during the war. Her Norwegian fiancé was an officer on a freighter carrying grain to Norway from South America. He mailed Schultz a letter from Morocco telling her he expected to arrive home in three weeks. Once his tour of duty was over, she would meet him in Denmark, where they would finally marry. Three weeks turned into three agonizing months that she remembered later as being "infinitely longer than the years that we had been separated."[2] Finally, the ship was officially reported as lost without a trace. Unofficially, her relatives informed her that it was torpedoed by a German submarine. At the time she thought it was the end of her emotional life. Going on without him seemed like more than she could bear. Schultz would mourn the loss for years.

Her experience was not uncommon. Many young men died in the war, leaving behind girlfriends, fiancées, and wives. It was not the first time that war had created a surplus of unmarried women, but the scale of the problem was new. It was so widespread in Germany, where more than two million soldiers and close to a million civilians died in the war, that Adolf Hitler promised in a 1932 campaign speech that his Third Reich would "make it easier for the maidens of Germany to find homes and husbands to support them." In her article on the speech in the *Chicago Tribune*, Schultz noted that hundreds of women cheered in response even though, as she pointed out, if the men hadn't existed before, there was no reason to believe the Nazis could produce them now.[3]

Soon after the United States entered the war, Schultz read an ad for a part-time job that sounded like a perfect fit for her skills and interests. A visiting Turk named Réouf Bey Chadirchi needed someone fluent in both German and French and familiar with technical legal terms.

Schultz's mother worried about her daughter working alone in an office with a possibly dangerous man. Teaching, especially in the private homes of the wealthy, was one thing. (Any reader of historical novels knows being a governess had long been an acceptable choice for gentlewomen who needed to support themselves.) Office work was one step further from the world in which young girls curtseyed to their elders and were escorted to and from school by a relative or family maid.

That world had already begun to fracture before the Great War shattered it completely. Growing numbers of single young women had entered the workforce, enjoying what early twentieth century German feminist and politician Gertrud Bäumer described as an "intermediary stage of personal independence" between adolescence and marriage/motherhood,[4] a stage that the teachers at the Lycée Racine had modeled for Sigrid and her classmates. Despite her mother's concerns, Schultz was a natural member of the league of New Women. She later said that despite her father's old-fashioned ideas about keeping women close to home, she "did not want to be kept under lock and key, seeing only those people of whom Father approved."[5]

Schultz was tempted not only by the nature of the work described in the ad but by what seemed to her a fabulous salary—500 marks a month (roughly $1,800 in 2020). With Hermann marooned in Hamburg, she was the only breadwinner in the family. (Hermann was still an invalid when Hedwig finally brought him to Berlin in 1922 and remained so until his death in 1924.) Working as a tutor did not pay well and the household budget was precarious; Schultz constantly looked for new opportunities to earn money. She was always afraid her tutoring clients would fire her because she was an "enemy alien," and the loss of one or two students could mean economic disaster. The Chadirchi job would give her a much-needed cushion.

Chadirchi was the mayor of Baghdad and a professor of international law in the university there: a "short, squat, quiet but witty and extremely wise man in his late forties" who seemed old to Schultz, then twenty-four.[6] Foreseeing the defeat of Germany and its ally, the Ottoman Empire, and not wanting to be in Baghdad during the aftermath of that defeat, Chadirchi came to Berlin under the pretext of studying international law at the University of Berlin. His interest was real, but he spoke no German. After an interview in which Schultz impressed him with her language abilities, he hired her to attend classes as his proxy.

Schultz happily took the new job, even though her schedule was already overloaded with tutoring sessions and the daily struggle to obtain food and fuel. It not only paid well, it also allowed her to continue her

education. In the morning she attended classes in history and international law. In the afternoon, she went to Chadirchi's office on Unter den
Linden and gave him a detailed report in French on the lectures she
heard that morning in German. She continued teaching her language
classes in the evenings. (She knew better than to put all her eggs in
one basket, especially when even ersatz eggs were hard to come by.)

The job also had an unplanned bonus: as a diplomat, Chadirchi
got extra ration cards. Together, he and Schultz practiced what she
called "charm put to practical use" to get as much for their combined
ration cards as possible. She collected both rations at the butter office,
which had a male staff who was susceptible to flirtation. Chadirchi
took the Schultz cards along with his own to the meat office, where
women distributed the diplomatic surplus, and bargained for as much
as he could get.

The work at the university was fascinating, but it also carried risks.
Schultz traveled outside the neighborhood to which she was restricted
each time she went to the university or visited Chadirchi's office. As
an enemy alien, she was not allowed to attend classes at the university.
Neither Turkish nor male, she nevertheless carried a special student
pass made out in the name of Réouf Bey. (Much later, Schultz told an
interviewer, "You should have seen the speed with which I showed my
pass to the guards.") The hazards were increased by the fact that she
was usually the only woman in the classroom, surrounded by German
veterans and soldiers on sick leave. Afraid that a less-than-perfect
accent might give her away as an American, she broke into a raucous
cough whenever another student spoke to her, making herself even
more noticeable.[7]

In addition to the formal, if unofficial, education she received at the
University of Berlin, Schultz also benefited from an informal education
in international politics, courtesy of Chadirchi and his friends, who
often visited his office while she was there. (It is possible his motives in
moving to Berlin included espionage.) She met Turkish diplomats and
military officers who were in Berlin on official business, high-ranking
Muslim clerics, German diplomats, and German-Jewish newspaper
editors and bankers.

Schultz earned her place in those meetings. She translated for
German visitors who could not keep up with the rapid conversation
in French and took notes when requested. In return, she learned more
about military and political developments in Germany than the government would have liked an enemy alien to know.

On the surface, the meetings in Chadirchi's office must have felt familiar to Schultz, similar to social gatherings in her father's studio before the war. But these meetings contained an edge of danger not present at Hermann's wine-fueled soirees, even when the conversation focused on contemporary politics.

On one occasion, she took notes of a conversation between Chadirchi and a Turkish colonel who was on a special mission to Berlin. The two had lunched at the Hotel Adlon with political officers of the German army's general staff and a middle-aged German civilian, whom Schultz later deduced was Heinrich Class, the antisemitic leader of the Pan-German League. Back at Chadirchi's office, where Schultz had arrived to report on the morning's classes, the two men wanted to compare notes on what they had learned without fear of being overhead.

Over lunch, the Germans had discussed their involvement in the three-sided civil war that had broken out in Russia in the aftermath of the February Revolution. Germany was supporting Lenin's Bolsheviks against the newly founded Russian Provisional Government and the monarchist White Army. They hoped the war would create enough chaos in Russia to ease the pressure on Germany on the Eastern Front. If Lenin failed to fulfill German expectations, Germany would instruct its agents to tap into Russia's long-standing antisemitism to create chaos from another direction.

Russian Jews had suffered systematic persecution under the tsars ever since the annexation of Poland in 1791 brought almost a million Polish Jews under Russian rule. More than sixty years later, Alexander II, who began his rule in 1855, instituted limited increases in freedoms for Russian Jews, but they did not last after his assassination by Russian radicals in 1881. Only one member of the group was Jewish, but Alexander's death was followed by a wave of anti-Jewish pogroms and the promulgation of a new series of regulations known as the May Laws, which tightened restrictions on where Jews could live, what property they could own, and how they could make a living. The May Laws were the most stringent antisemitic regulations put into place before those enacted by the Nazi government in Germany. Although the May Laws were passed as temporary regulations, they remained in effect until the Bolshevik Revolution of 1917. Before the revolution, many Russians already believed Russian Jews had invented Communism, and they equated Communism's international goals with those in *The Protocols of the Elders of Zion*, a fake document created by the Russian secret police in 1903 that became an international bestseller.

Now, as the civil war raged on, White Army officers portrayed the Bolsheviks as Jews, and encouraged pogroms by their troops. Given these circumstances, the Germans informed Chadirchi and his companion over lunch, it would be easy for German agents to inspire the Russian masses to overthrow Lenin and his organization as members of an international Jewish cabal.

Schultz stopped taking notes for a moment, horrified at the idea that Germany—or at least a coterie of its senior imperial officers—was prepared to cold-bloodedly provoke a pogrom and interfere in the outcome of Russia's civil war for its own benefit. At the end of the meeting, she sealed her notes in an envelope and told Chadirchi to store them in the safe of one of his diplomatic friends. She did not want to risk having a "snooper" find them in his office or, worse, being caught with them herself if a policeman stopped her on the street.

———— ✾ ————

During the years of the Great War, Schultz widened her circle of influential acquaintances, the start of what would become an extraordinary network of sources in Germany. In addition to her father's friends and her students' families, her circle now included well-informed newspapermen, young Foreign Service officers, diplomats from the Spanish embassy, which represented America in Germany after the United States entered the war, and as Schultz put it, "nice white-haired old baronesses."

Schultz's relationship with widowed and unmarried older women in the German aristocracy is an excellent example of the genuine social connection and political opportunism on which her later network was built. Many of these women lived in apartments stuffed with antique furniture, precious china, heavy silver, and other inherited treasures but had a difficult time making ends meet on inadequate pensions. Schultz and her mother also struggled during the war, but they made a point of sharing with these women whenever they had a windfall of food.

Over time, Schultz connected the information dots. She combined knowledge gathered from her own acquaintances with the political and military intelligence she heard in Chadirchi's office. Military officers spoke indiscreetly at tea parties given by their elderly aunts, ignoring the small, blonde, seemingly innocuous enemy alien in the room. A Spanish reporter passed along information he received from a Foreign Office man. A wealthy friend from an old and influential Swiss family, who dropped by the studio whenever he was in Berlin for ersatz coffee and gossip, shared sensitive details about military negotiations between the allies in Paris. When the father of one of her students found her in obvious distress at a headline trumpeting the number of ships Germany had sent to the bottom of the Atlantic in recent days—horrifying to the young woman who had lost the man she loved to German torpe-does—he comforted her with the information that several naval officers had admitted to him that the numbers were exaggerated.

Put together, Schultz's small pieces of information, gathered from many sources, gave her a picture of how the war was progressing that was very different from the tightly controlled news that appeared in the German papers.

Chadirchi, too, was gathering information about the advance of the Allied powers. At the end of September 1918, he decided it was time to leave Germany and go to neutral Switzerland.[8]

He turned out to be well-informed. A few weeks later, on October 29, German sailors mutinied in the port city of Kiel. Within days, the old Reich was dead, a new republic had been declared, and an armistice was in the making.

"And so then we waited until the negotiations were all over," Schultz remembered later. "And it was a pretty hectic time, because the revolution was not very easy."[9]

CHAPTER FOUR

"HOW TO MEET A REVOLUTION"

It is a wonderful thing when Spartacist
troubles and revolutions occur often. You
are getting used to them and you know
what to do.

—SIGRID SCHULTZ[1]

In the last days of October 1918, Germany's absolute monarchy was effectively dead. Despite the soon-to-be-ex-kaiser's conviction that the army would still follow him to victory, Germany's top military leaders insisted that the time had come to sue for peace. Negotiations for an armistice with the United States were underway.

At the same time, the (relatively) liberal-minded Prince Maximilian of Baden, newly appointed imperial chancellor, had joined forces with the leaders of the Social Democratic Party of Germany (SPD) to change Germany's constitution. Together, they were in the process of creating a true constitutional monarchy and reforming electoral laws, with or without the kaiser's support.

On October 29, the hope of an orderly transfer of power disintegrated. Sailors in the port city of Kiel mutinied against orders that were not just stupid but suicidal. The initial mutiny expanded into an uprising against their officers, the war, and the empire. Several days later, delegations of sailors traveled to cities across the country, spreading word of the revolt. By November 7, the mutiny had turned into a rebellion as striking workers and mutinous soldiers joined forces with the sailors.

Thousands of revolutionaries converged on Berlin on November 8, ready to demand both an end to the war and the creation of a new government.

⎯⎯ ❦ ⎯⎯

Sigrid Schultz had experienced violence in the streets of Berlin throughout the war.

"Butter riots" and violent demonstrations against merchants, farmers, and government leaders—the people whom Berlin's working classes blamed for the lack of food in the markets—were a regular occurrence, beginning as early as October 1915. In April 1917 and again in January 1918, when the government cut the food ration to a thousand calories a day, Berlin's metal and munitions workers took to the streets, demanding more food—and peace.

When Germany signed a separate peace treaty with the new Russian government on March 3, 1918, after the provisional government overthrew the tsarist regime, victory celebrations broke out on any convenient street corner. Some demonstrations were spontaneous; others were incited by a politician or policeman armed with a political poster and a loud voice. Such celebrations, official or unofficial, often became violent. Crowds turned on anyone who failed to join in the cheers quickly or enthusiastically enough to suit the excited celebrants.

Schultz had learned to skirt around the demonstrating crowds as she walked through Berlin's Tiergarten Park on her way to a tutoring session or classes at the university, far enough away to be safe but close enough to hear the speeches denouncing food shortages or assuring the audience that the "Teutonic race" would soon rule Europe. (Eavesdropping on what Schultz called the "oratory" was surely irresistible, given her fascination with politics.)

⎯⎯ ❦ ⎯⎯

The demonstrations in Berlin of November 8 and 9 were on a larger scale than those Schultz had experienced during the war, though for the most part they were no more violent.

Schultz and her mother did not know when they left their apartment on the morning of November 9 that what would become known as the November Revolution had reached Berlin. A friend of Hedwig's had spent the night. In the morning, they walked her to the zoo, located near them at the west end of the Tiergarten, where it was easier to catch a streetcar. The first clue that something was wrong was an encounter with a ferocious-looking Russian speaking broken German to a young soldier. Cars and trucks barreled up and down the main streets. Rumors flew, but no one could tell them what was happening.

If things were chaotic at the zoo end of the Tiergarten, they were significantly worse two and a half miles away, at the other end of the park. Tens of thousands of striking workers and mutineers gathered outside Prince Maximilian's chancellery. Thousands more were still marching into the city.

Faced with the real possibility that the newly formed workers' councils would call a general strike or that the crowd would storm the chancellery, Prince Maximilian announced the kaiser's abdication to the press at eleven thirty. (He informed the kaiser that he had unknowingly abdicated only after the fact.)

Maximilian turned the position of chancellor over to Friedrich Ebert, the head of the SPD, before noon. Ebert, a saddlemaker by trade, never expected to head the government. He was dedicated to improving the living conditions of German workers and giving them access to meaningful participation in the political process. He and his party supported constitutional reform within the existing system. Instead, they had government thrust upon them. After one day as chancellor, Ebert helped create the new German republic and was elected its first president several months later. Schultz believed Ebert was one of the few leaders who sincerely tried to bring about peace, not only in Germany but in Europe as a whole.

At two o'clock that afternoon, Philipp Scheidemann, another SPD leader, speaking without his party's authorization, proclaimed the end of the German Empire from the balcony of the Reichstag, the German parliament building. Several hours later, Karl Liebknecht, a radical Socialist leader, stood on a balcony of the royal palace and, also solely on his own authority, announced the creation of a Socialist republic.

While Scheidemann was declaring the empire dead, Schultz was on her way home from tutoring. As she crossed Charlottenburger Chaussee (now the Strasse des 17 Juni), which ran from the kaiser's palace in the center of the city through the Tiergarten toward Schloss Charlottenburg, a truck stopped next to her. A wild-eyed young man pointed a revolver at her head. Schultz held as still as she could: something about his expression told her he would shoot if she moved. But he veered off, as abruptly as he had stopped. Later she realized he must have been a member of one of the groups trying to seize control of the strategically important elevated station at the west end of the Tiergarten, near the Schultz apartment. The revolution was coming dangerously close to home.

❧

The declaration of a new government did not mean the revolution was over. As Schultz would later remember it, "The people had every reason to be desperate. They were cold and hungry and their soldiers had fought in vain."[2] Schultz and Hedwig were often cold and hungry too. With Chadirchi gone, and his 500-marks-a-month and diplomatic ration card gone with him, the Schultz family budget was once again stretched dangerously thin. The only improvement as far as Schultz was concerned was that Hedwig was back on her feet and able to help with the still onerous task of shopping, including forays into what Hedwig described in her brief notes about life during the revolution as "very discreet ways" of getting food (i.e., the black market).[3]

New waves of revolution and counterrevolution swept through Berlin and across Germany, beginning with an unsuccessful putsch on December 6, 1918, by members of the political right intent on restoring the monarchy and continuing through the first months of 1919, when a small group of Marxist revolutionaries who called themselves the Spartacus League, or Spartacists, rose against the Weimar Republic. Streets became battlefields. Leftist revolutionaries of all stripes fought the right-wing volunteer paramilitary groups known as the *Freikorps* for control of the government.

❧

The events of November 8 and 9, 1918, had little impact on most Berliners' daily lives.

The same could not be said of the subsequent revolutions that swept through Berlin in the first half of 1919. Gas, electricity, and domestic water were cut off again and again. In addition to standing in lines to buy food and other necessities, people, usually women, had to stand in line at public fountains to fill buckets when the water was off. Schultz learned to stockpile pantry goods, candles, and a few bottles of fuel in anticipation of the next violent outburst. (It literally made her physically ill when one Norwegian guest burned candles two at a time, with no thought for the future. Burning candles frivolously today meant no light when you needed it tomorrow.) At the first sign of an uprising, Schultz filled the bathtub, careful not to let it overflow—a hard-learned lesson that she shared in an undated, apparently unpublished satirical piece titled "How to Meet a Revolution." Then she hurried to the market to buy whatever perishables were available, a job that took hours because everyone else was doing the same thing.

Machine-gun fire, pistol shots, and grenade blasts became as familiar as they had been at the front in the war, sharp bursts of violence set against the routine sounds of Berliners moving about their business through the city. According to Hedwig, the Schultz home suffered a distinctive addition to the soundtrack of revolution—an organ-grinder playing outside their studio throughout the cold, sunless days of fighting. She couldn't bear street organs after that.

Traveling to her teaching jobs, Schultz walked a city torn by violence. She passed activists haranguing hungry crowds and hurried through streets made dangerous with cross fire between revolutionaries on one side and the Weimar army on the other. (As a result, Schultz never romanticized the Russian revolutions and the Communist governments that followed them, unlike many of her contemporaries. From her perspective, armed Communists and armed right-wing extremists looked much the same.) One of her regular routes took her through a section of Tiergarten Park that lay between two stations of the Berlin elevated train, the Zoo and the Tiergarten. For several weeks, revolutionaries and government troops fought bitterly for possession of the two stations, which were strategically important for control of the area. Hedwig would hear the shooting begin in the night and knew Schultz would soon walk through the contested area. "At that time, I learned to pray again," she wrote.[4]

When an officer was nearly killed in front of her, Schultz had had enough. She decided to stop teaching her pupils until things calmed down, no matter how much they needed the money.

—◦◦◦—

Today, the term "Lost Generation" is often used to describe the well-known circle of expatriate American writers and artists who gathered in Paris after the First World War. It applies more broadly to the generation born in the last decades of the nineteenth century and shaped by their experience of the war, described by the generation's chronicler, Malcolm Cowley, as people who "were in their teens when the twentieth century was in its teens."[5] A large number of them spent time in Europe after the war, a phenomenon made possible by America's strong postwar economy and inspired by America's new interest in the larger world.[6]

By that broader definition, Schultz was a member of the Lost Generation. Her experience was considerably different from that of most of the young Americans who poured into Europe after the war with little knowledge of its history, politics, or languages and spent time in Paris, Vienna, Moscow, or even Weimar Berlin, but she, too, was in her own way "lost." Schultz came out of the war exhausted, malnourished, heartbroken, and homesick for an America she had never really known.

Like other members of the Lost Generation, many of whom supported themselves with magazine or newspaper work while abroad, Schultz would find her calling in journalism, thanks to a trio of reporters from Chicago who arrived in Berlin with what she later described as the "glamor of rescuing angels," bringing with them a sense of family and home Schultz hadn't realized she was looking for.[7]

CHAPTER FIVE

FINDING HER OWN PEOPLE

Only someone who has lived abroad as an enemy alien in a country at war, cut off from friends, always aware that he or she may be arrested or interned if the local authorities want to, can realize what it means to see your own people again—especially in the joy of victory.

—SIGRID SCHULTZ[1]

It was March 4, 1919. The Great War was over. The victors were convened in Paris, negotiating peace terms. The new Weimar government had a shaky hold over a politically divided country, with both Right and Left challenging the centrist parties' ability to rule. The Spartacist revolt had been put down in January, only a few weeks earlier, but riots and street battles broke out almost daily in Berlin. Food was still scarce in German cities; the British would not lift the North Sea blockade to allow imports into the country until after the Versailles treaty was signed several months later. And the Schultz household's financial situation was as shaky as it had been at any time since the beginning of the war.

But for this one night, Sigrid Schultz refused to think about any of it. It was the final night of Berlin's Karneval week. As Schultz remembered it decades later, Berliners were determined to forget war, defeat, and revolution. The city had not yet reached the frenzied gaiety that marked the Weimar Republic at its height. But for that one week, there seemed to be a ball or a party everywhere she turned.

Schultz had been invited to attend a gala costume ball, thrown by a wealthy banker who was the older brother of one of her students. She was determined to set down her burdens for just one night. During the war, some of her father's wealthy contacts had occasionally invited Schultz to extravagant dinner parties that included game and produce sent from their country estates and luxuries such as black-market coffee—rare treats even when she had to swallow unpalatable politics alongside the pâté. But it had been years since she had been to a real party. There would be good food, champagne, and the chance to whirl across a ballroom floor. Even more exciting from her perspective, several Americans who had recently arrived in Berlin from Chicago would be among the guests.

⊗⊗⊗

That night, another round of bloody battles threatened the city. The previous day the Berlin workers' councils had called for a general strike to force the new government to make radical political changes. Although the council leaders urged the strikers to remain peaceful, as soon as the strike was called, armed revolutionaries seized some thirty Berlin police stations. Within an hour, Ebert's cabinet gave the defense minister, Gustav Noske, dictatorial powers. Noske immediately proclaimed martial law in the city. Thousands of Freikorps soldiers marched into Berlin and set up machine gun and artillery positions on the main streets. Skirmishes occurred whenever the two sides met.

With the strike in effect, public transportation was not running. Schultz knew it could be unsafe to walk to the party that night, but she had traveled the streets in dangerous times before. Some things were worth taking a chance for. Dressed in a tight-waisted, wide-skirted gown in the rococo style of eighteenth-century France, another time of violent revolution, her long blonde hair arranged into a high pompadour dusted with white powder, she hurried through the ice-cold night, past corners where trigger-happy Freikorps members and their revolutionary opponents had exchanged shots earlier that day. At one point, men carrying rifles stepped out of the shadows and followed her, whether they were threatening or protecting her she wasn't sure. When gunfire sounded from a side street, her silent escort ran toward the shots, leaving her alone once more.

When she reached her destination, a luxurious apartment on the Kurfürstendamm boulevard, Schultz put aside the dark, the cold, and the risk of running into a gun battle for the night. The host, Herr Sachs, had urged his guests to recapture the lost lighthearted spirit of parties held before the war. It appeared that they had succeeded. Costumed couples circled the room to the sounds of old-fashioned waltzes, lively two-steps, and perhaps a daring tango or two, from the fad that swept Berlin in the years before the war. (Even though the Weimar Republic is popularly associated with the cabaret culture of jazz and sexually explicit dances, this American music had barely reached Germany in early 1919. It would not have been played at a private ball only months after the end of the war.) At the edges of the room, guests clinked champagne glasses in merry toasts. No one seemed worried about riots, street battles, the imminent general strike, or the economic pressures on the working classes that fueled them.

Despite appearances, not everyone at the party had set aside thoughts of politics for the evening. Schultz didn't know it yet, but she had been invited as bait. Her host and many of his guests wanted to meet some of the American newspaper correspondents who had arrived in Berlin in the weeks since the armistice had been declared in mid-November. The Americans were there to report on the Weimar revolution and Germany's response to the armistice. Germany's political and economic classes were eager to talk to them. Two Chicago reporters, Richard Henry Little of the *Chicago Tribune* and Ben Hecht of the *Chicago Daily News*, had accepted Sachs's invitation, lured by the promise that in addition to a chance to talk to prominent Germans, they would meet an American "girl" who could give them an eyewitness account of wartime Berlin, the Weimar revolution, and the Spartacist uprising. (Schultz was twenty-six at the time.)

<hr />

Little and Hecht were on the leading edge of a change in the way foreign news was reported in the United States.

Before the Great War, most American newspapers considered on-the-ground foreign news coverage an expensive luxury. Some larger papers had correspondents in London, which was the center of American journalism in Europe. A few correspondents were stationed in Paris. (There were nine in 1907.) For the most part, American editors relied on the wire services, which had been founded in the mid-nineteenth century in response to the new technology of the telegraph (i.e., wire) to provide them with breaking international news.

The role of foreign news in American papers changed with World War I. After the United States entered the war on April 4, 1917, hundreds of American reporters made their way to Europe. Some were accredited correspondents, attached to the American Expeditionary Force (AEF). Others were visiting correspondents, in Europe on assignment for magazines such as *Scribner's* and the *Saturday Evening Post*. A few were free agents.

When the war was over, some newspapers chose to strengthen their foreign news coverage by establishing news bureaus in the major cities of Europe. America was playing a greater role in international affairs. Consequently, Americans were more interested in foreign news than they had been before the war.

———

The *Chicago Tribune* had a head start in developing its foreign news bureaus at the end of the war because of its Army Edition.

The Army Edition, launched by the *Tribune* from Paris in July 1917, was a four-page tabloid aimed at American soldiers stationed in France during the war. The *Tribune's* owner and publisher, Robert McCormick (soon to be Colonel McCormick), saw the paper as a way to provide soldiers with a blend of war and hometown news as well as popular features from the parent paper.

Anticipating a rush of Americans to Paris at the end of the war, McCormick, with his cousin and partner, Joseph Patterson, decided to build a European presence for their papers, the *Chicago Tribune* and the *New York Daily News*. In November 1918, a week after the armistice, McCormick gave flamboyant reporter Floyd Gibbons the job of creating two overlapping news organizations that built on the Army Edition framework: the *Tribune's* Foreign News Service and the European Edition of the *Chicago Tribune* and the *New York Daily News*, known as the Paris Edition.

The relationship between the two organizations was complicated, confusing, and occasionally contentious.

McCormick envisioned the Foreign News Service as an elite group of journalists reporting on the "most important assignment in history."[2] In pursuit of that vision, Gibbons hired reporters who had served in the Great War to head up permanent bureaus in London, Paris, and Berlin and to work as roving correspondents as needed. Secondary locations, including Vienna, Rome, and Constantinople, were home to bureaus, or at least full-time correspondents, whenever the news, or McCormick's whims, demanded it. In addition, much like the wire services, the *Tribune's* Foreign News Service drew on a network of local correspondents and freelance stringers in areas where there wasn't sufficient news of international interest for a full-time reporter. The *Tribune* paid local correspondents, American or otherwise, male and female, a retainer to be available when news was hot in their regions. Stringers received piece rates for articles when they were needed. The structure was constantly evolving, with correspondents themselves sometimes unclear on who was responsible for covering a particular story and who they reported to at any given moment. (Colonel McCormick contributed to the confusion, often giving instructions directly to his foreign correspondents without informing his managing editors.) Despite its structural uncertainties, the Foreign News Service successfully reported the news from across Europe, Latin America, and Asia, producing articles that ran in the *Chicago Tribune* and *New York Daily News* and subsequently were sold through a profitable syndication service to papers in smaller cities that wanted foreign news coverage beyond that provided by the wire services but could not, or did not want to, maintain reporters abroad.

By contrast, the famed Paris Edition, which operated from 1919 to 1934, was published for the benefit of the growing number of Americans who traveled abroad in the years between the wars. William Shirer, who worked there from 1925 to 1927, dubbed it "the world's zaniest newspaper"—a jab at the *Tribune's* subhead, "The World's Greatest Newspaper." The Paris Edition printed news from home for Americans abroad, news about Americans abroad, especially those in the expatriate colony on the Left Bank in Paris, and erudite reviews of the avant-garde literature, art, and music produced there. Its reporters, fueled by late nights and cheap wine, amused themselves by writing parody news features (at least one of which made it into print), phony column fillers, and announcements of the arrival and departure of fictional visitors for the society page.

Compared to its rival, the older, well-established *Paris Herald*, the Paris Edition was more literary, more irreverent, and more liberal in tone, taking stands on the issues of the day that stood in direct opposition to those espoused by its parent paper in Chicago, which were shaped by McCormick's own complicated, intertangled, and sometimes inconsistent political and intellectual positions. McCormick was isolationist, anti-Britain, and wary of Europe as a whole. He was hostile to the Eastern Seaboard in general and New York in particular. He was antisemitic in the same way he was Presbyterian—an inherited and unexamined belief. He was anti-Roosevelt (Franklin, not Theodore), an antipathy that ran both ways and would turn into a vicious feud during the Second World War. He was against Socialism, Communism, and most of the New Deal programs, which he believed were inherently Socialist, if not actually Communist, in nature. And he had his doubts about any form of entertainment that was not commercially viable, especially the "toot, toot, toot stuff" of opera. Except when he wasn't.

The Paris Edition's offices became a home away from home for Lost Generation luminaries like Henry Miller and James Thurber (both of whom worked there for a time) and Ernest Hemingway and F. Scott Fitzgerald (who liked to hang out there). It was also the training ground for a generation of foreign correspondents. For employees who caught the reporting bug, promotion from the Paris Edition to the Foreign News Service meant double the salary and an increase in prestige, though it may have meant a corresponding decrease in fun.

Little and Hecht were among the first American correspondents to arrive in Berlin after the war.

Dick Little was head of the *Chicago Tribune's* new Berlin bureau. He arrived in Berlin directly from the battlefields of eastern France, carrying only an Army musette bag and a typewriter. At fifty, he was a veteran war correspondent. He had covered the Spanish-American War from Cuba, Haiti, and the Philippines, the Russo-Japanese War of 1905 from Port Arthur on the Manchurian coast, and the Great War from Italy from 1915 to 1917. When the United States entered the Great War in 1917, he tried to enlist, but the army rejected him because of his age. Rather than applying for accreditation as a reporter by the AEF, he volunteered for another kind of war service, working with the YMCA, which provided canteens, classes, and entertainment for American troops on the front line.

Ben Hecht, later famous for his screenplays, such as *His Girl Friday* and *Scarface*, was half Little's age and a year younger than Schultz. He came to Berlin from Chicago's crime beat, accompanied by his wife, Marie, who was a reporter for the *Chicago Daily Journal* when they met.

They were as eager to meet Schultz as she was to meet them.

Schultz and her new friends had just raised glasses of champagne to toast their meeting, when she noticed the Chicagoans looking over her shoulder. She turned and found a group of gentlemen, some in formal evening attire, others in costumes, each bowing and deferring to the others. They reminded Schultz of the two main characters from the popular American comic strip *Alphonse and Gaston*, punctilious Frenchmen who never managed to go anywhere or do anything because each bowed and insisted the other go first.

Schultz thought it was hilarious. Little and the Hechts did not. They were frustrated by their inability to communicate with potential sources who were obviously interested in talking to them. The two reporters had already tried to converse with some of the Germans but found their English incomprehensible. And while Hecht spoke some German, Little claimed to know only two words: *ein* and *Bier*. As reporters, they depended on local stringers and tipsters to help them interview sources. Here on the dance floor, they were helpless.

Once she understood the problem, Schultz announced she would be happy to interpret for the group, just as she had translated at the meetings in Chadirchi's office. A few questions proved to her fellow guests that she could indeed translate, rapidly and accurately, between German, French, and English. After that, questions flew back and forth, with Schultz as the conduit between them.

While celebrating Berliners danced around them, a fluctuating group of Europeans—German businessmen and attorneys, retired military officers, French diplomats, and a Hungarian banker—besieged the American reporters in a corner of the ballroom, set apart by heavy brocade drapes. All of them were intent on telling the newsmen about the political and economic challenges facing the new-born German Republic and on learning what Americans thought about those challenges.

Occasionally an impatient wife dragged her husband back to the dance floor. Marie abandoned them for a turn around the ballroom whenever the opportunity presented itself. For her part, Schultz waved away the hopeful young men who invited her to dance. She was more interested in discussing politics than dancing the polonaise.

It was almost dawn when the European half of the conversation left the ballroom in search of hot coffee, which was still a luxury in postwar Germany, and *Pfannkuchen*, the jelly-filled doughnuts that are Berlin's traditional Karneval treat. Once they were gone, Schultz got her first lesson in American journalism. Ben Hecht grumbled about the all-night crash course in German history, saying the "milkman in Omaha" would not care. Seeing that Schultz was confused, Marie Hecht explained. Little and Hecht regularly reminded each other that everything they wrote "must be so clear or spectacular that even the milkman in Omaha understands it and finds it worth reading."

At that moment, the band swung into the waltz that traditionally marked the end of a Karneval ball.

As they left the party together, Little and Hecht teasingly accused Schultz of cheating them out of the eyewitness account of wartime Berlin from a young American that their host had promised them.

Marie Hecht laughed. "You'll get your story when you take her and me to tea at the Adlon."

Promising to meet again soon—three days at the latest—the four walked out to the Kurfürstendamm boulevard and went their separate ways in the icy dawn.[3]

The day after the ball, the pounding of field artillery, fired from the elevated Tiergarten station and a nearby water tower, broke into the quiet of the neighborhood where Schultz and her mother lived. It was the beginning of ten days of bloody street fighting.

Schultz decided to play it safe and canceled her classes—perhaps she felt she had taken enough chances walking to the ball the night before. She and Hedwig doubtless took their usual precautions in times of riots: filling the bathtub with water, setting candles where they were easy to reach, checking that the bunnies were safe in the hutch, and stuffing their most precious belongings into a satchel so they could grab them if they needed to run. Finally, there was nothing left to do but anxiously wait for the shooting to end. On and off all day, while Schultz tried to write notes on what she remembered from the conversation the night before, shells screamed over their apartment building and across the River Spree toward the Moabit neighborhood, an industrial and working-class area that was a center of leftist political activity. Machine-gun fire roared through the night, interrupted on occasion by combatants cheering a lucky hit. The windows were blown out in nearby buildings. The Schultz apartment remained intact.

For the next two days, the street battles centered first on Alexanderplatz, in the central city, then on the Potsdamer and Tiergarten stations. Both sides were armed with field artillery and mortars, which they used to alternately defend and attack the barricades and wire entanglements that turned city streets into the functional equivalent of trenches. The fighting was some of the bloodiest Berlin had suffered. By the end, Alexanderplatz resembled the French villages left battered by the end of the Great War; streets were strewn with the bodies of the dead and wounded.

On March 9, the workers' council ended the general strike, but the fighting continued as government troops drove the revolutionaries out of the city's center and Noske unleashed a bloody spate of public executions.

⁕

Several days later, when the worst of the violence in her neighborhood had run its course, Schultz ventured again through the riot-torn streets to the Hotel Adlon, determined to keep her promise to have tea with Little and the Hechts.

It was her first visit to the luxury hotel, which opened its doors in 1907 under the patronage of Kaiser Wilhelm and had entertained Europe's wealthy, noble, and notable ever since. While two bellboys, dressed in the hotel's signature sky-blue livery, hurried off to locate the Hechts and Dick Little, Schultz settled into an armchair and inspected the lobby, not knowing it would become as familiar to her as her family's apartment.

She later said that it felt like she had left a drab, cold Berlin behind and entered a brightly colored, international stage set. The ornately decorated lobby had suffered damage during the November Revolution and had been the center of a standoff between Spartacists and a group of Freikorps a few days before the January Uprising began. Now it was neutral ground. Politicians from all points on the Weimar political spectrum met in the hotel bar. Former members of the Russian aristocracy and representatives of Russia's postrevolutionary Provisional Government ignored each other when they crossed paths in the lobby. Diplomats from around the world, German bankers and industrialists, and foreign correspondents met there to make contacts, chase rumors, and spin political webs.

Schultz was amused to see the lobby was neutral ground in another way as well. On one side, stiff-backed dowagers dressed in what Schultz guessed was perpetual mourning, sneered over their teacups at a flutter of ostentatiously dressed "ladies" who sat nearby, more interested in catching the attention of the various Allied military officers congregated on the other side of the lobby than they were in their tea.

For their part, the officers seemed to be more interested in the bar than in the tea drinkers.

Schultz enjoyed speculating on the little dramas that played out in the lobby that afternoon, putting together stories from the details she observed, but she was happy to leave them behind when Ben Hecht appeared and shepherded her upstairs.

———

Over the past few days, the Chicago contingent had seen the revolution up close. As a result of their experiences, they had questions about Germany, past and present. Lots and lots of questions. Schultz was happy she could answer them.

While the "tea party" in the Hechts' room turned into another crash course in all things German, Ben Hecht got a wire from his paper's London office that enraged him—and Schultz got a second lesson in the business of journalism. Cable service to the United States from Central Europe was unreliable, so correspondents based in Berlin and other Central and Eastern European capitals sent their reports through their paper's offices in London or Paris. As a result, those offices exercised unofficial control over what news reached the United States. Based on information they received at the costume ball, Hecht had written a "think piece" describing the efforts of General Erich Ludendorff and his reactionary colleagues to increase the Allied powers' fear of the "Red Menace" and thereby lead them to see Berlin as a buffer between Soviet Russia and the rest of Europe. The London office insisted Hecht was underestimating the danger of Communism in Europe and refused to transmit his piece to Chicago. Schultz realized for the first time that getting the news out was as important as getting the story.

She left the hotel that afternoon determined to invite her new friends to the apartment to meet her mother and enjoy the soon-to-be famous Schultz hospitality.

———

Schultz almost canceled the party a few hours before their guests were due.

Early that morning, she had encountered a scene that upset her more than any of the violence she had witnessed during the revolution. An underfed cab horse collapsed on the street in an elegant district of the city. Men and women fell on the horse with axes and knives, butchering it where it lay. They ran past Schultz clasping chunks of meat and bone to their breasts. The elderly driver, almost as frail as his horse, tried at first to protect it from the scavengers with his whip. Finally, he took shelter in a doorway, weeping. Another man stood with him and assured the driver the horse was dead when it fell. The driver was not consoled. He had lost his income, and possibly his companion, in an instant. Almost as distraught over the incident as the driver, Schultz gave him what money she could and helped him to the nearest saloon for whatever comfort a few marks could buy.[4]

Hospitality had been an important part of Hedwig's life with Hermann, from their parties in Summerdale to their soirees in the Berlin studio. Throughout the war, Schultz and her mother had managed small gestures of hospitality, but with Hermann in Hamburg and their limited wartime resources, it had been a long time since Hedwig had given a real party. She had bustled around the apartment for days, making arrangements for their guests, polishing the silver Hermann had purchased at the Columbian Exposition in Chicago, and baking a cake, using flour Schultz acquired from the florist across the street in exchange for a bunny.

Worried that her mother would know something had happened, and not wanting to diminish Hedwig's pleasure in the party, Schultz hid in her bedroom, a small studio at some distance from the main apartment, trying to regain her composure before the guests arrived.

When the time came, neither Hedwig nor their guests noticed her agitation. They were all in a party mood.

Near the end of the evening, Schultz and her mother offered their guests a drink of good whiskey, from a carefully hoarded case a British client had sent Hermann before the war. Settling back to enjoy their drinks, the visitors complained about the quality of alcohol served at the Adlon bar. Then they shifted to a more serious problem: the unreliability of their "gunmen"—the journalists' nickname for their local translators and informants. Giving in to the temptation of a bad pun, they complained their gunmen weren't shooting straight with them. They kept back important news items or distorted them to reflect their own political views.

Drinks finished, the trio from Chicago left to check on the late news before sending out their final reports, part of the daily routine of all American newsmen stationed in Europe. As she showed them out through the garden, Schultz decided to tell them what she had seen earlier that day, partly because they had complained about things being kept from them and partly because she needed some sympathy. As she remembered it later, though, they were as shaken by the story as she had been. Their understanding and appreciation that she had shared her experience eased her distress.

through the garden, Schultz decided to tell them what she had seen earlier that day, partly because they had complained about things being kept from them and partly because she needed some sympathy. As she remembered it later, though, they were as shaken by the story as she had been. Their understanding and appreciation that she had shared her experience eased her distress.

A few days later, Schultz was on her way to have tea with Marie Hecht when she ran into Dick Little in the Adlon lobby. He had a bundle of German newspapers under his arm.

He took her into the Adlon reading room and handed her a newspaper. "Now is the time," he said, "for you to show that you understand highfalutin' German editorials by translating this for me."

The editorial he chose was a detailed discussion of the future German constitution. Knowing it was a test, Schultz translated the article carefully, stopping occasionally to explain a point that might not be obvious to an American. When she finished, Little exploded. Whether from laziness or duplicity, his "gunman" had left out critical passages when he translated the same editorial. What's more, Little ranted, every time he asked his assistant to make an appointment to interview an important German, the assistant claimed the man in question refused to talk to Americans.

Little gave Schultz a sharp look through his thick-lensed glasses. "Would you like to try your hand at a job as a combination interpreter and cub reporter?" he asked. "If you can get me the interviews I want, I'll make you the 'number two man' on the Berlin team."

It seemed to Schultz that everything in her life up to this point had been designed to prepare her for this job. She had the language skills. She knew how to look at current events within the context of the past. She had a network of sources that rivaled that of any native German tipster. And she was fascinated by politics. What better way to satisfy that fascination and use her skills than reporting from Europe for an American newspaper?

Schultz said yes—so quickly she didn't think to ask how much the job would pay until later. (She did have enough sense to tell him she would continue to teach her students in the evenings until her position as "number two" on the team was confirmed.)

Then she asked her new boss what interview she should track down first.

"Naval officers who will give me the German version of the Battle of Jutland," he answered.

Schultz didn't think that would be a problem.[5]

CHAPTER SIX

THE TRAINING OF A FOREIGN CORRESPONDENT

Tramping Berlin streets over barricades
was joy with your friends ex [from] home.
Stories just jumped up in your path.

—SIGRID SCHULTZ[1]

O ne of Dick Little's first assignments as the *Tribune*'s Berlin bureau
chief was to write an article on the German version of the Battle
of Jutland (May 31–June 1, 1916), which the Germans call the Battle
of Skagerrak.

It was the largest naval battle of World War I, and the only one in
which the British and German fleets directly confronted each other.
Britain and Germany both claimed to have won. In fact, neither side
had a decisive victory.

Colonel McCormick, who had been an artillery officer in the Great
War, was deeply interested in all things military. He was also no fan
of Great Britain, a position that would contribute to his isolationist
stance in the early years of the Second World War. McCormick suspected the British Navy's claim of victory at Jutland was overstated,
if not an actual lie.

Little had tried to interview someone at the Admiralty about the battle ever since he arrived, with no success. His "gunmen" all came back with
the same answer: the Admiralty would not give interviews to American
correspondents. The German Foreign Office gave him the same response.
By the time Little met Sigrid Schultz, McCormick was getting impatient.

Eager to prove herself, Schultz stormed the Admiralty Building late one afternoon, armed with her personal visiting cards and a note on the back of one of Little's business cards saying Miss Schultz was calling on the Admiralty on his behalf. She had carefully crafted a strategy to break through the German officers' resistance to talking to an American reporter.

The Admiralty Building was an imposing neoclassical structure built shortly before the Great War. It might as well have had a sign over the entrance saying "No Girls Allowed." Women, even those who worked in the building, were required to enter through the back. Schultz boldly came in the front door. Officers stopped in their tracks to stare at her—tiny, blonde, and undeniably female—as she crossed the Admiralty lobby and stopped at the front desk. She handed Little's card to the guard on duty and asked to be taken to the officer-in-charge of the press office. The guard, who was undoubtedly aware of the rules prohibiting such a thing, stared at the card dumbly. A ranking officer came to his rescue. After a glance at the card, he told the guard to take her to the press office. He then followed Schultz and her escort, disappearing into the office next door once she had been delivered.

The press officer politely offered her a seat, as if he were used to strange women appearing at his desk, and asked how he could help her. Politeness changed to icy hostility when she handed him Little's card. Schultz ignored the change in attitude and delivered her planned spiel: Perhaps Herr Little's previous assistants, being German citizens and consequently in awe of Germany's military officers, had hesitated to explain how the Admiralty's repeated refusal to allow him to speak with naval officers looked to an American reporter. (At this point, she probably opened her blue eyes wide, one of her favorite tricks for disarming recalcitrant male officials.) It would be—she paused, as if looking for the right word—embarrassing if Herr Little were forced to tell the owner of the *Chicago Tribune* that the Germans didn't want to talk to him because they knew they had lost the Battle of Jutland. An unstated threat added punch to her words: the Colonel would doubtless share that position in his newspaper, which reached four hundred thousand readers in a five-state region on weekdays and seven hundred thousand on Sundays—many of them of German descent.[2]

The officer shouted, "No, we won that battle!" Perhaps he pounded his fist on the table between them. Schultz doesn't say.

He made so much noise that the officer who had followed Schultz upstairs came into the room. He glared at the younger man, lowering bushy eyebrows over steel-blue eyes. "No one is allowed to use that kind of tone here," he told his subordinate. He glanced back at Schultz. "What this young lady said was certainly disagreeable, especially to a man who fought in the Battle of Jutland. On the other hand, I think we should consider her statement quite seriously."

It took a little more "palavering," as Schultz loved to say, but the deal was done. Schultz left the Admiralty with a promise that two officers would be detailed to talk to Herr Little about the battle.

The next day, two German officers in full regalia called on Little at the Adlon and scheduled an appointment to meet with him. Thereafter, Schultz and Little met with the officers every second day for two hours until early April.[3]

Schultz had earned the position of "number two man" at the *Tribune*'s Berlin bureau.

Schultz and Little were grateful the naval officers could only give them two hours a day, because Berlin was hopping with news stories in March and April 1919. As Schultz would later say, "That early year of 1919 was fabulously interesting because all the elements of the next twenty, thirty years were right there, visible."[4]

Paris drew members of the Lost Generation in the years immediately after the war. But Weimar Berlin—politically tense, bawdy, and creative—had its own allure. The third-largest city in the world, with a population of four million, Kaiser Wilhelm's stodgy, rather provincial capital became an international crossroads in the years after the war. Lilian Mowrer, wife of the Berlin bureau chief for the *Chicago Daily News* and a journalist in her own right, wrote in her memoir that Weimar Berlin reminded her "of a huge railway station; it was the stopping-off place between eastern and western Europe; everyone traveling from Paris to Moscow, sooner or later, came there."[5]

Weimar Berlin was the darker counterpart of interwar Paris, known for sex, drugs, and provocative cabaret acts. With the well-earned reputation of being the most licentious city in Europe, Berlin drew an international community of artists, political dissidents, journalists, intellectuals, and members of the Lost Generation engaged in what a later generation would term "finding themselves." It was a period of enormous, almost hyperactive, creativity. Artists of all types—in film, music, photography, the visual arts, and the many forms of theater that flourished in the city—drew energy from the prevailing sense that the social norms had been broken twice, first by the war and later by the revolution. As a result, anything was possible.

At the same time, Berlin was a political hot spot. The new Weimar Republic created an innovative and far-reaching social security net, but it did so with its back to the wall. The years between the wars were marked by repeated economic crises, constant street battles, and frequent, occasionally violent, political challenges from both the monarchist and nationalist Right, which had overlapping but not identical platforms, and the most extreme elements of the Socialist and Communist Left, which were even more divided than their counterparts on the extreme right. Over time, Lost Generation writers with a nose for news, like William Shirer, came to the conclusion that Berlin, not Paris, was the place where the news was being made.

⁂

Because Little did not speak German, he took Schultz along for many of his interviews. They became a regular sight walking the long hall of the Reichstag building that ran from the deputies' reading room to the deputies-only restaurant. Germans who insisted they didn't want to talk to Americans found their objections eroded when faced with the comic sight of Schultz sandwiched between a large German and Dick Little, who was a lanky six foot, six inches tall. Watching her scurry to keep up and translate at top speed as they walked was as good as a vaudeville act.

Weimar politics required negotiation and compromise between political parties. Centrist parties were committed to maintaining the republic as a democratic state. The monarchists and their close cousins, the pan-German nationalists, were opposed to the Weimar Republic, though their members held seats in the Reichstag because they knew refusing to participate in Weimar politics would leave them out of the decision-making process. The various shades of "Reds," who ranged from slightly left of the Social Democrats to full-blown Bolsheviks, were a constant disruptive force. No one party was able to hold enough seats in the Reichstag to form a government alone. Ebert's Social Democrats, then Germany's largest political party, built an alliance with the liberal German People's Party (DVP) and the Catholic Center Party. Known as the Weimar Coalition, this alliance successfully created governments for much of the period, though its hold on power was always tenuous.

Together, Schultz and Little interviewed leaders of every German political party. Schultz also translated for Little in meetings with Germans who stood on the front lines in the street violence that was a regular feature of Berlin politics. Whether they were interviewing an idealistic young German lieutenant who believed he and his men were fighting to save the world from Communism or a dozen equally idealistic Communists determined to avenge the deaths of their comrades at the orders of German officers, Schultz translated Little's questions and their answers as carefully as she could.

Little had already taught Schultz the importance of accuracy. More than once he turned down what Schultz thought would be "sensational yarns" because he couldn't find credible evidence they were true.[6] For example, German officers and tipsters regularly warned Little and the other foreign correspondents that Russia was poised to invade Germany. Most of the foreigners in Berlin seemed to believe it was true, and yet no one presented proof. Little wasn't willing to accept the story without confirming it from more than one source—a lesson Schultz would follow for the rest of her career. With no reliable source on the Russian threat, Schultz and Little spent evening after evening at Berlin's cavernous glass-and-iron Silesian Station, interviewing people as they arrived in Berlin from eastern Germany and eastern and southeastern Europe. No one they interviewed reported Russian troops massing near the borders. No proof, no story.

***

As Dick Little reported his way through the riots, mass meetings, street battles, and political tangles of 1919, Schultz "trotted by his side, an eager cub reporter."[7] Working with Little, Schultz got a crash course in reporting from a man whom Ben Hecht described as "a veritable Knight of Journalism."[8]

The exchange of knowledge went both ways. The arrangement with the Admiralty was Schultz's first victory in what would be an ongoing test of her creativity and determination in arranging interviews for Little—and providing the background information for those interviews. At some level, she translated not just the language but Berlin itself.

Having Schultz as a combination translator, "gunman," and cub reporter gave Little an advantage over other foreign correspondents stationed in Berlin. Enough of an advantage that several weeks after she began working for the *Tribune*, Ben Hecht offered her a regular job with the *Chicago Daily News*, which paid much better salaries than the *Tribune*. She turned him down, though she could have used the money. (With Hermann still ill in Hamburg, Schultz was supporting two households.) But she knew Hecht wasn't scrupulous about accurate reporting. Moreover, she had seen him lash out at an informant in public and didn't believe he had the patience to train her as a journalist, the way Little was.

Over and over Schultz demonstrated her ability to get an interview or find an unusual angle on a story by taking a backdoor approach when the front door wasn't working.

For example, in the weeks before he hired Schultz, Little repeatedly applied for interviews with army officers who had taken part in important battles during the war. The press divisions of both the Foreign Office and the army's general staff responded to each request with the same reply, transmitted through his "gunmen": the army's officers were far too busy to be interviewed by an American. Once she was a member of the *Tribune* team, Schultz saw arranging those interviews as a personal challenge. Instead of repeatedly trying to go through official channels, hoping to change "no" to "yes" by sheer obstinacy, she took advantage of personal contacts that no other American correspondent in Berlin had. On carefully chosen days, she dropped in for tea with the aristocratic old ladies she and her mother had befriended during the war, bringing treats that ensured her welcome. The ladies knew nothing about politics or battles, but they had younger male relatives—nephews and grandnephews, sons and grandsons—who had served in the war. Now many of those relatives were stationed in Berlin and they called on their delighted older relatives on a regular basis. (Schultz cynically speculated their main purpose in visiting was to make sure they inherited the old ladies' prized heirlooms. Of course, she, too, had an agenda for her visits.)

Sipping ersatz tea from precious Meissen china, Schultz listened to her hostesses tell stories about a past when they mingled with dukes, kings, and sometimes, the kaiser himself. When their military relatives dropped in to pay their respects, Schultz gave them tidbits of the American gossip that was important social currency in German military and political circles and sowed the idea that it might be important for officers to talk to an American correspondent. The process was slow, but eventually it resulted in an interview with Major Gerd von Rundstedt, who would become a field marshal under Hitler.

In March 1919, every correspondent in Berlin wanted to interview General Erich Ludendorff.

As deputy chief of the Imperial German army's general staff, Ludendorff was responsible for much of Germany's military strategy in the later years of the Great War. In March 1918, he launched a massive offensive on the Western Front, with the objective of crushing the Allied powers' armies before the Americans arrived. When that offensive failed, he joined Field Marshal Paul von Hindenburg's call for an armistice. After he learned the proposed terms for the armistice, he reversed his position and demanded Germany resume military action. Ludendorff resigned on October 26, a few weeks before the armistice went into effect, and fled to neutral Sweden.

Now Ludendorff was back in Berlin and living in a suite in the Hotel Adlon, which housed most of the Allied diplomats who were stationed in Germany and much of the foreign press corps.[9] Both groups were eager to talk to Ludendorff; he was equally eager to avoid them.

The Ludendorff suite was in a separate wing of the hotel, with a private entrance on Wilhelmstrasse, which meant that neither Ludendorff nor his wife had to walk through the hotel lobby, where they would be subject to ambush by diplomats and journalists. The hotel management prided itself on protecting their guests' privacy and made sure the private entrance was manned at all times by porters and hotel detectives. Nonetheless, on several occasions, Schultz convinced a friendly porter to look the other way while she slipped past him in exchange for a can of sardines or a few American cigarettes. (Small luxuries, and even basic necessities, were still hard to come by in 1919, and the staff of the Adlon was not immune to temptation.) She cornered the general several times, but he refused to talk, walking away from her as quickly as he could without abandoning his dignity.

Finally, Schultz found a way to learn Ludendorff's plans without talking to the general himself.

One afternoon when Schultz and Dick Little returned to the Adlon from the Reichstag, they found the lobby full of excited correspondents. Little took one look at them and said, "They think they have a scoop." If it was a big story, Little and Schultz needed to know before their filing deadline.

Leaving Schultz to find her own sources of information, he headed toward the bar, hoping he could coax his competitors' "gunmen" into sharing what they knew for the price of a glass or two of whiskey. Looking around the lobby, Schultz noticed two of the Adlon regulars, a wealthy political dilettante and dabbler in the arts named Arnold Rechberg and his sister. They came to the hotel twice a day: once at noon for an aperitif and again for afternoon tea. Rechberg would settle his sister at a table and then saunter across the lobby looking for someone to bore with his theories about the war and the peace. His current favorite topic was the Red hordes that he claimed would soon pour into Germany as a first step toward world conquest—also a favorite theme of Ludendorff's.

Normally, Schultz wouldn't have found their presence in the lobby unusual; they were as much a fixture as the double row of bellboys bowing to guests as they entered. On that day, though, the Rechbergs seemed to be unusually pleased with themselves. It occurred to Schultz that Rechberg, who had served as an aide-de-camp to the Imperial Crown Prince, was a natural monarchist and possibly one of Ludendorff's cronies.

When Rechberg headed toward the back of the hotel with a self-important strut, Schultz joined his sister at the tea table. Because the woman often looked lonely, Schultz had always made a point of speaking to her—genuine kindness to otherwise neglected people was a cornerstone of Schultz's network of friends and sources. Now those small acts of kindness paid off. The older woman was happy to see Schultz and, as always, ready to chatter about her brother. He had just enjoyed a long conversation with General Ludendorff, discussing important matters, she told Schultz. Now "Brother" was meeting the general in a salon off the private Wilhelmstrasse entrance to arrange interviews with him for some American and British correspondents.

The promise of interviews with the elusive general would explain why the journalists congregating in the lobby were so excited. Excited herself, Schultz flagged down a bellboy and gave him a note for Little explaining the situation. She suggested he try to get to the salon through the kitchens.

Taking her own advice, she smiled her way past the kitchen staff, through a darkened banquet hall, and into a small rococo salon, where Rechberg stood alone. He began talking as soon as Schultz walked in, without questioning why she was there. He was thrilled, *thrilled*, to have learned from Ludendorff himself that General Sir Neill Malcolm, the highest-ranking British military authority in Berlin, had promised British cooperation with Ludendorff's plan to assemble a

German army of three hundred thousand men in the east to fight the Communists. (The Versailles treaty, which would limit the German army to one hundred thousand men, had not yet been completed.) At the same time, Rechberg was also distraught. Ludendorff had just left, swearing he would not talk to the "international journalistic rabble that was Jewish or controlled by Jews"—the same rabble that was waiting in the hotel lobby for Rechberg to produce his promised interviews. He would walk right into them when he went back to the lobby to take "Sister" home.

Schultz offered a solution, if Rechberg would promise to introduce her boss to Ludendorff. He could leave through the private entrance. She would escort his sister to the front of the hotel, where he could pick her up in a cab. Then, Schultz asked where she should take his sister if he had to leave without her, making sure she got his address in addition to his gratitude.

Schultz kept her part of the bargain, but neither she nor Little were willing to rely on Rechberg keeping his promise. After giving the couple time to recover from the afternoon's excitement, they headed to the Rechbergs' apartment, where they found Rechberg, wearing a sumptuous dressing gown and lounging in a big easy chair while his sister fussed over him. When the reporters walked in, he straightened up into the stiff posture of a Prussian officer, and popped his monocle back in. Rechberg was proud of his association with the general and happy to expand on what he had told Schultz about Ludendorff's plans.

It turned out Little wasn't interested in the details of Ludendorff's plans to convince the Allied powers to allow him to set up a new German army. As he told Rechberg, he had known about them for weeks. (Thanks to the Germans who lectured him at the Karneval ball, a source he had no intention of sharing with Rechberg.) He *was* interested in who was supporting Ludendorff. Rechberg was happy to share everything he knew, and to hint about what he didn't know.

Back at the Adlon, Little decided they needed to get some English reactions to Ludendorff's unverified claims before he wired the story to Chicago. As luck would have it, a number of British and French officials were leaving a dinner at the hotel just as Schultz and Little arrived. The British officials were adamant that General Malcolm, whom they saw every day, had made no promises to Ludendorff.

Quotes from a general who had been so important during the war were still news, Little told Schultz, even secondhand and accompanied by denials from credible sources, especially when they were an exclusive.

———— ⊶⊷ ————

Schultz's on-the-job training with Dick Little ended in August 1919, when the *Tribune* reassigned him to Russia, where Soviet and White Russian forces were engaged in a bloody civil war. He had been at the Berlin office for less than a year.

While attached to the White Russian army, which was trying to recapture Petrograd from the Soviets, Little was injured by an artillery round. He received a severe scalp wound and an injury to his leg that left him with a permanent limp. He returned to Chicago, where he edited a popular column titled "A Line O' Type or Two" until he retired in 1936. Schultz remained in touch with him until his death in 1946.

Little always said discovering her was one of the things he was proudest to have done in journalism. Schultz, for her part, always considered him her "father in journalism."

CHAPTER SEVEN

MUSICAL CHAIRS

Miss Schultz . . . has developed into a reliable field correspondent although of course being a woman she is not
available for all assignments.

—HENRY WALES, Paris bureau, Foreign News Service,
to Robert McCormick, November 18, 1922[1]

Although small, her production has been reliable and often
exclusive. Noteworthy for responsiveness to emergencies
in Germany and to requirements of home office. Energetic,
nose for news, straight reporter, alert.

—JOSEPH PIERSON, *Tribune* cable editor,
to Robert McCormick, January 24, 1924[2]

After Dick Little's departure, the *Tribune*'s Berlin bureau experienced a constant churning of chief correspondents.

Colonel McCormick moved his correspondents across Europe
as easily as he moved the colored pins with which he tracked them
on a large world map in his Chicago office. Moves were triggered by
major stories, by McCormick's often inaccurate belief that he could
sense when and where a story would break, and sometimes by a correspondent's own actions. (One of Schultz's later bosses, George Seldes, the Berlin bureau chief on and off between 1920 and 1925, set
off correspondent musical chairs twice—in May 1923, when he left
Moscow in a well-publicized protest against the Soviet government's
censorship of foreign correspondents' stories, and again in July 1925,
when Benito Mussolini's government kicked him out of Italy for, as

he put it, honest reporting.) The only constants were John Steele, who headed the London bureau from 1919 to 1935, Henry Wales, who was permanently based in Paris (with an occasional trip to cover breaking political events in countries where the *Tribune* had no reporters), and Sigrid Schultz herself, whose reliable presence in Berlin provided an anchor for the entire system.

Little was replaced by Parke Brown, a *Tribune* political reporter who was attached to General Pershing's headquarters during the war, traveled with the American Army of Occupation into Germany after the war, reported on the Paris Peace Conference, and remained at the Paris bureau after the Treaty of Versailles was signed on June 28, 1919. Schultz later described him as a conscientious and hardworking man who was a joy to work with, something she would not say about all her colleagues.

Schultz played much the same role for Parke Brown and the chief correspondents who followed him as she had for Dick Little, using her language skills, her understanding of German culture and history, and her ability to find unconventional ways to access sources. As George Seldes put it, she got the facts and he wrote the report.

Riots, attempted revolution, and street battles between government forces, Reds, and monarchists remained constant elements of Berlin life, with machine guns hidden in doorways, ready for use. But Schultz spent less time climbing barricades and running after active shooters with her later bosses than she had with Little. Much of the work was routine. Seldes estimated foreign correspondents spent 90 percent of their time at their desks, scanning newspapers and government handouts, reading reports from the wire services, and working the telephones, not to mention writing. An assistant correspondent added semi-clerical tasks to the mix: keeping the log of future assignments, maintaining—or in Schultz's case, initiating—contact with possible news sources, transmitting stories to the home office, and checking that the transmissions went through.

In March 1920, Schultz got her first chance at reporting a major story on her own, though her role was not publicly acknowledged. Parke Brown was in Hamburg covering the second of two plebiscites that would decide whether the province of Schleswig would be under German or Danish rule. It was a hotly contested issue that everyone expected would be the big news story of the week. As a result, Schultz was the *Tribune's* "man on the spot" in Berlin when a civil servant named Wolfgang Kapp and a cabal of German army officers attempted to overthrow the Weimar Republic.

On February 29, 1920, the German defense minister, Gustav Noske, under Allied pressure, ordered that two powerful Freikorps brigades be deactivated. Both had been active in Munich and Berlin during the Spartacist uprising, and their leaders were violently opposed to the idea of a democratic German government. One commander, Hermann Ehrhardt, refused to disband his unit. Worse, General Walther Lüttwitz, the army's commander in Berlin, announced he would not accept the loss of such an important military asset. In a meeting with Noske and President Ebert on March 10, Lüttwitz not only demanded that the order to disband the Freikorps units be revoked but also that the National Assembly be dissolved, new elections be held for the Reichstag, and he be named the supreme commander of the German army. In response, Noske and Ebert told Lüttwitz they expected his resignation the next day.

Instead of resigning, Lüttwitz went to Ehrhardt and asked if his brigade was prepared to occupy Berlin. Ehrhardt asked for another twenty-four hours to put things in motion.

Lüttwitz then contacted Kapp and a group of conspirators who had been toying with the idea of establishing an authoritarian government that would restore the imperial federal structure, minus the emperor. (Their goal could be described as "government by the upper bureaucracy for the upper bureaucracy.") Lüttwitz asked them to be ready to take over the government on March 13.

Ehrhardt marched his troops into the center of Berlin on the evening of March 12, 1920. The regular army, which had put down leftist uprisings in January and March without compunction, refused to defend the city against the Freikorps.

Without the army's support, the cabinet fled, leaving ten minutes before the Freikorps arrived to occupy the chancellor's office. By six thirty on the morning of March 13, the rebels were in possession of Berlin, or at least the government offices. Kapp declared himself chancellor and formed a provisional government, ensuring the revolt would be known as the Kapp Putsch rather than the Lüttwitz Putsch. Lüttwitz became the commander in chief, the minister of defense, and the real power in the provisional government.

When news of the coup reached Chicago, McCormick ordered Floyd Gibbons and other experienced *Tribune* reporters to Berlin to cover the story. What sounded reasonable from Chicago proved to be difficult to execute in Europe.

It is easy to forget that Friedrich Ebert and the cabinet members who belonged to the Social Democratic Party were skilled artisans before they were politicians—and union men to the core. As they fled Berlin, they called for a general strike to defeat the putsch. The trade unions stepped up. The strike began in Berlin on March 14. By the next day it had spread across the country. Twelve million workers went on strike, including the rank and file of the government bureaucracy. Shops and factories closed. Gas, electrical, and water service was cut off. More importantly, at least from the perspective of reporters trying to get to Berlin, the streetcars and railroads stopped running.

Instead of trying to make her way home through street battles between Freikorps members and striking workmen, Schultz chose to stay at the *Tribune* office in the Hotel Adlon. (Machine-gun fire in front of the Adlon helped her make up her mind.) She had a supply of candles, which she stuck in bottles to work by, and a small stash of food hidden in the bathroom for just such emergencies.

Several times, Schultz slipped out the back door of the hotel and headed toward Wilhelmstrasse, where most of the government buildings were located, hoping to learn the latest news. Once she made it as far as the intersection of Wilhelmstrasse and Unter den Linden, only to find her way blocked by field artillery and barbed-wire entanglements. When she tried to bypass them, two machine-gun-toting soldiers stopped her and pointed to a sign stating anyone going further would be shot. Another time, she got as far as the Prince Leopold Palace, when a correspondent for the United Press yanked her into the doorway of the German Foreign Office just as a burst of machine-gun fire swept the street.

Floyd Gibbons, who had made his way as far as Cologne, managed to get a call through to Schultz at the Adlon, even though telephone service had been reduced to emergency calls only. The connection was bad and it was her first long-distance phone call. In an effort to be heard, she allowed her operatically trained soprano to creep up the scale. Eventually she realized that was the wrong approach and forced her voice into an unnaturally low register. Once Gibbons could hear her, she reported that battles were being fought in the street right outside the Adlon, and corpses had been dragged into the hotel lobby. The *Tribune's* first story on the putsch ran on the front page of the March 14 edition, with a screamer headline across all columns but no byline. Details in the piece suggest that much of the material came from Schultz.

Parke Brown made his way back to Berlin, despite the general transportation strike, and Schultz resumed her duties as "number two." But she had gotten a taste for reporting. When Floyd Gibbons reached Berlin a few days later, with information on the impact of the putsch in Ruhr, he asked if she took dictation. She lied and said no. Telling the story many years later, she said she thought it was the only time she refused to do some work that she could have done, "but when you know what you want you must sometimes have the courage to take a chance and gamble and drop the working girl meekness."[3]

The strike successfully brought the putsch to an end. After considerable negotiation between the revolutionary leaders and the four major political parties, the legitimate government returned to power. Hermann Ehrhardt was allowed to remain in command of his brigade, which was permitted to march out of Berlin as a military unit.

Schultz and Parke Brown watched from the windows of the *Tribune* office as the Ehrhardt Brigade marched in formation down Unter den Linden toward the Brandenburg Gate on their way out of Berlin. A crowd stood on the sidewalk outside the hotel and jeered at the soldiers as they passed. When they reached the corner of Unter den Linden and Wilhelmstrasse, the rear guard turned, raised their rifles, and fired at the heckling crowd.

Conflicts between evacuating troops and unarmed crowds continued outside the hotel over the course of the day, with increasing civilian casualties. When Schultz was finally able to go home, she had to climb over bodies of the dead and wounded to get out of the Adlon lobby—described in the *Tribune's* in-house employee paper as a "grewsome [sic] moment."

After a year on the job, Parke Brown, like Dick Little before him, was transferred from the Berlin bureau to report on a political hot spot—in his case, Poland, where war with Russia over the new state's eastern frontier was coming to a head. His replacement, George Seldes, traveled to Berlin from a dead-end assignment in Stockholm, the result of one of McCormick's bad guesses about where the next big story would occur. He arrived in late July, after Parke Brown had already reached Warsaw, and complained to McCormick that he had to start with "almost no information about news sources, methods of conducting the office or the usual routine."[4] Schultz surely set him straight on all of it.

Over the next few years, Schultz worked at different times under Seldes, Larry Rue, and John Clayton as they moved from assignment to assignment, following the news in Constantinople, Rome, Moscow, or the Baltic states.

As time went on, her bosses spent more time away from Berlin, tracking special stories, and Schultz played a more important role in the office. One of those occasions gave Schultz her first chance at reporting a big story under her own byline.

In the fall of 1922, society pages and political reporting overlapped in the story of the former kaiser's second marriage to Hermine Reuss of Greiz (modern Thuringia), which was to occur in Huis Doorn, his home-in-exile in the Netherlands on November 9. (No one ever mentions it, but it was also her second marriage.) As the wedding drew near, correspondents all over Europe plotted ways to get insider details about the ceremony.

George Seldes, the Berlin chief correspondent, was in Moscow. Schultz was once again doing the work of acting bureau chief without benefit of the job title or the salary.

On October 6, she wrote to Floyd Gibbons, suggesting ways to get someone into the wedding, including a tongue-in-cheek suggestion that they stage an airplane accident in the Huis Doorn grounds. She had already reached out to "all kinds of princely people" with the hope of getting their reports and photographs from the event. She planned to send a "legman" to the prospective bride's home region, hoping to bribe one of the princess's servants or former governesses. She thought it would be easy: "The princess is very stingy and pays almost no wages."[5]

As October drew to an end, Henry Wales, who was managing the Foreign News Service from the Paris office in Gibbons's absence, wrote to McCormick to get clarity on plans for covering the wedding. He expected Larry Rue to arrive in Berlin any day and had planned to send either Rue or Schultz to Doorn. However, he informed McCormick, with some irritation at having received the news secondhand, he learned from Miss Schultz that a Colonel Thomason had wired directly to Chicago and offered to cover the event for the *Tribune* for $1,500—roughly equal to $24,000 today. Thomason claimed to have an invitation to the wedding and planned to relay the story to his wife, who would be waiting for it in Utrecht. Miss Schultz, who tended to know this kind of thing, told Wales she doubted any American had been invited to the ceremony. Wales ended his letter saying he assumed the matter would have been resolved by the time McCormick read it.

Rather than resolving the matter one way or another, McCormick and Wales assigned the story to different people. McCormick gave Thomason—whom cable editor Joseph Pierson dubbed "our $1500 gamble"[6]—the assignment on his proposed terms. Wales, hedging the *Tribune's* bet, decided to send Schultz to Doorn to cover the event as well.

***

Schultz had trouble getting the necessary documents to leave Germany, but when the day came, she was one of the crowd of reporters besieging the castle at Doorn. She was frustrated. Her only informant in the castle had passed along stories that Schultz, and every other reporter there, had already read in the Dutch papers. It was her first big out-of-town assignment and she couldn't bear the idea of being "licked." Then her luck turned.

The day was cold and clammy. The little hotel where Schultz was staying was poorly heated. She went down to the basement kitchen for a pitcher of hot water, hoping the warmth would help her write the few details she had been able to gather. There she found a group of wedding guests, still hungry after a scanty meal at the formal reception, raiding the kitchen because they didn't want to deal with the journalists who were hanging out in the hotel dining room. One of the guests, an elderly lady who recognized Schultz's face but had clearly forgotten she was one of the journalists they were trying to avoid, waved her over and made space for her at the table. Schultz sat. Without giving herself away, she listened to the woman and her friends discuss the wedding.

Finally, Schultz managed to get away from the group, who were still not aware they had been talking to a reporter. She rushed to file her story at the local post office, smugly certain she had scooped every reporter there.

Her smugness was short-lived. On the train back to Berlin she learned most of the other reporters had made arrangements to file their stories through the larger post office in nearby Utrecht. They told Schultz her story would never get through in time to make the morning edition. While "the boys" bragged about their wonderful inside stories,

Schultz sulked. She had more accurate material—and more of it—than any of them. But it wasn't worth anything if it hadn't gotten through.

Still unhappy when she reached Berlin, she went straight to the office from the train, where she found one of the rare and valued cables of congratulation that McCormick sent his reporters for a job well done—her first. Expecting the crowds of reporters who descended on Doorn, the Dutch had organized a special telegraph service there, with English-speaking clerks who could clear copy quickly and efficiently. The office in Utrecht, which was not used to dealing with press interest in the royal exile, was unprepared for the volume of copy. Wires sent from Utrecht were held up, sometimes for hours. Schultz had scooped everyone, including Colonel Thomason, whose arrangements to get the story failed completely.

⸺ ◦⸭◦ ⸺

John Clayton was the last Berlin bureau chief that Sigrid Schultz called boss.

Clayton had been a foreign correspondent for the *Tribune* since the beginning of the Foreign News Service. He was hired by Colonel McCormick himself at the end of the war, in which he had served as a flight instructor in the Army Air Force. Like most of McCormick's foreign correspondents, Clayton had spent the intervening years traveling. He reported from India in 1920, where he uncovered a plot by Indian nationalists to assassinate the Prince of Wales. In 1921, he was one of several *Tribune* reporters sent to Russia to uncover the extent of the famine there. In 1922, McCormick sent him to Constantinople, where trouble was brewing between Greece and Turkey, with a little help from Great Britain.

Clayton was invalided out of Constantinople in November 1922 after he contracted a dangerous case of typhoid. When he recovered enough to go back to work in February 1923, he was assigned to Berlin. George Seldes warned Schultz that the *Tribune* grapevine said Clayton had wanted the Berlin position as a permanent posting for at least a year and that he was maneuvering to displace the current bureau chief, Larry Rue.

If Seldes was correct that Clayton wanted a permanent post in Berlin in November 1922, the appeal of the assignment soon wore off. The following October he complained to McCormick that "life is not pleasant in Berlin today." He was not exaggerating.

Berlin had been considered a cushy assignment when Clayton arrived. Along with Geneva, it was seen as a less arduous posting where correspondents could recover from health problems, to which all of them were prone as a result of the stress of dealing with war zones, bad food, constant travel, physical danger, and censorship, which was not limited to having copy subjected to the censor's ubiquitous blue pencil. Correspondents working in countries with totalitarian governments in the years between the war faced imprisonment, physical threats, or being thrown out of the country when they angered hostile governments.

A year later, hyperinflation had the country by the throat. In the summer of 1922, the exchange rate was 400 marks per dollar. By January 1, 1923, the mark's value had dropped to 7,000 marks per dollar and sank at an increasing speed thereafter. By mid-November, the rate was 1.3 trillion marks to the dollar.[7] American correspondents, paid in dollars, were protected from the worst of the inflation, but dollars could not protect them from the erratic food supply caused by the mark's volatility.

Hyperinflation was accompanied by a general slump in business, declining exports, and rising unemployment. Berlin and other German cities were rocked by food and unemployment riots, many of which contained a violent antisemitic element. Cries of *"Strasse frei!"* (Clear the streets!) became familiar as the police were called out to control the mobs.

On November 8, 1923, two weeks after Clayton's letter to McCormick, an obscure politician named Adolf Hitler, egged on by General Ludendorff, attempted what Clayton described in a front-page article as a "comic opera monarchist revolt in Bavaria."[8]

Hitler's Beer Hall Putsch was the only major event in the rise of the Nazis that Schultz missed. She spent that fall in the United States for a well-earned furlough, the first time she had been "home" since she had left at the age of eight. She sailed back to Europe from New York on November 2. Her absence may have been one reason Clayton was finding life in the Berlin office hard. Schultz was used to running the office without a bureau chief, but none of her bosses were accustomed to working without her as backup.

Despite his complaints, Clayton headed the Berlin bureau until April 1924, when he happily turned the office over to George Seldes and relocated to Vienna.

Clayton returned to Berlin as bureau chief in February 1925, a few days before Friedrich Ebert checked into a hospital with what he believed was the flu. It proved to be appendicitis. The official report claimed there was no reason to worry about the president's condition. With all reporters banned from the hospital, there was no obvious way to verify how sick Ebert was.

In what she later described as a case of "journalistic luck," Schultz had a bad case of bronchitis (a recurring ailment throughout her life) when the news that the Weimar Republic's first president was in the hospital reached the *Tribune* office. Her voice was gone and she was shivering with fever, but she had gone to the office anyway, convinced that the best cure for bronchitis was work and also concerned that she not be written off as physically incapable of doing the job. As she would write much later, "It is never very good when people suddenly start feeling anxious about the poor little working woman's health. Many a time I carried on with fever or the 'flu or whatever ailment hit me at the time, because I did not want anybody to be tempted to say 'naturally, women are not as strong as men.'"[9]

Faced with the hospital ban on reporters, Schultz decided to use her illness to get the "dope"—her favorite word for hard-to-get information. She called the hospital where Ebert was being treated, exaggerated her "raucous sick voice," and arranged to be admitted as a patient.

Once in the hospital, Schultz managed to talk herself into a room on Ebert's floor. The doctor who examined her was more concerned about her heart than her lungs. He insisted she needed at least ten days of bed rest. A rest cure probably sounded good given her run-down physical condition. Unfortunately, it would not allow her to move around the hospital to get information about Ebert. Schultz took a chance and confessed she was there to get the Ebert story. Instead of throwing her out, the doctor made a deal with her: he would play reporter and get her the information she needed if she would rest quietly.

Schultz never found it easy to rest. Just as she had during her days at the lycée in Paris, she would work hard and play hard until her body forced her to stop, then she would retreat to a health spa for several weeks "on vacation," or better yet, in conjunction with traveling for a story.

Schultz spent a week in the hospital "watching Ebert die to get a scoop for the paper."[10] Two days before the president died, while official press releases were still reporting that he was fine, Schultz called in the story that he was dying from a burst appendix.

The first story using her material appeared on February 25, with the headline "Ebert Sinks: In Crisis as Fever Mounts" over John Clayton's byline. (The *New York Times* was still reporting steady improvements in Ebert's condition on February 27.)

Clayton also got the credit for subsequent stories. Once again, Schultz gathered the information and her boss got credit for the scoop.

When Clayton returned to the Berlin bureau in 1925, he made it clear he wanted the assignment to be permanent. He'd had "a bellyful" of traveling. Now that his children were older, he was ready for a position where he could make a home.

Writing much later about Clayton's term as bureau chief in 1925, Schultz claimed he "spent a great deal of time taking care of his health in an elegant suburb and improving his golf game while I cabled most of the news under his name."[11] The evidence of his correspondence and his bylines don't support this. It is possible that, fifty years after the fact, Schultz confused Clayton's actions in 1925 with a health-related leave of absence he took in the middle of his earlier Berlin assignment in 1923. At that time, he was assigned to Geneva, where, by his own account, for six weeks he played eighteen holes of golf every morning, covered the Geneva conference in the afternoon, and kept regular hours. (A luxury no correspondent enjoyed in Berlin.) Meanwhile Schultz ran the Berlin bureau, with all the responsibility, none of the authority, and Clayton second-guessing her from a distance.

Throughout the summer and fall of 1925, Clayton traveled through Central Europe, reporting from Poland, Bulgaria, Transylvania, and the Locarno Pact conference in Switzerland. While he traveled in pursuit of news outside Germany, Schultz once again ran the office on her own and earned bylines on important stories in Germany, including those surrounding Field Marshal von Hindenburg's election as president, a critical moment in the history of the Weimar Republic. The popular war leader was nominated by the monarchists and accepted with great discomfort by the centrist parties. He rejected the nomination twice before he reluctantly agreed to run for president after Ebert's death in May 1925. Hindenburg was elected by an enormous margin—an emblem of just how far the Weimar Republic had drifted from its revolutionary roots. And though he swore to uphold the republic's constitution, he was not at heart a republican.

In late October, McCormick asked whether Clayton would like to move to Rome on permanent assignment as a replacement for Larry Rue. A week later, what had previously been phrased as a possibility became an instruction: "Wish Clayton proceed take over Rome Bureau leaving Schultz on carrying Berlin."[12]

Not surprisingly, Clayton objected.

Decades later, Schultz told several versions of Clayton's efforts to keep the Berlin assignment. They vary in their details and conflict with the existing correspondence between Clayton and McCormick, but the broad outlines are always the same. In each case, she reads the draft of a telegram to McCormick in which Clayton makes the argument that Schultz should not be given the Berlin office. The reasons vary, but all relate to her being a woman. She confronts him, sometimes in company with his co-conspirators, John Steele and Henry Wales, in the *Tribune*'s office, sometimes alone in the Adlon bar. She threatens to expose him with his frequent absences from the office if he sends the telegram, having kept copies of the stories she filed under his name. (In one version of events, she points out that it would be easy to prove which stories were hers because his were always neatly typed and hers were definitely not.) And then she congratulates herself that the telegram was not sent and that Clayton subsequently left without a fight. (In one account, she claims that when confronted with the truth, John Steele was ashamed of how he had been manipulated and was thereafter her ally.)

In fact, Clayton did fight the change in appointment.

The day after he received the telegram, he responded with a long letter that boiled down to "Berlin is more important, and like most of us I am selfish enough to want the most important job." He did not argue that Schultz was not competent to do the job, as she claimed in her various accounts. Instead, Clayton suggested McCormick send Schultz to Rome in his place, on the grounds that she spoke Italian and, moreover, she could do the job at less expense—a statement he made as if it were a truth that required no explanation and that was undoubtedly based on her status as an unmarried woman. He had discussed the idea with Steele and Wales, and they agreed it would be "an excellent arrangement."[13]

McCormick's response left no room for argument. Clayton was to leave for Rome immediately after the Reichstag had approved the Locarno treaties. Rue was prepared to turn over the Rome bureau on January 15. As for Clayton's suggestion that Miss Schultz take Rome?

It was totally unacceptable. The potential danger was too great: "there are apt to be riots and revolutions and news of street fighting."[14]

Unlike Berlin?

On December 26, 1925, John Clayton finally conceded his term as the Berlin bureau chief was over. He sent McCormick a telegram saying he would leave Berlin on the night of the thirtieth, arriving in Rome on the morning of January 1.[15]

Despite what appear to be fundamental inaccuracies and inconsistences in Schultz's memories of the events that preceded Clayton's departure, one idea at their heart rings all too true: her assertion that, as a "working girl," "you quite often have to fight for your rights."[16] It would not be the last time that she felt a male colleague looking at her job with a covetous eye.

CHAPTER EIGHT

FRONT-PAGE GIRLS, STUNT REPORTERS, SOB SISTERS, AND MOB SISTERS

They are the front-page girls who somehow have weathered storms of prejudice—the odd creatures who have been pictured as doing things only slightly more impossible than they all have attempted at one time or another.

—ISHBEL ROSS, *Ladies of the Press:
The Story of Women in Journalism by an Insider*, 1936[1]

Sigrid Schultz is frequently described as the first woman to be the foreign bureau chief of a major American newspaper, a title that she claimed for herself loudly and often in later years. It is not as monumental a claim as it seems at first glance, given that foreign news bureaus as an institution were established in 1919, shortly after the end of World War I.

Moreover, it might not be true. The same claim is made about Schultz's longtime "frenemy" Dorothy Thompson, who became head of the *Philadelphia Public Ledger*'s Berlin bureau at much the same time—a counter-claim that infuriated Schultz for much of her life. In fact, the question of which woman held the distinction is meaningless. As Schultz admitted in a letter to her former boss and old friend, George Seldes, in 1973, the two women's appointments as bureau chiefs occurred within a few weeks of each other. If you drop the qualifier "for a major American newspaper," the title belonged to neither of them. Mary Boyle O'Reilly became the London bureau chief for an American news syndicate, the Newspaper Enterprise Association (NEA), in late 1913.

Whether she was the first or not, Schultz was the only woman to head a foreign news bureau for most of her career. And she held the position at a time when few women worked as what her contemporary Ishbel Ross called "front-page girls," a term Schultz would have categorically rejected, along with "girl reporter" and even "newspaperwoman." Her preferred title was newspaperman.

∾

Women became journalists in increasing numbers in the mid-1880s—part of the wave of "New Women" who challenged traditional limitations on middle- and upper-class women in many ways, all of which centered on ideas of female autonomy. Seeking the financial independence that made other forms of autonomy possible, women entered the workforce not only as professionals but as shop girls, secretaries, typists, and telephone operators. (It should be pointed out that the idea of women working outside the home was new only in the middle and upper classes. Women from the lower classes and women of color had often worked outside the home. In addition, women whose families farmed or worked as artisans generally played an active role in the family businesses. It is all too easy to filter women's history through the lens of privilege.)

US Census figures prove that the visible increase in newspaper-women was not an illusion based on male fears and vocational insecurities. In 1870, the Census reported that 35 women worked as reporters and editors; by 1900, thirty years later, out of a total of 20,098 reported journalists, 2,193 were women. According to historian Alice Fahs, this underrepresented the number of women working as journalists, because many women worked for newspapers on an occasional basis as "stringers," who were paid on space rates rather than as salaried reporters.[2]

For the most part, women were limited to reporting "soft news"—fashion, society news, and other traditionally female domains—but a few pushed their way into jobs as beat reporters, news service staffers, and even editors, usually of the women's pages. A number of women were assigned stories on sensational criminal trials, especially those with a female angle. (Editors assumed women reporters, known as "sob sisters," would include subjective observations related to the emotional aspects of a trial—observations they believed a male reporter might miss—as well as factual reporting.) A handful caught the public imagination as "stunt girl" reporters, who went undercover as workers in textile sweatshops, patients in public hospitals, and in the case of Nellie Bly, an inmate in a mental institution, becoming part of the story as well as reporting it. (Their male counterparts were called investigative journalists. There was a reason Schultz called herself a newspaper*man*.)

⸺⸎⸺

The Great War provided new opportunities for women journalists.

Some were already in Europe when the war started and were among the first to report from the front lines. Mary Boyle O'Reilly of the NEA hurried to Belgium from London a few days after the war began, carrying a change of clothes, emergency rations, and $500 in gold. She filed her first report on August 11, a week after Germany marched into neutral Belgium—a graphic account of the aftermath of battle that was only possible because combatant nations did not yet have press controls in place. May Birkhead of the *New York Herald* and Carolyn Wilson of the *Chicago Tribune*, both of whom wrote society and fashion news from Paris, added war correspondent to their job descriptions. Birkhead, a seamstress who stumbled into a thirty-year career as a journalist with a firsthand account of the sinking of the *Titanic*, wrote feature stories about the war and later reported on the Versailles peace conference. Wilson, who continued to write her illustrated fashion column throughout the war, filed thoughtful political analyses and reported pieces from both sides of the front, described by the *Tribune* as "the news of the battle front as a woman sees it."[3]

No women received official press accreditation with the American Expeditionary Force (AEF) during World War I, but a number of female journalists reached the front as "visiting correspondents." Soon after the war began, the *Saturday Evening Post*, which had the largest circulation of any American magazine at the time, sent popular novelists Cora Harris and Mary Roberts Rinehart to Europe as reporters. (Rinehart was the first journalist to visit the frontline trenches.) Freelancers, veteran newspaperwomen, reporters for women's magazines like *Good Housekeeping* and *Ladies' Home Journal*, and journalists with assignments from general interest magazines, like *Scribner's* and *Collier's*, followed in their footsteps.[4] Their shared assignment was to cover the "woman's angle" of the war, by which editors probably meant human-interest stories. Women journalists expanded that mandate to cover more than life at the home front, reporting from the trenches and frontline hospitals as well as from wartime capitals.

Perhaps the most unusual of these was self-styled "girl reporter" Peggy Hull, who arrived in Paris at the same time as the AEF. After her arrival, Colonel McCormick hired her to contribute chatty pieces to the *Tribune*'s Army Edition. Under the heading "How Peggy Got to Paris," Hull wrote about her experiences as an unofficial guest of General Pershing and the AEF at an unnamed training camp that was easily identifiable as La Valdahon, at least until the accredited reporters made a fuss about the access she was enjoying and got her kicked out.

After the war, it was easier for women to get newsroom assignments back home, though they remained a minority. For example, several contemporaries of Schultz's, dubbed "mob sisters" by historian Beth Fantaskey Kaszuba, made their way into the *Tribune*'s newsrooms covering the crime beat during Prohibition.

At the same time, women of the Lost Generation came to Europe, and, like their male counterparts, they wrote to support themselves and to understand their European experience. A few became important correspondents with international reputations, most notably Dorothy Thompson and Anne O'Hare McCormick, the first woman to win a Pulitzer Prize for journalism. Others who were less well known also used their European experience as a step up in decades-long careers as journalists and authors. Irene Corbally Kuhn, for instance, already had several years of newspaper experience in Syracuse and New York City when she headed to Europe. Like so many others, she landed at the *Chicago Tribune*'s Paris Edition, where she wrote fashion and society news and feature articles, including a series on the American Army of Occupation in Germany. She went on to report for the International News Service in Honolulu and Shanghai before returning to the United States, where she worked for various publications over many years.

Still others worked as local correspondents, stringers, and freelancers. The *Tribune* hired several women in this capacity. In fact, soon after Schultz took over as Berlin bureau chief, George Seldes hired an experienced newspaperwoman named Enid Wilkie to do the routine bureau work for the Vienna offices. Before the *Tribune* hired her, she worked for the *New York Times* in The Hague during the war, transferred to Vienna after the war, and subsequently, was replaced by a male correspondent. Writing to McCormick about her appointment, Seldes reported "Wales and Clayton, who know her work for years, say she is very good."[5]

He didn't even add "for a woman."

CHAPTER NINE

THE "RIGHT MAN" FOR THE JOB

Dear Kollege [sic], This is just a line to tell you how thoroughly pleased I was to hear of your appointment. Without any aspersions on your predecessors, most of whom I know and who are my friends, it's an open secret that you've really been No. 1 for a long, long time. If anybody ever deserved this recognition, you're IT. Best of luck to you in your new old job!

—FREDERICK KUHL, United Press, Berlin, January 20, 1926[1]

My dear Miss Schultz: I just had a letter from Louis P. Lochner, telling me you had been made chief of the Tribune bureau. My heartiest congratulations. It is a change in title alone, for you have been the man behind the guns for a long, long time. But after all there is more satisfaction in the title. I hope this one has come to you along with an increase in salary to make it all the more acceptable.

—CHARLES STEPHENSON SMITH,
Associated Press, London, February 23, 1926[2]

When Sigrid Schultz became the chief correspondent of the Berlin bureau, the *Tribune's* Foreign News Service boasted nearly thirty foreign correspondents, located in what the *Tribune's* public relations staff described as "the frontiers of the news," with reporters in Constantinople, Shanghai, Manila, and Buenos Aires, as well as Berlin, London, Paris, and Rome.[3] (But not in Moscow. *Tribune* reporters became personae non gratae in Russia after George Seldes made his well-publicized exit protesting Soviet censorship in 1923. They remained unwelcome through World War II.)

Only a few days after Schultz began her new position, McCormick described her initial territory in a memo to all European-based correspondents, in which he reminded them who was responsible for covering the news where. Her beat was limited to Germany and whatever news came her way from Poland. This was a considerable reduction from the territory Clayton had covered from Berlin, which included Estonia, Latvia, Poland, Denmark, Czechoslovakia, Lithuania, Austria, and Hungary. By the end of the year, her territory had expanded, including not only Germany, but at various times Poland, Hungary, Czechoslovakia, the Balkan states, and Austria. (Austria in particular was a moving target. Sometimes local correspondents reported to Berlin, and at other times, Vienna approached the status of a bureau in its own right.)

<hr />

The consensus among her contemporaries was that Schultz had done the work of the *Tribune*'s "No. 1" correspondent in Berlin for a long time. In fact, as early as September 1922, a map in a *Tribune* ad touting the Foreign News Service showed Sigrid Schultz holding down Berlin, though she would not be the bureau chief for another four years.

Despite this seemingly widespread acceptance that Schultz was the "right man" for the job, things weren't that simple.

Looking back through the rosy lens of time, Schultz often stated she had never suffered discrimination because she was a woman. On those occasions when she recalled indignities she had experienced as a "woman in a man's job" at various times in her career, she treated them as humorous stories, focusing on a victorious twist at the end rather than the humiliation of the moment.

For instance, soon after she became bureau chief, Schultz arrived late to a banquet of important economic leaders. She showed her invitation, but the functionaries who were checking people at the door would not let her in: no women allowed. She took out a business card, wrote on the back "Are two hundred men scared of one woman?" and insisted the gatekeepers take it to the press officer in charge of the event. He came out laughing and escorted her into the room. "One big boss after the other came over to interview the strange woman," Schultz said, "and from then on I never had any trouble seeing world leaders."[4]

Schultz was not alone in sugarcoating her memories. Journalism historian Linda Lumsden, writing about the women who reported hard news at the national and international level in the 1920s and 1930s, noted "their relentlessly sunny reminiscences about how they functioned in an atmosphere of sex discrimination." Drawing on Carolyn Heilbrun's classic discussion of the prohibitions that have shaped how women write about their lives, Lumsden claims that nostalgia often masks repressed anger. She suggests the women she writes about were unintentionally dishonest because openly expressed anger was implicitly forbidden to them in the male-dominated world of journalism.[5]

For that matter, expressing anger even in the mildest form was sometimes explicitly forbidden. After an interview in which Schultz spoke up when a subject was condescending toward her, Dick Little told her while people (by which he meant men) might accept a sharp rebuttal from a man, an outspoken woman with a sharp tongue was in danger of being labeled a shrew, which would not be helpful in the newspaper game. Unlike most of Little's lessons on journalism, this was one Schultz regularly ignored.

No matter what Schultz said later, at the time she was not always so sanguine about her position as a woman in the Berlin press corps. In her letters she regularly described having to deal with barriers to doing her job, subtle microaggressions, and open clashes with men in the workplace. Gregor Ziemer, headmaster of the American School in Berlin, who worked part-time for Schultz from 1928 until her departure in 1941, later noted she was often on the defensive about being a woman. He once heard her say, "It's not easy to be the only woman correspondent in Europe, among all the big-shot males who look upon me as a freak, if not a threat." And, he pointed out, when she thought a man was after her job, she could be thoroughly ruthless.[6]

⸺

Schultz's first battle with the Chicago office following her promotion was one that women continue to fight almost a hundred years later. She had to argue that her pay and expense allowance should equal that of the full-time male correspondents.

J. H. Hummel, business manager for the *Tribune*'s overseas operations, was known to the foreign correspondents as "Give-'Em-Half" Hummel for his habit of arguing with reporters about their expense accounts.[7] When Schultz raised the question of equal pay, he trotted out a list of reasons why she should not receive as much as her male counterparts. The men had wives and children to support. And since her home was in Berlin, she did not have the expense of maintaining separate addresses in Berlin and the United States, as the men did. She lived in a leased apartment with her mother, which was cheaper than renting a room at the Hotel Adlon, as her male predecessors had—and she could entertain in her home rather than in public venues.

After four months with no progress, Schultz went over Hummel's head to D. M. Deininger, the *Tribune's* business manager in Chicago, whom she had met during a visit in 1923. He had told her to come to him if things went wrong. They were wrong now, and she was asking for his help. She did not point out that she had a widowed mother to support, as much her dependent as any male correspondent's wife and children. But she howled—not in laughter but in anger—at the idea that Berlin was her home: "Berlin is not more my home than it is theirs—just because I have been here without interruption while they have been traveling does not cut down the price of rent, heat, food, and entertaining for me."[8]

Two months later, things were still not resolved. She reached out to Deininger once again. She had used her Christmas bonus and borrowed money from her mother to cover expenses that her predecessors had been allowed to charge to the office. Now her credit sources were exhausted.

It was a full year before Schultz and Hummel reached an agreement, of sorts. When Hummel said their arrangement placed her on exactly the same basis as other correspondents, Schultz reminded him it was the same basis only in principle. In fact, she received a smaller expense allowance than her predecessors because she had a long-term lease on a prewar apartment and artist's studio, which reduced her living and entertaining costs. She was currently fighting to keep that lease, which had been in her father's name before his death in May 1924. If the housing authorities succeeding in ousting her, she would be back to renegotiate.

CHAPTER TEN

ON THE JOB

My most vivid image of Sigrid Schultz is that of an eager, energetic, fiercely intense woman in a serviceable but colorful and becoming tweed suit, and low-heeled shoes, pounding away on a noisy typewriter, concentrating on her newest story.

—GREGOR ZIEMER, "Sigrid Schultz,"
Lost Generation Journal IV, no. 1 (Winter 1976)[1]

Our only lady-correspondent manages The Tribune's important bureau in Berlin. . . . It is a bit startling to reconcile someone so small, fair and jolly as Sigrid Schultz with the distinguished cable reports of political, economic and social news of Germany. But a strong personality and a keen mind are behind her gay blue eyes.

—*THE LITTLE TRIB* (in-house publication
for *Tribune* employees), October 1928[2]

Sometime between late morning and early afternoon, Schultz would burst into the paper's cramped office, a suite of three small rooms with a small storage space above them located off the lobby of the Hotel Adlon, with windows looking out over Unter den Linden. She would already have spent several hours in pursuit of a breaking story or chasing a rumor, even though her workday would extend well past midnight. As she told a young reporter in an interview for the *Tribune*'s in-house magazine in 1957, "I never knew an eight hour day, much less a five day week. And since extra time off would have meant missing some exciting story of the day, I shied away from leisure in the past as I do now."[3]

Once in the office, Schultz spent the first hour at her desk, planning the day's work and smoking a decorative little clay pipe—a habit she picked up after she was made bureau chief. She had hoped her new salary would allow her to indulge in the Turkish and Egyptian cigarettes she enjoyed, but she quickly deemed it too expensive, even with the favorable exchange rate that allowed foreign correspondents to live more lavishly than they could at home.

With that quiet hour over and, with luck, the first pipe smoked without interruption, the rush was on. Schultz always moved quickly, as if she were literally chasing a story, perhaps a remnant of the days when she half-ran to keep up with Dick Little's long-legged stride. When developments warranted, she changed her plans abruptly, wadding up pages of carefully written copy and then dashing off after the new story.

The arrival of the daily cable from the Chicago office that listed which stories appeared on the front page set the tone for the day. (The only recognition more prized by a *Tribune* correspondent than a front-page story was a personal cable of congratulations from McCormick on a story.) "When Sigrid had made front-page news," Ziemer recollected, "we—that is her researcher, Herr von Schimpff, Erich Weidner the office boy, and I were sure the mood in the office that afternoon and evening would be optimistic. When Sigrid was pessimistic, gloom lay like a fog over the place."[4]

According to Ziemer, Schultz had a few tricks that she used when she got too tense, or when one of the recurring ailments that troubled her over the years struck. Sometimes she'd lie flat on the office floor, not moving. ("Nobody else moved either," Ziemer remembered.) On other occasions, she would go to a movie. It didn't matter what was playing, or whether she arrived at the beginning, the middle, or the end. She'd watch for an hour, then leave: "By that time she'd have hatched four or five new assignments, a dozen new ideas, and decided what to do about [propaganda minister Joseph] Goebbels's latest Lie."[5]

On quieter days she and her staff would work on feature stories, write what she called "situationers" (background information on German politics, society, or culture that editors in Chicago could use to fill out cable stories when the news was running hot), and compose the always undervalued "mailers," stories that had a low enough priority that they could be sent to Chicago by mail.

Then she would get word of a new story and rush off again, small low-heeled shoes beating a tattoo as she raced out the door.

In the late afternoon, the *Tribune* office would fill up with what Thomas Ybarra, correspondent for *The Times* of London and later for the *New York Times*, described as a "low herd of loafers representing all the papers." They crowded the room, talking, smoking, and generally making a mess, until "Miss S. Schultz gave up in despair the idea of working" and joined the conversation.[6] At some point, that conversation would move from the *Tribune* office to the Hotel Adlon's bar, the unofficial clubhouse for foreign correspondents, a place to meet sources, share gossip, stumble across stories—and drink.

When Schultz first joined the *Tribune*, and for several years thereafter, she was uncomfortable hanging out with the boys in the bar. She had been raised to believe it was unladylike for a young woman to go into a bar unless chaperoned by her husband or her father. Her "father in journalism" was not an adequate substitute, though you could argue that the foreign press corps as a whole served as her chaperones. Certainly in the early years, they were quick to give her all the dirt when a would-be swain whom she didn't know well invited her to a party. It was "quite amazing and equally educational," she remembered later. "Men are quite energetic and revealing when they assume the role of chaperone."[7]

As bureau chief, Schultz decided it wasn't a good idea to continue to refuse to join her colleagues at the Hotel Adlon's bar—too much of the community's business happened there. The first time she bought a round at the bar, on February 27, was so momentous that she noted it in her diary; it felt like she had finally entered the world of full-rank correspondents. But she had no interest in replicating the hard-drinking style for which her male counterparts were known. Her father had taught her to appreciate good alcohol, and when finances allowed, she would purchase several dozen bottles of a wine she enjoyed or a small keg of good whiskey for the Schultz family cellar. Hermann also taught his daughter to know how much alcohol she could handle: less than that of her much larger male colleagues or, for that matter, Dorothy Thompson. Schultz's solution was a secret agreement with the Adlon bartender: when she asked for a "Schultz," he would pour her a nonalcoholic drink that looked like the real thing so it appeared that she was matching the others drink for drink. If anyone else ordered a "Schultz," they got a similar-looking drink with "the kick of a mule." She later remembered one occasion when she attended a party held at the bar in Floyd Gibbons's honor: "I could see his one eye almost falling out of his face as I joined in one round of drinks after another," she wrote. When she was called to the telephone, he jumped up as if he expected her to fall and then watched in surprise as she walked to the phone booth "in perfect harmony."[8]

The Adlon bar was not the only social component of Schultz's workday. Night after night, especially during the fall and winter social season, Schultz attended official events and nonofficial parties, nurturing the social contacts that provided her with many of her best leads. Even the dullest events provided material for a story.

When the functions were over, or the last drink was downed, she returned to the office, driven by the inexorable schedule of the Chicago printing presses. In order to meet the deadline for the morning paper, she had to call in the news to the Paris bureau by 1 a.m. If extraordinary news was breaking, she could file a story by cable as late as 8 a.m., but only if the news was truly extraordinary. At the exorbitant cost of a dollar a word, to cable or not to cable was always a hard choice. Schultz and her colleagues had to balance the value of a possible scoop against the headache of defending the decision to spend the money on cable fees.

There was another reason for Schultz to stay late. Politicians and diplomats would drop into the *Tribune*'s office to chat after attending an event at the Adlon.

Foreign minister Gustav Stresemann was a regular visitor, and one she valued highly. A successful businessman before he entered politics, Stresemann was the head of the liberal German People's Party (DVP). After a brief term as chancellor in 1923, he had served unchallenged ever since as the Weimar Republic's foreign minister, and would do so until his death at the age of fifty-one in 1929. At least one evening a week Stresemann would drop in around eleven, on the pretext of asking about the photographs displayed in the office window. Even with her 1 a.m. filing deadline looming, Schultz was always willing to drop everything for a good talk with Stresemann, who was unusually aware of the importance of working with foreign journalists and often a source of a good tip, sometimes for publication, sometimes in confidence.

Schultz understood well the importance of talking to people outside the formal framework of interview and press conference.

Even before her promotion, the Schultz home, like Hermann's studios in Paris and Berlin in the days before the war, was the stopping place for Americans who traveled through Berlin: foreign correspondents, *Tribune* employees traveling abroad, and an ever-growing circle of friends—and friends of friends. Frazier Hunt, correspondent for the Hearst group's Universal News Service in the years between the wars, remembered that though "the cramped Adlon Bar ... was Berlin's number one American Club, the real niche for countless Americans centered in Sigrid and Mamma Schultz's studio."[9] Dorothy Thompson offered a slightly different version of the Schultz hospitality in a radio broadcast in 1938: "She lives in a studio apartment with her mother, an old lady beloved by 'boys' from one end of Europe to the other, and Sigrid's greatest asset is that she knows how to entertain delightfully in a simple and Bohemian manner, and by way of setting an excellent table and being able to create a jolly atmosphere, has become intimately acquainted with a great many persons in key positions."[10] Or as William Shirer put it many years later, "You met a lot of nice people. They had wonderful food."[11] Not a small thing in Germany in the 1920s and 1930s.

Thompson did not give Schultz credit for her courage, energy, and knowledge of languages, history, diplomacy, and politics—all qualities Thompson believed were essential to the modern foreign correspondent. But she clearly understood Schultz's parties were a powerful tool as well as genuine hospitality.

From the start, Schultz knew the value of entertaining as a means of building relationships with sources and getting stories, and she never underestimated the role played by her mother's personal charm, and her cooking,[12] in creating the "jolly atmosphere" that Thompson described. Together she and Hedwig threw popular "bean-parties," at which they served copious amounts of Mamma Schultz's famous baked beans, and *Bier Abende* (beer evenings), informal gatherings that had traditionally been stag events until Schultz became part of the foreign correspondent corps and proved she could handle her beer as well as any of her male counterparts. Their events always included a wide mix of guests, who reflected the often-stated idea that Schultz seemed to know everyone: German nobility, politicians, and industrialists; diplomats, including members of the American embassy "who were just a little bit snooty about correspondents" but had good stories and were worth cultivating as sources; performers, artists, and intellectuals of all nationalities;

German friends and fellow journalists. Eleanor Painter, a star of the Ziegfeld Follies in her youth who now sang at the Berlin Opera House, was an occasional guest. So was movie heartthrob Ramon Novarro, in Berlin studying voice with Painter's husband, baritone singer Louis Graveure. (Novarro attended her parties under his real name, José Samaniego. When one of her female guests realized who he was, Schultz became "the most popular woman with the ladies of the Berlin embassy crowd."[13]) Other guests included novelists Paul Gallico, Katherine Anne Porter (who later claimed Schultz was a Nazi "honey-trap"), and Edna Ferber; critic and playwright Alexander Woolcott; dance pioneer Ted Shawn; and Schultz's "play uncle" Oscar Mayer. Those who fancied themselves expert cooks would congregate in the kitchen, showing off for the crowd. Sigrid later said of Hedwig, "One of the funniest sights she ever saw was her daughter in the kitchen mixing dough for a pie of some kind, while a Hungarian newsman was busy cooking a real goulash and an English diplomat mixing his best salad."[14] Her guests ate, drank, and talked with enthusiasm—and pumped each other for information regarding the news of the day.

CHAPTER ELEVEN

LOVE AND LONELINESS

I know all about loneliness—much more than I care to.

—SIGRID SCHULTZ, December 15, 1928[1]

Writing much later, Gregor Ziemer gave detailed accounts of Sigrid the Planning Reporter, Sigrid the Boss, Sigrid the Career Gal, and Sigrid the Journalist, but he faltered when he reached Sigrid the Woman.[2] Nobody knew much about that Sigrid, he told the reader. She was lovely to look at—when she bothered. She knew how to make the most of "her small, compact, lively body"—when she wanted to. There were rumors, he said, that she had been engaged, even married, and was disappointed in love. No one knew for certain. And, according to Ziemer, no one dared ask. And yet, at the time Ziemer came to work for Schultz, she was involved in a serious romantic friendship for the first time since the death of her young fiancé eleven years earlier.

It is, perhaps, not surprising that Ziemer failed to notice the relationship. Schultz was thirty-three, and over the years, she had enjoyed casual flirtations under the eye of Berlin's foreign press corps. To the casual observer, her relationship with Carl O. (Denny) Dennewitz could have looked much the same.

The evidence for Schultz's romance with Dennewitz is limited to fifty-some letters in the Schultz archive and a few terse comments in the daily logs that she kept erratically over the years. (Schultz sometimes skipped entries for weeks at a time, seldom indulged in self-reflection, and was often cryptic, even before Nazi surveillance made keeping a diary a risky habit.) These sources leave many unanswered questions:

When did they meet? How far did the relationship go? (There was at least one memorable kiss.) And what went wrong?

Dennewitz was the managing editor of the Gary, Indiana, *Tribune* when America entered the Great War. He left the paper to enlist in the army as an airplane mechanic. After the war, he spent two years working for the Red Cross in Europe and then returned to journalism as a foreign correspondent. He initially worked on the Berlin staff of the *New York Herald*. In 1924, he was reassigned to the newly named *New York Herald Tribune*'s Paris bureau, where he was one of the hard-drinking journalists who hung out at Harry's Bar and called themselves the "International Bar Flies."

By 1926, Dennewitz was back in Berlin as a correspondent for the *New York Times* and the *New York Sun*. Several months later, he was transferred to Warsaw. In February 1927, he left the *New York Times*—and sailed back to the United States. After that, with the exception of two brief interludes in 1928 and 1933, his relationship with Schultz was limited to correspondence.

Dennewitz first appeared in Schultz's daily log on January 1, 1926. In the confusion of Clayton's leaving for Rome and her own promotion to Berlin bureau chief, Schultz had uncharacteristically failed to make plans for New Year's Eve. She was more than willing when Dennewitz dropped into the *Tribune*'s office late on the afternoon of the 31st to invite her to what he warned her could be a wild party.

Years later, in one of the many drafts of her unfinished memoirs, Schultz described the mid-1920s as a period when "people were still living at top speed trying to catch up with the fun they had missed in wartime and fun they might miss in the upheaval that was bound to come."[3] She could well have been describing that New Year's Eve with Dennewitz and the months that followed. That night they dined at the glamorous Hotel Tiergarten, where they danced until midnight, then went on to the party. (Schultz noted in her log that the party was dull compared with the scene at the Tiergarten.) They hung out with Austrian actor and director Eddie Polo, the alcoholic *New York Times* bureau chief Lincoln Eyre, and his wife, German movie star Dina Gralla, from two until four o'clock in the morning. Dennewitz finally took Schultz home at seven thirty on New Year's Day.

It was not the first, or last, time that Sigrid danced until dawn with a fellow foreign correspondent or a tourist passing through Berlin. What was new was that evenings with Denny became a regular part of her life. He would meet her at the *Tribune* office. Once she had filed her report for the day, they would go to dinner, sometimes at the Schultz apartment, or have drinks at the Adlon bar. Occasionally they spent part of the evening with others—one evening he and several other correspondents taught her to shoot craps. (She gleefully reported that she won 75 marks, then took the boys to the office for whiskey before going "home with Denny," a recurring phrase that can be interpreted several different ways in the absence of more detail.) Often they talked into the early morning.

Their relationship continued after Dennewitz was transferred to Warsaw in the late spring or early summer of 1926, with all the difficulties inherent in such a separation. Schultz visited him in late July, with the excuse of gathering material about Marshal Józef Piłsudski, who had led a successful coup against the newly formed Polish republic in May of that year. Dennewitz returned to Berlin in September and again in October. In many ways these visits resembled the time they had spent together before his reassignment, though they were punctuated by arguments triggered by unmet expectations on his part and insecurity about his reputation as a ladies' man on hers.

Writing to Schultz from Warsaw, Dennewitz listed a litany of frustrations. The news was thin. The weather was unpleasant. He was trading colds with the *Tribune*'s local correspondent. He was waiting for Adolph Ochs, owner and publisher of the *New York Times*, to decide where he would assign Dennewitz next, if at all. On December 23, Dennewitz wrote that he would not make it to Berlin for Christmas at the Schultz home, but he expected to be there in six weeks, when "all the delayed enjoyment of a holiday season will be knocked for a St. Valentine's day."[4]

Schultz did not wait for Valentine's Day. She joined him in Warsaw, where they spent a second New Year's Eve together, five days of heavy drinking, late nights that rolled into early mornings, "evening drama," and reconciliations. They attended a grand ball and spent one night in her hotel room with a friend who composed songs on the fly for Dennewitz to sing to her.

In mid-February 1927, Dennewitz returned to New York, where he tried unsuccessfully to find work as a journalist. (He stopped in Berlin on February 14, but did not contact Schultz until the next day—not quite the Valentine's Day celebration she may have hoped for.).

For the next two years, they wrote long letters back and forth.

Denny complained about the state of journalism in the United States and the expense of living in New York. He described his efforts at building a public relations agency.

Schultz shared newspaper staffing troubles, roadblocks in tracking down stories, news about mutual acquaintances, and leads on newspaper jobs for Denny. She told him silly anecdotes about her dog. She reported on a grand roulette party she threw at the house and an even grander champagne party she threw at the Hotel Adlon for "the boys."

Sometimes, Schultz let down her mask and shared just how lonely she was. In one letter, she told him their friend Hans Albers, a cabaret comic and popular German movie star between 1930 and his death in 1960, took her out on occasion after his performances, saying the only way to get a grin on her face was to provide her with a plate of oysters and Denny as a dinner companion: "he couldn't get you since you were in America but he could get the oysters." Schultz ended that letter, a long screed of local gossip, newspaper troubles, and news about mutual acquaintances, with the sad comment that "by the length of this letter you can judge that I am lonely for a good talk."[5]

More than once, she complained about exhaustion, in terms that sound remarkably close to depression to the modern reader, and let him know how much she missed him. But she didn't share just how bad things had gotten in her relationship with the *Tribune*'s business office.

Finally, in June 1928, Schultz admitted to Dennewitz that it had been a "nasty" year with "black streaks so broad they almost overshadowed bright ones."[6]

The previous fall, about six months after Schultz had resolved the question of her salary and expense allowance, she found herself at odds with Robert Schwinbold, the *Tribune*'s advertising manager in Berlin, over what she described as "the invasion of the Berlin newsfield by the Berlin business department."[7] With the cooperation of J. H. Hummel, her adversary in the salary debate, Schwinbold began to chase news stories for the business section of the Paris Edition. When she and her staff called on the German Foreign Office and the American embassy in pursuit of the news, they were told those offices had already given the information, or invitations to press conferences, to Schwinbold.

"Schwinbold cannot even spell correctly, much less write [a] story, though I admit he is an excellent advertising getter," Schultz complained to a friend of her mother's, peace activist and Hull House reformer Lillian Kohlhammer.[8]

Things got ugly quickly after Schultz sent Hummel a letter objecting to Schwinbold's arrangement with the Paris office. Schwinbold responded with a long, ranting, and incoherent letter to Hummel, in which he charged Schultz of making unjust accusations against him and his staff. He then sent copies of the letter to Schultz and to various departments of the *Tribune*. The main idea of the letter was summed up in one sentence: "Shame on Miss Schultz to write such lines. She is not a credit to womanhood when she writes such charges."[9] Soon thereafter Hummel visited the Chicago office, where he praised Schwinbold for his undoubted ability at selling ad space, and, Schultz told John Steele, "did everything under the sun to convey the impression that I am a professional fussmaker."[10]

The constant conflict left Schultz so drained that she had to force herself to do her work, and then crawl home "too weak for words."[11] When she finally gave in and went to the doctor, he prescribed "a tragic diet of noodles and rice and similar fattening food" to repair "the ravages of irregular eating hours and hectic newspaper life." The treatment did not leave her feeling full of energy—yet—but at least she no longer had to grit her teeth just to finish the day's work.[12]

The controversy ended with both Schultz and Schwinbold still in Berlin, their differences papered over temporarily but fundamentally unreconciled. After the fact, she wrote to Dennewitz that things had been so difficult that she considered resigning, but she loved her work and thought her resignation was just what Hummel and Schwinbold wanted: "I swallowed hard and stuck—but how cheap it made me feel and how thoroughly ill I was!"[13]

———— ∞∞∞ ————

At the same time as the fight with her colleagues in the Paris and Berlin business offices, Schultz found herself in trouble with the German Foreign Office press department for a piece she wrote about President von Hindenburg's eightieth birthday celebration, in October 1927.

The celebration took place in the massive Berlin stadium, opened on the occasion of the former kaiser's silver jubilee in 1913 and intended to house the 1916 Olympics, which had been canceled due to the war. The press office placed the foreign correspondents in stands at a distance from the president, no doubt hoping to control what they had access to, and consequently, what they wrote. While most correspondents stayed in their assigned places, Schultz did not. Instead, she headed toward the president's box, where Field Marshal August von Mackensen and other octogenarian generals who had served under Hindenburg in the war waited for the president, resplendent in their luxuriant white mustaches and prewar uniforms. She was sure the president would stop to greet von Mackensen and thought their meeting might make a story.

When Hindenburg reached the box, Schultz was close enough to him that she could see how tired he was. She told Dennewitz "the poor old dear" was exhausted: "five more minutes and he would have wept like a baby."[14]

Schultz was slightly more diplomatic in her article about the event, but only slightly. The piece opened, "It was a weary old man who walked up the steps to his box in the Berlin stadium today amid the cheers of 40,000 jubilant school children and 80,000 enthusiastic adults assembled to celebrate his eightieth birthday." She went on to describe his drawn face and the way he leaned on his walking stick to hide his weariness. He shook hands with his old war comrades without saying a word: the five-mile drive from the presidential residence to the stadium, through streets lined with hundreds of thousands of cheering Germans, left him too tired to speak.[15]

"Twas best story I wrote syear [sic]," Schultz wrote to Dennewitz in heavy cablese—an improvised shorthand which foreign correspondents used to reduce the costs of sending cables to their home offices. Cable companies charged by the word, so reporters condensed some words and left others out altogether. Writing in cablese was such an engrained habit that Schultz peppered her personal correspondence with it, especially in letters to other journalists. Thus: "It was the best story I wrote this year" became "Twas best story I wrote syear."

The German Foreign Office was not pleased with the story. When they complained about the piece, she asked them whether or not it was true that Hindenburg was shaky. Her favorite reply when she was in trouble with a censor, even under the Nazis, was to question whether she had written anything that was untrue and promise to have the *Tribune* issue a "beg your pardon" (the in-house term for a correction) if they could prove that it was.

The Foreign Office's press officials admitted her report was true but said she "lacked tact." When they pointed out that other correspondents stayed put "in the little boxes allotted to them," she answered that she was paid to see as much of the truth as she could find, not to stay wherever someone put her. One press officer threatened her with expulsion over the article. Schultz told him to go ahead. It would be marvelous publicity and shipping companies would fight for the honor of providing her passage home.

The attempt to stifle her backfired. When she complained to Stresemann, he responded by adding her to the invitation list for dinners his wife hosted in what had been Chancellor Otto von Bismarck's dining room. These dinners were limited to twelve people, she told McCormick, and "famed for their political importance and no pressman, foreign or German, has ever been admitted—I've been at them twice in the last two weeks."[16]

———

In the fall of 1928, with the office safely in the hands of what she confided to Dennewitz was the first competent assistant she ever had, Schultz went "home" for several weeks. She had not been back in the United States since her brief stay in 1923.

There is not much information about what she did when she was there. A chatty article in the *Little Trib*, the *Tribune's* in-house publication for employees, documents that she visited the home office in Chicago. On October 15, she reported on the difficult landing of the first commercial passenger flight of a zeppelin across the Atlantic at Lakehurst Airfield in New Jersey. And at some point, she met up with Dennewitz. It's not clear how much time they spent together or what happened between them.

In December, Schultz took a chance. How big a chance is hard to say; there are no details on how she left things with Denny. She mailed him two stuffed animals, which she described in a separate letter as "the Zoo." One, a dog she bought for him in Paris, was a straightforward, slightly silly Christmas present from one dog lover to another. The second, a fancy giraffe, was a more daring gift. She instructed him to take the toy to his private quarters, slash it open about three inches below the neck, and dig inside until he found something small and hard. It was a ring her father had given her years ago as a "luckbringer." Now she wanted to pass on the luck to Dennewitz.

It was the first letter Schultz had written Dennewitz since her return. Her health had been wonderful while she was in the United States, but her energy dropped once she was back in Berlin. She found she needed to be "stingy" with her strength, in part because she had to "slay dragons of all varieties" on her return. Lincoln Eyre's sudden death had left his wife, Dina Gralla, alone, destitute, and subject to rumors in the gossip-happy Berlin foreign press community. Understanding Gralla's loneliness all too well, Schultz appointed herself the young actress's champion.

Schultz had to slay dragons on her own behalf as well. She found her colleagues had tried to take advantage of her absence and she "ran [up] against the 'woman in a man's job stuff' right and left." It took a while to reestablish her position, but by the time she wrote to Denny, she thought the worst was over.

She also endured teasing from fellow *Tribune* correspondents John Steele, Henry Wales, and Larry Rue, who came to see her in Berlin on her return. Together they decided a man was the only explanation for her glowing health after the rigors of a trip to America. They even agreed on the man and practically married her off—"and between you and me," she told Dennewitz, "they hit on the right one."

Schultz may have wanted to shelter their continued relationship from gossip by the foreign correspondent community, many of whom had assumed it had ended when Dennewitz left for America. The year before, Schultz had watched Dorothy Thompson suffer under the public scrutiny of her affairs by "the boys" during the end of her first marriage and her romance with writer Sinclair Lewis. Affairs and infidelities on the part of male correspondents were accepted without comment. Women were held to a different standard.

Whatever her reasons, Schultz chose neither to confirm nor deny their speculations. Instead, she teased them back, accusing them of male conceit. "Must there always be a romance as [the] most important factor in life?" she asked them.

Then she turned the question around to Dennewitz, "Now I ask you, Denny, must there?" Describing herself as the "most monogamous woman in creation," she told him that sometimes she thought she could "just pass out of life out of sheer loneliness." But she refused to wallow. Life had too much promise to give up, she told him. And until those promises came true "theres [sic] the job, trying to mother Dina a bit, mother my own family and stray dogs of all descriptions."[17]

—————⟨∞⟩—————

But those promises didn't come true. Not with Dennewitz. Something went wrong between them.

It is clear some of their letters have been lost. It is equally clear that there was a long period in which they did not write.

They picked up their correspondence again in 1933. Dennewitz wrote in April, in response to a Christmas card that reached him via a common friend, Frazier "Spike" Hunt, in which Schultz complained he hadn't written her a single line. At first his tone was humorous. He indignantly claimed he had written—copiously—and received no letters in return: "No letters about long vigils—galley proofs—telephone calls—ear biting—think pieces—personal contacts—the yarn filed at last. The keg. The glowing stove. The lovely guests. Farewell to Mother's pie. The quiet studio." Then the tone shifted: "A kiss. Forgotten by you; not by this sap, who didn't hoist you to the pedestal that you deserved." Friends had come between them, sticking the rapier into her with the idea that they were helping him. He had written her about the ring in the past. Now he had more to tell her. Lots more. He signed it "Always and always."[18]

Schultz's response was shorter, more serious, and more cautious. She had not received any letters from him. Those same friends who had stuck rapiers in her had knifed him as well, she told him: "only I did not take it seriously—nor will I."[19]

They met again that September, when Schultz made another trip to the United States. Their first encounters were not a success. Dennewitz was stiff and formal. Their conversation was boring. Somehow they worked past their discomfort. Schultz wrote to her mother that they had been together most of the time for several days. "Am I grateful?" she wrote. "I am! . . . Love the whole world for the first time in my life."[20]

Dennewitz mailed two last letters in December 1933: Christmas greetings sent on two different ships in the hope that one would reach her. He ended one "Love again, and double isn't too much if both these letters reach you." He ended the other "all that an old colleague and a true friend and—well, maybe a sweetheart, could wish on this occasion."[21]

The cautiously renewed promise of those letters was never fulfilled. Dennewitz died suddenly of meningitis, after collapsing in Floyd Gibbons's New York apartment on November 1, 1934.

CHAPTER TWELVE

"THE FASCISTI ARE VERY RESTLESS"

While the financial magnates of the world are bickering about the billions of gold dollars of reparations which Germany must pay, a new wave of unrest has seized the country.

—SIGRID SCHULTZ, February 24, 1929[1]

The Hitlerites have increased their activities in Silesia, where many clashes took place in the last 24 hours. The latest Fascist war song echoed for the first time in the Jewish district of Gleiwitz. "Heads are rolling—Jews are howling" is the chorus of the song, which created such an uproar that it took police some time to restore peace.

—SIGRID SCHULTZ, June 22, 1932[2]

Seen from today's perspective (or that of, say, 1939) the rise of the Nazis was the most important German news story between 1925 and January 1933, when Hitler became chancellor of Germany. But in 1925 the Nazis were not yet a significant political power. In fact, the term *Nazi* did not come into common usage until the 1930s. The *Tribune* used the word for the first time on March 1, 1931, in the headline of an Associated Press article. The term was clarified in the article: "the Nazis, as the National Socialists are called." Schultz used the term for the first time six days later—in quotation marks. Prior to 1931, the *Tribune* variously referred to Hitler's followers as Fascists, the National Socialist Party, and, increasingly, as "Hitlerites."

In 1925, what Germans call *Die goldenen zwanziger Jahre* (the Golden Twenties) was at its height. The economy was on its way to recovery, with the passage of the Dawes Act in 1924, which put the German economy under foreign supervision and stabilized the mark. The political landscape was relatively calm, on the floor of the Reichstag if not in the streets, under the strong leadership of Gustav Stresemann. The country was enjoying an artistic and intellectual blossoming that was dynamic, challenging, and transgressive.

But that paradoxical sense of stability and movement was an illusion, which began to crack in 1929.

A severe cold wave swept through Europe in mid-February, bringing with it the lowest temperatures in one hundred years. With waterways frozen solid, river barges could not transport coal and other necessities to major cities. Schultz reported that potatoes, the primary food stuff for many Berliners, froze on their way to market. Store owners complained that eggs, oranges, and bottled beer exploded in their half-heated shops. A week into the deep freeze, prices for potatoes and coal rose by 50 percent, causing the Berlin government to ration both household staples. As they had during the Great War, Berliners lined up at markets to buy supplies and rioted when the supply chain failed. To add to the misery, on February 15, the gas mains in Berlin froze, plunging the downtown streets into darkness; the lights stayed off because artificially thawing the pipes could cause explosions.

While Berliners shivered in the dark, the German government suffered a cabinet crisis. Unable to form a stable coalition, the Reichstag's leaders considered dissolving parliament, hoping a general election would give one party a working majority. It was a dangerous tactic. Some feared a dictator would seize power if the Reichstag was dissolved. Other Germans actively hoped that "a German Mussolini" would rise up and lead the country out of its economic and political woes. There were numerous candidates for the job of dictator from all points on the political spectrum, but most of what Schultz styled "pigmy Mussolinis" were right-wing extremists. "The Fascist Hitler" was one among many, and not one of the most powerful, in Schultz's estimation.[3]

When the American stock market crashed on October 29, 1929, it took the German economy with it. American banks and businessmen had made huge loans to the German government and to German businesses. Those loans helped fund Germany's reparations payments, paid for new factories and assembly lines, and subsidized postwar reconstruction. Following the crash, American bankers called in their short-term foreign loans, with devastating results for Germany.

By the spring of 1930, the German economy was in a self-reinforcing downward spiral. With credit no longer available, factories reduced production and businesses closed. As a result, workers lost their jobs. With unemployed consumers unable to buy their products, more businesses failed and factories further reduced production, sending the economy on another spin down into the vortex.

In 1928, 1.3 million Germans were unemployed. By 1932, the number had risen to almost 6 million—40 percent of the labor force.[4]

Germany's economic free fall proved to be a boon to both the Communists and the National Socialist Party. As unemployment rose, the hungry, the frustrated, and the desperate sought solace in the promises of political parties at both extremes. The Communist Party's membership increased from 117,000 to 360,000 between 1928 and 1932; 80 percent of the new members were unemployed. The Nazi Party's membership increase was even more dramatic, from 109,000 in 1928 to more than one million in 1932.[5] Berlin's workers had historically looked to the Communists and Socialists for leadership, Schultz told her readers only two weeks after the markets crashed. Now, as those leaders were failing them, the working classes were listening to the National Socialists' promise of a nationalist utopia.[6]

⁂

"The fascisti are very restless," Schultz told McCormick in March 1930, but he did not need to worry. Possibly remembering the difficulties she and other journalists had faced in the Kapp Putsch in 1923, she had made plans for getting the story out of Berlin in case of a coup. She arranged for American-owned ships, anchored at Hamburg, to be used as wireless stations. It would be faster to send messengers to Hamburg than to send them to one of the borders. In short, she assured McCormick, "We are all set for putsches of any kind."[7]

Schultz had cause for concern. The reason the Fascisti were restless was clear. Germany's economic and political situation was getting worse.

On March 29, 1930, Hindenburg appointed a new chancellor, Heinrich Brüning, a Catholic conservative and the leader of the Center Party.

He attempted to solve Germany's economic problems by enacting defla-
tionary policies that were the opposite of Roosevelt's New Deal. Rather
than introducing work-creation and other capital-intensive programs
into the economy, he reduced state expenditures and urged businesses to
slash their labor costs: a policy that could be summed up as "everybody
tighten your belts and things will get better." Unfortunately, most people's
belts had already been tightened as far as they could go.

Brüning's coalition government could not create legislative consensus among the twenty-nine parties represented in the Reichstag. In July,
he tried to invoke Article 48 of the Weimar constitution, which would
allow him to rule by decree. When that failed, he persuaded President
von Hindenburg to dissolve the Reichstag and call for new elections,
apparently believing he and his policies would find widespread support
at the polls from a population sinking deeper into economic misery as
the financial crisis worsened under his leadership.

⚬⚭⚬

American newspapers gave more attention to the 1930 Reichstag elections than they had to any German news story since Field Marshal von
Hindenburg ran for the presidency in 1925. Beginning in mid-August,
a month before the September elections, hundreds of American newspapers in small cities and smaller towns ran the same three think pieces
issued by different wireless services, which all included a discussion of
the increased profile of the National Socialist Party, and the dangers
attached to it.

The most popular, an Associated Press piece just two paragraphs
and fewer than 150 words long, appeared in newspapers from Pennsyl-
vania to South Dakota. Its sole subject was Hitler and his political program, particularly his plan "to disfranchise [sic] or drive from Germany
all the Jews." The anonymous author suggested that before proceeding
with that plan Hitler should "inform himself as to what happened to
Portugal when that country drove out all the Jews, sending them to
Holland and England, and what happened to Holland and England
after the Jews arrived, in the way of prosperity."

Two longer pieces, one by Milton Bronner, of the Newspaper
Enterprise Association and the other by J. C. Oestreicher of the Hearst-
owned International News Service, focused on the possibility that the
National Socialists and the Communists would win enough seats to
disrupt the long-standing centrist Weimar Coalition and fundamentally

change the complexion of the Weimar Republic. Both pieces discussed the fact that the divided nature of German politics meant that parties governed by coalition; the National Socialists were the only party whose platform they considered in any detail.

The two papers that Colonel McCormick saw as the *Chicago Tribune*'s primary competitors, the *New York Times* and the *Chicago Daily News*, both emphasized what Edgar Ansel Mowrer, the Berlin bureau chief of the *Chicago Daily News*, described as "the almost undecipherable confusion of parties." Neither paper attempted to help their readers understand the differences between those parties, nor did they discuss the National Socialists as a serious threat to the republic. Mowrer, who would go on to win a Pulitzer for reporting on the rise of the Nazis, limited his analysis to grouping the twenty-four parties on the ballot as of September 12 into three categories. He acknowledged that both Hitler's "brown-shirted National Socialists" and the Communists at the other end of the political spectrum were likely to win additional seats, which would weaken the ruling coalition. Guido Enderis, who was promoted to Berlin bureau chief for the *New York Times* in 1928 after Lincoln Eyre's death and was generally considered to be a better office administrator than a reporter, concentrated on the technicalities of how a party earned a place on the German ballot rather than what the parties stood for. As late as September 12, he continued to hold the position that those technicalities would automatically eliminate both Hitler's Fascists and the Communists from consideration in forming a new government coalition. He assured his readers that a moderate coalition would remain in power, and the biggest problem the new Reichstag would face was a shortage of chairs for the newly elected deputies.

By contrast, on August 31, 1930, with the elections for the new Reichstag only two weeks away, Schultz analyzed the position of the seventeen parties then on the German ballot in a long article in the *Tribune*. She told her readers bluntly that the outcome of the election was important to the entire world. Radicals, Communists, and Fascists battled against the "quiet, unspectacular" supporters of the Weimar Republic for control of Germany. In a long section on what she alternately called Fascists and Hitlerites, titled "Threatens Pogroms," she made clear what Hitler and his followers wanted and how dangerous they were. The Fascisti wanted to overthrow the government and establish a dictatorship of "truly Germanic men," she wrote. They openly threatened pogroms against Jews and "other alien elements in Germany."

They had proved over and over that they were willing to club down political opponents when they couldn't argue them into submission.

Schultz's story was an important assessment of a critical event, but it ran on page 39 of the *Tribune*, next to "Jolson Plans to Make German Talkie" and "Facts in Case of Mae West, Mystery Star." The odds are good that readers of the entertainment section were more interested in Al Jolson and Mae West than in warnings about political extremists on the other side of the Atlantic.[8]

The results of the September election surprised everyone. The National Socialists held twelve seats in the Reichstag before it was dissolved. Hitler estimated they would win 60 seats in the election. Instead, they won 107 of the 470 parliamentary seats, making them the second-largest party in the Reichstag. As Schultz pointed out, Hitler emerged from the election as one of the most powerful men in Germany, even though he was not a German citizen and could not legally hold office.

With the Hitlerites in a position of real power in the Reichstag for the first time, Schultz decided she needed to give "the wild men who got themselves elected to the Reichstag" a closer look.[9] She asked her assistant, Alexander von Schimpff, a dapper, monocle-wearing whippet of a man with ties to both British and Prussian nobility, to find a ranking member of the National Socialist Party whose table manners were good enough that she could invite him to the informal dinners she and her mother hosted on Sundays—parties harder to navigate socially than official banquets because of the mix of guests and the lack of formal protocol.

Her idea was to build a connection with a useful source. She succeeded better than she could have hoped. Von Schimpff suggested Captain Hermann Göring, a former World War I flying ace who would become one of the most powerful officials in Nazi Germany.

Schultz invited Göring to lunch at Pelzer's, a small, excellent restaurant located near the Hotel Adlon. At lunch, Göring displayed the enthusiasm for food for which he became known. She later said the bill was terrific, but there was no doubt about the excellence of Göring's table manners. After a second lunch at Pelzer's, she decided she could risk inviting him to the house.[10]

The first time Schultz invited Göring to her home, she threw a big party, including members of the American and British embassies who wanted to meet him, with the idea that he would be less noticeable in a crowd. After dinner, he backed her into a corner, where he told her about the greatest experience of his life to date. Early in the Great War, when he was still a cavalry officer, he killed a French soldier with his saber, an event he described in vivid detail. He may have expected a squeamish reaction from Schultz, but she had lived through the revolution of 1918 and the uprisings that followed. She understood the violence of war in a way that a woman recently arrived from the safety of the United States would not. She just looked at him and said, "Interesting." If that was the greatest experience of his life, she thought, it told her everything she needed to know about how the Nazis thought. As she would tell Colonel McCormick soon after Hitler became chancellor, "They confuse manliness with brutality."[11]

Göring became a frequent guest in the Schultz home in the days when the Nazis were still increasing their political power. He, and later his staff, reciprocated by giving her news, though she had to sift the facts from the propaganda.

⸏⸏⸏

The newly elected Reichstag opened on October 13, 1930, against a backdrop of violence.

Thousands of Hitlerites threw stones at the police cordon surrounding the Reichstag building and tried to force their way in. The police fired over the heads of the mob, until it scattered. Undisciplined groups of what Schultz described as "underfed, shabby toughs" ran through Potsdamer Platz and Leipzigerstrasse, both important shopping districts, yelling *Deutschland erwache! Juda verrecke!* (Awake, Germany! Death to the Jews!) and smashing the windows of Jewish-owned stores—a foretaste of things to come. More young men ran through the side streets, throwing stones at the windows of smaller stores. On Alexanderplatz, Hitlerites and Communists fought, until the police arrived and attempted to disperse them with rubber truncheons.

Inside the Reichstag building, Schultz watched Hitler's followers march single file into the fifth Reichstag's first session wearing their brown shirts, which Chancellor Brüning had banned earlier in 1930 in an attempt to control the various paramilitary movements. Unlike later Nazi gatherings, where the uniforms were, well, uniform, each of the Hitlerite deputies created his own version of brown-shirt style. Schultz reported that the only consistent features were Sam Brown belts and red and white armbands with swastikas on them. Their haircuts in particular were "fantastic," by which she meant strange, not wonderful.

Once the National Socialist members entered the Reichstag, Hitlerites and Communists whistled, booed, and shouted invectives at each other through the roll call. The members of the centrist parties that made up the Weimar Coalition hunched between them, expecting catcalls to escalate into battle, as happened so often on the streets. Thanks to orders given by Hitler and the Red leaders, the first session of the new Reichstag ended without blows in the parliament building, though the fight continued outside its doors well into the night.

Two days later, the new Reichstag began its regular parliamentary work. The National Socialist threat was now business as usual.[12]

The violence that accompanied the opening of the Reichstag set the tone for the months to come. Riots on the streets were so routine and yet so bloody, that political parties often arranged for the presence of a Red Cross unit when organizing a demonstration. According to an official report that Schultz shared with her readers, in Prussia alone the police were called out to quell riots 2,494 times in the twelve-month period from March 1930 to March 1931.[13]

Given the wealth of material, Schultz chose which riots she reported on with care. She often used them to explain the larger political and social context of Depression-era Germany. Using this technique, she described heckling on the floor of the Reichstag, explained Chancellor Brüning's coercive and ineffective measures for reducing the costs of living and production, and introduced *Tribune* readers to the six million men who belonged to paramilitary organizations controlled by political parties, including the Reichsbanner, made up of members of the Social Democratic Party (SPD), Hitler's Brownshirts, and the Steel Helmet, an organization of World War I veterans that began as monarchists and nationalists but became aligned with the Nazis over time. (The regular army was limited to one hundred thousand men by the terms of the Treaty of Versailles.) She gave equal consideration to violence at the hands of Reds and Fascists. She also gave her readers glimpses of the National Socialist Party's growth as a political force.

Despite the restraint Schultz showed in choosing which riots to report on, the *Tribune's* editorial desk feared Chicago readers had a limited appetite for such stories. In December 1930, George Scharschug, who had replaced Joseph Pierson as cable editor, followed a compliment on her story on riots related to the Berlin showing of *All Quiet on the Western Front* with the statement: "Berlin riots are becoming almost a joke. They happen so frequently."[14]

Schultz agreed that "Berlin riots are too frequent to be really thrilling." She promised to limit coverage of them even further, though she expected a spree of "hotter" riots by February or March that might be worth space in the paper. Nonetheless, she pushed back a little: "Time and again I have seen the A.P. [Associated Press] or the U.P. [United Press] slip a little riot over on us and so I surmised they still had some charm."[15]

Several months later, Schultz took the Chicago news desk to task for adding incorrect information to one of her stories, presumably drawn from a news service account. The article claimed that Communist rioters fired from the rooftops into a massed formation of police, leaving sixteen people dead. She contacted Scharschug as soon as the paper reached her, two weeks after its publication: "I am sorry to have to report that the attached slaughter story is not true." The wire agency that reported the false information could have discovered the story was a fake with a little effort. Her office had investigated the rumor twice: on Sunday, August 9, when the rumors began, and again the following day. The reported death toll was wrong. There wasn't even one death as a result of Sunday's clashes, let alone sixteen.

Schultz described her "riot organization" so that the Chicago office would understand how carefully she investigated such stories. They got local news through the Telegraph Union service and the Ullstein press conglomerate, owner of one of the great European wire services. She had a mole in another German news conglomerate—the Scherl papers, owned by Alfred Hugenberg, leader of the right-wing Nationalist Party—who watched for stories not carried by the wire services. She had informants in police headquarters, and in the Nazi and Communist Parties as well—and she took care to maintain those relationships. Schultz explained, "The dinners we give them to encourage their willingness to talk don't appear on the expense account, but they give us the necessary contact. Should a policeman, Nazi or Communist get killed, I can assure you we hear about it! The victims' friends are only too glad of the opportunity of denouncing their 'wicked' enemies."

In addition to her outrage at what she bluntly described as "faking," she was also annoyed that the *Tribune* was giving riot stories from the wire services prominent placement. After his admonition in December that Berlin riots had become a joke, her office had cut back on the number of "fight messages" they filed. If the Chicago office wanted more riot stories, she would send more but they would be authentic news, "not New York fabrications."

"I know there are lots of stories from Berlin that could be jazzed up," she went on, "... but I always understood that the Tribune wants accurate and reliable news that we sincerely believe or know to be true, after investigating it. I believe our readers prefer this 'safe and sane' if unspectacular reporting—or am I wrong?"[16]

Two days later, she wrote to Scharschug again. The faked story with its sixteen dead had reappeared, this time in the Sunday edition. She was furious. The erroneous articles had caused the foreign press office to cancel a rare official interview she had scheduled with Chancellor Brüning—an important opportunity wasted. The articles wouldn't affect her private conversations with the chancellor: "I see Brüning quite often informally, but he rarely speaks for publication," she told Scharschug. In fact, Schultz was scheduled to have dinner with the minister of the interior that evening, and Brüning promised to try to drop by for coffee.[17]

It still stung.

Over the course of 1931, the number of stories Schultz filed about the actions of Hitler and his followers increased in frequency, but she consistently applied her philosophy of "safe and sane" reporting to those stories, despite the temptation to do otherwise. "One can make glorious creepy stuff out of the Hitlerites," she told Scharschug, "but we believe we are acting more in the interests of the paper if we stick to facts as closely as we can and not strain for the glory of a big flashy story that sounds grand one day and makes you feel foolish the day after."[18] The day would soon come when "creepy" would be a mild description of Nazi actions, but for now even the most astute political observer found it difficult to be sure whether the Nazis were a political aberration or truly dangerous.

Schultz met Hitler for the first time at the Hotel Kaiserhof, where he stayed when he was in Berlin before he became chancellor. She was at the hotel for a scheduled meeting with Göring. When Hitler came into the lobby for tea, Göring introduced them. Hitler loved sweets, hence the afternoon tea break. He also liked to kiss women's hands—a habit Schultz attributed to his Austrian background. But, she said, there is an elegant way to kiss a lady's hand and a non-elegant way. Recounting the incident later, she said Hitler "gave me that kind of a hot kiss with his staring at you at the same time, which is a bad way of doing it." The kiss with "soulful stare" had always repulsed Sigrid. She froze. In response, Hitler froze too. (She would later claim he had a superb instinct for whether people responded to him or not.) Thereafter, when the occasion demanded, Hitler gave Schultz a "good manly handshake."[19]

Despite their mutual distaste, Schultz had a rare, private interview with Hitler on December 4, 1931. Hewing to the *Tribune's* preferred style of "no editorializing," she quoted Hitler at length without commentary for much of the interview. Hitler stated he would be a fool to try to take over Germany through violence: "It will be mine within a very short time, anyway, since every election brings my party closer to an absolute majority." He asserted that under his control Germany would no longer pay war reparations. He described his party's involvement in street battles as a bloody war and made the unsubstantiated claim that "communist assassins" had killed and wounded thousands of his followers. He declared, at length, that the Nazis' main mission was to destroy Communism, which he described as the scourge of nations. Speaking of his absolute control over his party members, he said, "My will is done"—a grandiloquent statement often misquoted as "My will be done" in histories of the period.

Hitler was convinced that he would hold absolute power in Germany in a year at the latest. He missed by a month. His lieutenants were more optimistic and less accurate—they believed he would rule Germany by February. Schultz's personal assessment of Herr Hitler, borne out by the interview as a whole, was that "his confidence in himself is staggering."[20]

Several weeks later, Schultz reported that Hitler, "like the sovereigns of yore," issued a New Year's Eve proclamation. Describing himself and his party members as knights fighting for Germany's welfare, he boasted of the Nazi Party's growth: "We started with seven members. Today we have 15,000,000 followers. Only one more step and we shall be the German nation. Awake, Germany!"[21] In the two articles combined, Schultz gave *Tribune* readers a portrait of Hitler as someone they should take seriously.

Schultz was not the first American journalist to interview Hitler. Hearst correspondent Karl H. von Wiegand, interviewed the "German

Mussolini" in 1922, and again in 1930 and in June 1940, a few days before German forces occupied Paris. But, according to CBS radio commentator Hans V. Kaltenborn, she was one of no more than a dozen "newsmen" who had exclusive interviews with Hitler during his years in power—many of which, Schultz would point out to Scharschug, "had special strings tied to them."[22] With the exception of Dorothy Thompson, who described Hitler as "the very prototype of the 'Little Man'" in an article that appeared in *Cosmopolitan* in March 1932, all of them recognized Hitler's potential importance, even when Americans back home did not.[23]

⁂

Only a few months later, Hitler was on the verge of making his prediction that he would soon hold absolute power in Germany come true. President von Hindenburg's seven-year term of office was up and a presidential race was underway—an election which Schultz, and those Germans who opposed Hitler, saw as a fight to "avert the threatening reign of Fascism."[24] The election was officially a four-person race, but in reality, there were only two candidates that mattered: Hitler, not a citizen and technically not eligible to run for office, and the duty-driven eighty-four-year-old President von Hindenburg.

Schultz reported every stage of the campaign. She gave her readers vivid accounts of mass meetings, what she described as "idealistic" young Nazis marching and singing military songs from the Great War, trucks outfitted with loudspeakers broadcasting election messages at busy Berlin street corners, the new use of airplanes as campaign vehicles, and an occasional free-for-all between Fascist and Communist orators, who competed for the attention of jobless men and women as they waited in snow and sleet outside the labor office to collect their dole. She explained how critical the women's vote was to the election. In one long article, she shared the twenty-five planks of the National Socialist platform in painstaking detail. In another, she summarized the competing parties' positions, concluding that their mutual antagonism explained the desperate fighting, with fists, daggers, and revolvers that disrupted German towns every night. (It wouldn't have been a German election without a street fight or three.) And over and over, she hammered home her belief that the election was a matter of life and death for the Weimar Republic—the story was too important and the stakes were too high for her to remain impartial. Over the course of the campaign, her articles often made the front page, where they competed with the Lindbergh baby's kidnapping for column inches, "scare cap" headlines, and readers' attention.

After a scant two weeks of campaigning, Germans went to the polls on March 13. Hindenburg received 18.65 million votes, or 49.54 percent of the popular vote. Hitler received 11.34 million votes, a 30.12 percent share, but still considerably less than the 21 million the Hitlerites predicted he would receive.[25] Despite Hindenburg's dominance at the polls, the German constitution required a run-off election if no candidate won more than half the popular vote. Hindenburg missed victory by 0.5 percent.

The run-off election was scheduled for the second Sunday in April. No one doubted how it would end. Hindenburg defeated Hitler again, this time with a sufficient margin to win the presidency.

It was a classic case of "win the battle, lose the war" for those who had embraced Hindenburg's candidacy as the only defense against Hitler.

Over the next nine months, German politics were marked by interparty intrigues. Hindenburg, who was increasingly under the influence of his son Oskar and other members of the nationalist and monarchist opposition, fired Brüning as chancellor, appointed monarchist politician Major Franz von Papen in his place, fired von Papen, appointed defense minister General Kurt von Schleicher in December, and refused to appoint Adolf Hitler on two occasions. Hitler refused to join coalition governments under von Papen's leadership, causing Germany to go through another general election on July 31, when the Nazis received 37.3 percent of the vote, and again in November, when the Nazi percentage fell to 33.1 percent—not enough to form a wholly Nazi government but still enough to be a major player in the chancellorship sweepstakes.

More than once in this period, Schultz experienced backlash as a result of her reporting on the political chaos. The German Foreign Office once again threatened her with expulsion, this time because she didn't show more sympathy to Chancellor von Papen, whom she regularly (and accurately) described as leading a "cabinet of junkers." Once again she reminded them that her expulsion would make a dramatic story, in which the German government would play the villain's role. At a more personal and frightening level, she received anonymous letters from both Hitler and von Papen supporters, threatening her with death if she failed to understand the greatness of their respective leaders. It was a new experience for her. "They are so thoroughly obscene," she wrote to McCormick, "I hesitate to send them on."[26]

Finally, Hindenburg, worn down by the political wrangling and losing his clarity of mind and purpose, asked Hitler to form a government.

At half past eleven, on the morning of January 30, 1933, Adolf Hitler was sworn in as chancellor of the Weimar Republic, placing his hand on the Weimar constitution as he took an oath to protect the German people and the laws of the German nation.

When the ceremony was over, Schultz returned to her office and sat down at her typewriter. She needed to file her first story about the new chancellor by one, in time to run in the morning edition. It was front-page news for sure.

"National Socialist banners with the Fascist swastika sign waved over hundreds of buildings today," she began.[27]

CHAPTER THIRTEEN

WHEN PUTSCH COMES TO SHOVE

We'd say she has her share of excitement.

—*THE TRIB*, July 1934[1]

Surely by this time, Germany has learned
that censorship is not a good thing and will
be anxious to let you tell the full truth.

—GEORGE SCHARSCHUG
to Sigrid Schultz, July 18,1934[2]

Hitler's term as chancellor opened with a nighttime parade through the capital that soon turned riotous. Thousands of Nazi supporters marched in massive columns across the Tiergarten, under the triumphal arch of the Brandenburg Gate, past the French embassy, and down Wilhelmstrasse. André François-Poncet, the French ambassador and one of Schultz's most reliable sources in the diplomatic corps, described the torches the Nazis brandished as they passed the embassy as "a river of fire"—a fitting start for a regime that would often be marked by flame.[3] By contrast, Schultz told her readers, the inhabitants of the Communist districts "were sullen and agitated, ready to fight at the drop of a hat." Clashes between Nazis and Communists were inevitable and violent. "It was evident," Schultz concluded in a massive understatement, "that Hitler's ascendency has sharply divided the nation."[4]

Hitler moved quickly to close that divide and secure his power. Like his predecessors in the chancellery, he did not control enough seats in the Reichstag to create a single-party cabinet, even counting his monarchist allies. Instead of building a coalition, as other chancellors had done before him, he convinced Hindenburg to dissolve the Reichstag two days after he appointed Hitler as chancellor, with elections scheduled for March 5, 1933—the sixth federal election in eleven months.

Writing to McCormick in anticipation of the election, Schultz told him that under the "unbalancing influence of the unbalanced Hitler and Papen" conditions in Germany were more dangerous than they had been in years. (As far as Schultz and most Americans in Berlin were concerned, Hitler seemed like "a cheap hysterical actor," but it was impossible to ignore that millions of Germans had fallen under his spell.) The Nazi storm troopers were bored and restless. There were secessionist movements in Germany's southern states. "Desperadoes" in both Germany and Poland plotted to provoke war. And Hindenburg's age and failing memory made him a puppet in the hands of both his own son and vice chancellor Franz von Papen.[5]

In the weeks before the elections, Schultz reported almost daily on attacks—political and physical—on Hitler's opponents. Communists, Socialists, and Catholics all took a hit, though the Communists were the primary target. One attack aimed at all of Hitler's political rivals was a decree curtailing the freedom of the press and freedom of assembly, signed by Hindenburg at Hitler's urging on February 4. Titled "For the Protection of the German People," the decree called for six month's suppression of newspapers, with heavy fines for publishers found guilty of "excesses." The decree was aimed at German newspapers, but the Nazis' desire to curtail freedom of the press would soon extend to foreign correspondents as well.

⚬⚭⚬

Schultz was at her desk when she heard the fire alarms sound at nine o'clock on the evening of February 27, 1933. She and her staff rushed out of the office and followed the fire engines, which raced toward the Reichstag building, two blocks away. As she ran through the Brandenburg Gate, slipping on the ice-covered sidewalks, flames burst out of the Reichstag and licked their way up to its huge glass-and-gold cupola. Sparks rained down on Bismarck's statue in the neighboring square. The cupola's framework cracked and threatened to collapse into the main parliamentary session room below.

Every fire company in Berlin arrived to fight the fire. The police threw a heavy cordon around the square as a safety precaution.

Thousands of people stood in the slush and snow on the other side of the cordon, shivering as a sharp wind blew in out of the west, and watched from the Tiergarten as the firemen attempted to save the blazing Reichstag building.

At 11:45 p.m., just as the fire companies prepared to leave, flames flared up again and the fire spread to the rooms surrounding the main chamber. It was one in the morning before the chief of police finally announced the fire was under control. Schultz had missed the deadline for calling Paris with the news, but this story warranted the cost of sending a late cable in time to meet the morning edition. She was probably composing the lead in her head as she hurried back to the office: "Fire of incendiary origin partially destroyed the massive $6,500,000 Reichstag building last night . . ."[6]

The Nazis blamed the Communists for the conflagration even before the fire was under control. Schultz, like every other correspondent in Berlin, believed the Nazis were responsible for the fire, though none of them included their suspicion in the stories they filed.

Thanks to Dick Little's training, Schultz always hesitated to publish suspicions she couldn't prove. In this case, her caution proved to be wise for reasons beyond journalistic ethics. The following day, the German government issued a decree that rescinded rights German citizens had enjoyed under the Weimar constitution, including freedom of expression. As Schultz pointed out to her readers, this included the foreign press.

The decree gave the police the right to spy on residents' mail, telegrams, and phone calls. It did not take long after the passage of the acts rescinding German liberties for correspondents, and other foreigners living in Berlin, to realize they were under surveillance. Their telephones, at home and at the office, were tapped. Their German friends' phones were tapped. Their letters were read. Schultz was sure her maid reported everything she did to the authorities.

A few days later, the government issued another decree, increasing the penalties for and giving descriptions of "treasonous acts," including publishing news that was not in the Reich's best interest to release— whether true or not. Schultz's favorite defense against government unhappiness with her articles—that she hadn't reported anything but the truth—would be less useful going forward.

On March 7, the German government made the consequences for the foreign press explicit: foreign correspondents who misrepresented the internal situation in Germany would be deported. How that would play out in real life no one yet knew.

⁂

The March 5 election was the last multiparty election held under Hitler's rule. Despite the threats and violence unleashed by the Brownshirts against their opponents in the lead-up to the election, the Nazi Party won only 43.9 percent of the seats in the Reichstag—not enough to rule as a majority party. Instead of trying to put together a coalition government, the Nazis pushed a set of bills called the Enabling Acts through the Reichstag on March 23. The acts gave Hitler the ability to rule by decree and made control of the Reichstag irrelevant.

Hitler used his new power to remove his political opponents from office at all levels of government and to crush any organization that represented a potential threat. The police arrested thousands of members of the Communist Party, rendering it powerless. The Nazis banned the SPD, which had been the dominant party throughout the Weimar Republic. Other parties dissolved themselves rather than face persecution at the hands of the storm troopers. The Nazis broke up the independent trade unions, which had been a powerful political force in the early days of the republic, and replaced them with the Nazi-controlled German Labor Front. By the end of the first year of Hitler's rule, the Nazis had dismantled the political landscape of Weimar Germany.

Throughout 1933, Schultz reported on how the Nazis tore German society apart with the aid of the Enabling Acts. In article after article, she informed her readers about laws attacking the rights of German Jews and about growing violence against Jewish store owners.

In addition to reporting on attacks on Jewish-owned stores, Schultz occasionally gave in to anger and crossed a boycott line. In September 1933, for example, at the end of the annual Nazi rally in Nuremberg, brown-shirted Nazis and their civilian counterparts instituted an unofficial boycott against Jewish stores in the city, using a combination of intimidation and force to keep would-be customers out of the stores. Schultz was in Nuremberg, reporting on the rally. Walking down the main street, she saw storm troopers gathered in front of a jewelry shop whose owner was Jewish. She marched into the store and bought a few silver butter knives from the terrified shop owner. When she walked out, parcel in hand, the storm troopers greeted her with curses. Never easily cowed, and probably still riding the energy rush of anger, she turned on them and told them she was an American and Americans respected the rights of people. Of course, as she admitted to an interviewer later, it was still early days in the Nazi regime and no one knew yet just how bad things would get.[7]

Schultz reported on incidents that are now part of the accepted narrative of Nazi Germany, such as the infamous book burning that took place in the square outside Berlin University and in other cities across Germany on May 10, and on other serious incidents that are less widely remembered, like the arrest of three thousand labor leaders and the seizure of trade union assets on May 3. She often wove several stories together, hiding significant information in the middle of less dangerous content. For example, the headline on an article dated March 21, 1933, focused on a Nazi raid on Albert Einstein's country home, ostensibly in search of weapons. The body of the piece dealt primarily with the passage of the Enabling Act—not a small story but not one that would endanger the correspondent who wrote it. Two substantive, even subversive, sentences were buried in the middle: "Authorities have announced that the first concentration camp for communists will be opened Wednesday at Dachau, near Munich. It will accommodate 5,000 Reds now in jail, as well as other political prisoners."[8] It was one of the earliest references to the concentration camps in an American paper. This sandwich technique made it less likely that pro-German readers in the United States and members of Germany's foreign press office would catch statements critical of the regime. Unfortunately, it also meant the kind of reader who skimmed the headlines, or perhaps only the first paragraph, missed important information.

⸙

Despite the constant surveillance, there was no official censorship on press cables in 1933, though occasionally a cable critical of the regime would mysteriously fail to go through. Instead, supervision of the press occurred after the fact. Once a story was published in America, the local German consul or one of the numerous German citizens living in the United States would contact the agencies involved with controlling the press if he found something objectionable in it. Then, sometimes weeks later, the journalist in question would be called into the Foreign Office, the foreign press division of the Propaganda Ministry or, worse, the Geheime Staatspolizei, which would soon become known as the Gestapo, from its acronym, GSP.

On June 11, 1933, Schultz received her first summons to the Gestapo office, framed as a request that she call at the GSP headquarters between eleven and twelve any day that week.

The Nazis had arrested two members of the foreign press corps in the months since Hitler became chancellor, but Schultz was not worried about the summons. After all, the Weimar government had taken her to task more than once when she wrote articles not to their liking. Even when they threatened her with expulsion, she had always successfully defended herself on the grounds that everything she wrote was true.

Nevertheless, she put the American embassy on notice before she visited the Gestapo headquarters the next day. Alfred Klieforth, the first secretary of the embassy, offered to go with her, but she told him she "did not feel fidgety about anything" and was willing to "face the lions" alone. All she asked was that the embassy be prepared to take action on her behalf if she hadn't returned after two hours.

The summons turned out to be a nonevent, at least for the moment. When she arrived at noon, the officer who had requested her presence was not there.

Annoyed, Schultz sent him a note: she was extremely busy and would not come back without a definite appointment.

Four days later, she received a call from the Gestapo asking whether the coming Monday would suit her, and if so, to name a time—"all in best parlor manners," she wrote to Colonel McCormick immediately after the call. She had been careful to avoid "agents provocateurs and such" and consequently felt quite safe being called into the "lion's den." In fact, she hadn't planned to write him about the summons until the matter was settled the following week, but friends were leaving Germany that night who were willing to carry her letter. Who knew when she would have another safe courier?[29]

On Monday, Schultz telephoned the American embassy and once again arranged for a secretary to wait in his office until he heard from her.

She presented herself at the appointed time. The Gestapo official who had "invited" her to the office, in what would become standard operating procedure when dealing with foreign correspondents, left her waiting for an hour and a half.

Once the official made himself available, Schultz learned she had not been called in because of her hard-hitting stories about the Enabling Acts and attacks on German rights. Instead, he pressed her about a story from April 25, which began with an account of Kiel University students who had demanded the resignation of twenty-eight professors, all of them Jewish, liberals, or alleged Communists. It was an ugly story but moderate compared to others that had appeared in the *Tribune* under her byline.

"The authorities are greatly displeased with the story," the Gestapo official told her, perhaps shaking the newspaper clipping under her nose. "Where did you get your news?"

It was public knowledge, she told him. The story appeared in at least three semi-official German newspapers that she could remember offhand. Moreover, she interviewed leaders of the German students, who were in Berlin for a convention. She helpfully pointed out that the story also referred to two killings, which she had taken from the police records.

The official warned her that correspondents were personally responsible for the news they sent out. The fact that it was published in the German press was no defense.

And then her appointment was over.

"Some official thought a little summons to G.S.P. might prove intimidating, which was an extremely foolish thought," she told McCormick. "I have always made it a point to stick to facts as closely as humanly possible and I don't see how anybody in his senses could object to factual reporting."[10]

In coming months, the foreign press community as a whole would learn that the truth was no armor against a government that was *not* entirely within its senses.

―⁂―

Instead of censoring articles before they went out, the Nazis attempted to control the information that reached reporters.

They established two daily news conferences for foreign reporters. The Ministry of Foreign Affairs, which had been a source of official information under both the German Empire and the Weimar Republic, ran the first, at one in the afternoon, in a long, ornately decorated room where Bismarck had once held forth. The newly founded Ministry of Public Enlightenment and Propaganda, sometimes referred to by correspondents as "Joseph Goebbels's Lie Factory," ran the second.[11] The primary value of the second conference as far as many correspondents was concerned was the opportunity to see previews of the weekly German newsreels before they were released to the public.

The news conferences were carefully staged performances. A half dozen spokesmen, described by United Press reporter Howard K. Smith as "confident, cocky little bureaucrats who were overbearing with [self] importance," held forth on diplomatic, military, and economic issues, with facts buried in layers of propaganda.[12]

In addition to the press conferences, correspondents who were lazy or too new in Berlin to have contacts of their own could get help from the foreign press office in the form of lists of sources, copies of periodicals, and appointments for relevant interviews. Schultz viewed such help with suspicion, even during the Weimar Republic. She had spent years building up her own news pipeline, which was the envy of other correspondents. "Where Sigrid got her news tips nobody ever really knew for sure," Gregor Ziemer later recalled, "—from friends among the German nobility, political party leaders, churchmen, governmental officials, labor leaders, educators (She knew more people in more walks of life than any other two journalists put together.); from analyzing all the leading German newspapers daily; from informants she hired; from casual conversations; from guests at her home. More generally, sheer instinct seemed to point her in the right direction."[13] Those sources became even more important under the Nazis.

⸙

The German press also was a source of official raw material for news stories.

Reading local newspapers had long been part of the tool kit of foreign correspondents. Whether in Berlin, Paris, or Warsaw, correspondents typically began the day reading the local papers.

When the Nazis came to power, German newspapers became less useful as a source. Within months of Hitler's appointment as chancellor, Germany no longer had a free press. The Nazis shut down hundreds of opposition newspapers. They seized papers owned by the Communist and Social Democratic Parties as well as Jewish-owned publishing companies. The few "independent" papers that survived were effectively under the control of the Propaganda Ministry, which handed down detailed instructions about what could be published and in what form at daily press conferences for German papers, separate from those for the foreign press. Failure to comply could result in fines, dismissal, or imprisonment. As a result, according to Louis Lochner, Berlin bureau chief for the Associated Press, "The reading of papers now became a game of looking for slip-ups by some careless or incompetent editor, or spotting a significant item in an obscure corner of the paper, and of reading the fine print in which decrees were published in the official section of the sheet."[14]

As far as Schultz was concerned, by the end of 1933, the German press was dead. Jewish journalists and anyone who did not support the Nazis had fled or been purged from newspaper staffs. Those reporters who remained were required to be members of the Nazi-controlled Reich Press Chamber, which kept registries of "racially pure" journalists and editors. "It is ridiculous to speak of the men running German newspapers now as newspapermen," Schultz wrote to Colonel McCormick. "They are low ranking state officials ... A few old-timers are left in the German newspapers because their knowledge is needed but they are under strict supervision of the newcomers and they know it. Many of the so-called newspapermen were file clerks and such who got the jobs of the former independent scribes because they were Nazis."[15]

It was treason for a German to give a foreign correspondent any news that was not flattering to the Reich. Nonetheless German informants risked their lives to tell Schultz and other journalists the truth about what was happening in Nazi Germany. Schultz later reminisced that she would be awakened in the middle of the night by pebbles thrown against her bedroom window: "it would be someone with news that he had not dared to bring around in daytime because of the watchful Gestapo."[16] More than once, she had to choose between the story and the source: "I know it is true but I could under no condition name my witnesses or sources."[17]

One place where Schultz and other members of the foreign press corps met possible sources under the noses of the Nazis was Die Taverne, an Italian-ish restaurant near the Hotel Adlon run by a large, gregarious German named Willy Lehman and his slender Belgian wife. Journalists arrived, one or two at a time, around ten or eleven o'clock, after filing their stories and stayed until early morning. Norman Ebbutt, chief Berlin correspondent of *The Times* of London from 1925 to 1937, when he was expelled on falsified charges of espionage, presided over the conversation at the large round corner table that Lehman reserved for them. Schultz wasn't the only woman at the table. A Mrs. Holmes, described by William Shirer, himself a regular, as "a beak-nosed woman of undoubted intelligence," had a regular seat next to Ebbutt.[18] Two other women, Mary Deuel and Dorothy Oechsner, often accompanied their husbands, reporters for the *Chicago Daily News* and the United Press.[19] Martha Dodd, the ambassador's daughter, who fancied herself a writer, came when she could. But Schultz was, as Shirer described her in his diary, "the only woman correspondent in our ranks, buoyant, cheerful, and always well informed."[20]

A dozen or more foreign journalists met at the restaurant most evenings to enjoy late night meals, talk shop, and complain about life in Nazi Berlin. They also (cautiously) pooled information. Before the Nazis came to power, correspondents had walked a fine line between being rivals and being colleagues. They were eager to protect their sources and guard their scoops. At the same time, correspondents stationed in the same foreign city had no one else to depend on. They covered for each other when they were out of town and shared information they knew wouldn't run in their own papers. The need to cooperate grew more urgent under the Nazis, causing correspondents to create what Schultz described as "the funniest little international combines of newspaperers [sic] . . . working together."[21]

The journalists' *Stammtisch*, or table for regulars, and its use as a point of contact was no secret. "Everybody else in the restaurant is watching them and trying to overhear what they are saying," Christopher Isherwood wrote. "If you have a piece of news to bring them—the details of an arrest, or the address of a victim whose relatives might be interviewed—then one of the journalists leaves the table and walks up and down with you outside in the street."[22]

Secretaries from various foreign embassies would make an appearance. So would Nazi press officials, "special German newspapermen barely tainted with the Nazi smell," and, on rare occasions, Gestapo chief Rudolf Diels—all hoping to find out what the correspondents had learned that day.[23]

⸎

The Nazis put more than four hundred anti-Jewish laws and regulations into place between 1933, when Hitler became chancellor, and the beginning of World War II in 1939. Most of them were passed at the national level, but cities and states also got in on the action. The first major act, which excluded Jews from positions in the German civil service, was passed on April 17, only twenty-five days after the Enabling Acts went into effect.

Schultz had written about what she called Hitler's "terror plan" to drive Jews out of Germany as early as November 1931.[24] Now, with Hitler in power, she published hundreds of articles dealing with the passage of antisemitic laws and violence against Germany's Jewish population between March 1933 and December 1940—openly reporting on the Nazis' fanatical hatred of Jews at some risk to herself, to the extent that she could do so without endangering her sources.

It is unclear how much Schultz did to help German Jews in a more immediate way. Later in life, she was evasive on the subject. Alan Green, interviewing her for the William E. Wiener Oral History Library in 1971, directly asked whether she was able to help any of the Jews who were trying to leave Europe while they still could in 1933, either through her office or her connections. In response, Schultz downplayed her efforts as "advising" them. She was frustrated by her Jewish friends who did not believe what was happening—or at least did not believe it could happen to them. She told Green she had "a heck of a time telling them: 'Get out.'" In one case, soon after the Nazi invasion of Czechoslovakia, she sent a young journalist to warn a friend who had previously worked at the Czechoslovakian embassy in Berlin to get his family out before it was too late. His answer: "Don't send any more people to see us because that endangers us." They died at Theresienstadt.[25]

Like other foreign correspondents in Berlin at the time, she helped friends get exit permits, gave them money when she could, and occasionally hid someone in her apartment for a few days. Glimpses of individual actions appear in her letters, and in letters she received after the war from those she aided. She helped Fritz Elsas, former mayor of Berlin, sell a valuable stamp collection to raise money to get his family out of Germany, though ultimately they were not able to leave. She arranged for Hansi Burg, the Jewish girlfriend of actor Hans Albers, to marry a Norwegian so she could get an exit visa. (Schultz later tried to reconnect Burg and Albers after the war in what she described as "a kind of Cupid act."[26]) She pulled strings on behalf of musician Hans Rosenwald, obtaining first his release from the Oranienburg concentration camp and then an exit visa for him; she remembered the case vividly because she was subsequently called into the Gestapo headquarters, where she was charged with being Jewish herself on the grounds that otherwise she would not "go to bat for Jews" the way she did.[27]

Quentin Reynolds, who arrived in Berlin in 1933 as a correspondent for the International News Service, claimed that she did more than simply react to requests for help. She sometimes orchestrated escape plans for people she knew.

When Reynolds mentioned to Schultz that he couldn't afford to live at the Hotel Adlon, where he was currently staying, she had a solution: a furnished nine-room apartment overlooking the Tiergarten that was within his budget. The apartment's tenant, Hans Lederer, had been fired from the University of Berlin because he was Jewish. The professor and his wife gave Reynolds a tour of the apartment, including a study lined with some five thousand books, many of them in Japanese. Then they left him alone with Schultz to close the deal. Schultz told him the professor could get a job teaching in New York, if he could get out of Berlin. She had already helped the Lederers get their exit permits. The only problem now was money.

"I want you to buy his books for a dollar a book," she told Reynolds.

Reynolds objected. He had at most $400 in his account and didn't read Japanese.

Schultz shook her head and gave him a look of exasperation that told him he was missing the point. "You buy them with a rubber check, just to satisfy the American authorities that Lederer is solvent," she explained. "Once he gets to America, you send him his books and he tears up your check."

The deal was done. Schultz had a lawyer draw up a bill of sale, then Reynolds signed the biggest check of his life. "I had a feeling that I was buying stock in her personal underground railroad," he concluded.[28]

Schultz's feelings on Jewish immigrants to America were more complex than her interaction with Reynolds would suggest. At the same time that she was helping people she knew, she also had concerns about who was allowed into the United States.

In a letter to George Scharschug, written while sailing back to Europe in January 1939, she told him that she had called on friends in the State Department while she was in Washington "to ask them to try to pass some kind of regulation, some instructions, enabling the consuls to give preferential treatment to those immigrants who could be business assets and to reject those who quite obviously, though their papers are in order, will never fit into the American picture, who will never become real Americans."

Her fear was that the arrival of those "hapless immigrants ... who could never adapt to America" would "make it easy for the antisemitic groups to spread their propaganda."[29]

As the year went on, Schultz became more and more cautious about what news she sent and how she sent it. She gave important or controversial material to friends to carry out of the country. When possible, she "hopped" across the border, sometimes for only a few hours, into Holland, Switzerland, Czechoslovakia, or Austria to mail reports herself. Prague was a particular favorite. She told McCormick that Czechoslovakia seemed "incredibly wholesome" compared to Germany, or even Austria, where it was already dangerous to send information to Chicago due to the strong Nazi presence there.[30]

Her letters to the Chicago office were filled with discussions of new arrangements she was making to gather the news, and concerns about old arrangements that were failing. Because the Nazis continued to monitor letters, she learned to divide her stories into parts, with the hope that at least some of the information would get through. Sometimes she prearranged codes for writing about specific dangerous subjects. She no longer kept copies of stories "which might seem unpleasant" in the office. The newest Gestapo tactic was to lure correspondents away with invitations to an event, then search the office while they were gone, "and possibly 'forget' some document or find something they brought along while we are not in."[31]

Schultz regularly argued with the Chicago office that it was more reliable to send stories by cable than to telephone them through Paris or London. Over the summer of 1934, the office phones would break down every few hours and callers would be told they were not answering the phone. Schultz believed Gestapo interference was the cause. When the telephones worked, it was safe to assume the Nazis were recording their conversations. Moreover, things sometimes got garbled by telephone: "in the story of Schleicher's funeral the telephone transmitted 'Comradly [sic] assassination' instead of 'cowardly assassination.'" In another case, Hindenburg's son was "curiously compromised" instead of "seriously compromised." For the most part, the garbled messages were no more than annoying, but it was possible that serious errors could occur.[32]

Telephoning stories had additional risks. Sometimes circumstances forced Schultz to telephone what she described as a "dynamity" story—one with the potential to blow up—through London or Paris. The London office was less dangerous because they simply transmitted the story to Chicago for publication in the United States. By the time copies of the paper made their way back to Berlin two weeks later, the story was stale and the Germans didn't get too excited about it. Paris was a different matter. Until the Paris Edition was sold in 1934, the Paris office had a newspaper to put out and sometimes used Schultz's stories to fill its pages. She regularly asked them to tone down her stuff if they printed one of the stories she relayed through them. More often than not, they printed her copy verbatim while it was still hot, after which threats would "sizzle in the air" in Berlin for a time.[33]

Behind every precaution Schultz took with transmitting her stories lurked the threat of deportation, arrest, or the concentration camps.

Schultz was more daring in her private reports to Robert McCormick, which she mailed from outside Germany or entrusted to friends, than she was in her stories for publication. In those reports, she shared what she thought about Hitler and the Nazis in addition to what she could prove. On one occasion, she told McCormick that conditions in Germany reminded her of the religious wars that had torn the region apart in the sixteenth century, with one third of the country made up of "sincere fanatic believers in the new religion" of Hitlerism.[34] She often referred sarcastically to the "darling, darling Nazis" or the "darling SS," particularly when they pulled what she called "little stunts" against members of the foreign correspondent community. She talked about the cruelty of the storm troopers (SA) and described "little Joe Goebbels" as rabid. Writing from Prague, she reminded McCormick of his own words: "You called the Nazi chiefs 'gangsters' in your series on Germany. I don't believe there is a word in any language that describes them more accurately." The word had particular resonance in Chicago only two years after the end of Prohibition and Chicago's gangland Beer Wars.[35] As she bluntly told George Scharschug, "I'm afraid I dislike Nazi dictatorship."[36] Dislike would harden into hatred as Nazi "massacres" grew more brazen.

Early in the morning on Saturday, June 30, 1934, Hitler and Schutz-staffel (SS) units swooped down on the resort town of Bad Wiessee near Munich, where Captain Ernst Roehm and other top SA leaders were gathered. Hitler arrested Roehm and ordered many of his companions shot, launching a nationwide attack on storm troopers and anyone Hitler considered a political foe. Roehm was executed on July 1, after considerable vacillation on Hitler's part. The massacre lasted through July 2. On July 3, the government issued a law that retroactively made the murders legal, calling them an emergency action to save the nation.

Every foreign correspondent in Germany had been expecting trouble between Ernst Roehm's brown-shirted storm troopers and the more conservative Reichswehr forces. But none of them expected Hitler to take matters into his own hands.

Caught by surprise, Schultz and her competitors scrambled to cover the story. Schultz filed her copy at the last possible minute on Sunday morning, after almost twenty-four hours of tracking leads, visiting storm trooper barracks, assessing reactions of the crowds in the streets, and parsing official statements on the night's events. In her daily log, she noted that she was so tired she could weep. Her article ran in the Sunday morning paper, the headline in scare caps across the entire front page: "HITLER CRUSHES OUT REVOLT."[37]

Schultz's initial story quoted extensively from Nazi sources on Saturday's events. In the following two weeks, Schultz produced eleven detailed articles about what became known as the June Blood Purge and the Night of the Long Knives. Ten of them ran on the front page. She continued to draw on official news releases from the chancellery, the Nazi headquarters in Munich, and Hermann Göring. But she also quoted unnamed "reliable sources" and "the best informed circles," eyewitness accounts of arrests and executions, and rumors on the street. She dug more deeply into Hitler's continuing attacks on those he pronounced enemies of the Nazi government and tracked the rising number of executions that followed the initial massacre. She analyzed the new laws promulgated in the aftermath of the purge. She contrasted official pronouncements—hedged with carefully chosen verbs such as "asserts" and "claims"—with the unofficial reports and death toll estimates that continued to circulate. She took a chance and reported on Hitler's state of mind before and after the massacres. As the story continued to unfold, Schultz reported that "Nazis themselves whisper to the inquiring foreigner," giving names of prisoners and rumors of deaths.[38]

On July 4, Schultz was once again called in to the Gestapo headquarters, one assumes because of her ongoing reports on the deaths. She was not the only foreign correspondent to incur the Nazis' wrath. On July 10, propaganda minister Joseph Goebbels broadcast a bitter attack on members of the foreign press for their coverage of Hitler's bloody purge of the Nazi Party. He threatened correspondents who misrepresented actions of the German government in the future. He ended his diatribe by declaring that the German people "turned from these lie fabricators with nausea and horror."[39]

⚬⚬⚬

The first expulsion of an American journalist occurred six weeks after Goebbels issued his threat.

President von Hindenburg died on August 2, 1934. The next day Hitler named himself Hindenburg's successor, combining chancellorship and presidency into one office with a new title: Führer. Hitler arranged for his elevation to be confirmed by a so-called free plebiscite—which was anything but free—on August 19. (He would use this technique more than once to give his actions an air of legitimacy until he no longer cared about the world's opinion.)

On August 24, Dorothy Thompson, famous in her own right as a journalist and also as the wife of Nobel Prize–winning novelist Sinclair Lewis, was ordered to leave Germany with one day's notice. The expulsion notice stated that her "invitation to leave" was due to her "numerous anti-German articles in the American Press," specifically her unflattering assessment of Hitler in *Cosmopolitan* two years earlier. "Reasons of self-respect forbid German authorities to grant you further hospitality in Germany." The American consul was told that if she did not leave voluntarily, she would be escorted over the border by two police officers.

Always flamboyant, Thompson turned her departure into an event. Many of the foreign correspondents in Berlin and much of the American expatriate community gathered at the train station to see her off. They gave her an armful of American Beauty roses as a farewell token.

Thompson's expulsion made the headlines in America, including a front-page article in the *Tribune*, in which Schultz compared the actions of the American government to those of the Russian and French governments in similar circumstances. When Germany arrested a Russian correspondent, Lilli Keich, and threatened her with expulsion, the Soviet government arrested and expelled a group of German correspondents from Moscow in retaliation. When Germany threatened the French correspondent Camille Loutre with deportation, the French ambassador warned Germany that for every French correspondent ousted four Germans would be ejected from France. "The Germans reconsidered," she told her readers. By contrast, the American embassy had merely asked for an extension of the date of Thompson's expulsion.[40]

Thompson was the first American journalist to be formally expelled from Nazi Germany, but prior to that, more than a dozen foreign correspondents left Germany during the first year of Nazi rule, either as a result of direct Nazi pressure or because they were warned that it would not be safe to stay. Between 1934 and 1937, another thirty-seven were expelled or left because of what George Seldes described as "real or imagined compulsion."[41] William Shirer, who arrived in Berlin as a correspondent for Hearst's Universal News Service a few hours after Thompson left, summed up the feeling of many: "All through my years in Berlin I was conscious of walking a real, if ill-defined, line. If you strayed too far off it, you risked expulsion."[42]

Schultz had walked that line during the Weimar Republic and was determined to walk it successfully under Hitler's rule as well. A year after Thompson's expulsion, she wrote to Seldes, "If you come to Germany you might get kicked out and coin a fortune out of it as Dorothy did—it certainly was a good business transaction for her." Schultz knew that path wasn't for her. "I suppose it's good publicity," she told him, "but I'd hate to miss the show even if I do scowl and gnash my teeth a lot and explode occasionally much to poor Mother's distress."[43]

CHAPTER FOURTEEN

LET THE GAMES BEGIN

She was short in stature, tall in ideas; often on the defensive as a female, but utterly fearless; tactful, stunningly blonde (before her hair turned white), smiling, but tough when it came to digging out stories, and treating with frank skepticism every news release concocted in Joseph Goebbels' Lie Factory, the Propaganda Ministry.

—GREGOR ZIEMER[1]

On March 10, 1935, a two-page story by Sigrid Schultz, titled "New Goose Step for 6.5 Million Germans" ran as the cover story of the *Tribune*'s illustrated Sunday magazine, *The Graphic*, which resembled magazines such as *Collier's* and *Liberty* in form and content.

In the weeks prior to March 10, Schultz and other members of the Berlin foreign press corps covered stories such as the return of the Saar coal region to German sovereignty, Anglo-German diplomatic talks regarding currency, Protestant churches' denunciation of Nazism as pagan, and the introduction of German television. Even when they included serious analysis of the issue under discussion, as Schultz's articles often did, such pieces were inherently narrow in scope.

Writing for magazines allowed a different style of reporting. Correspondents were able to sink into stories that would at best merit a few column inches in the daily papers. For example, Schultz's good friend Thomas Ybarra wrote several deep-dive stories for *Collier's* in which he analyzed aspects of life in the Third Reich in 1935, including a piece on the *Hitlerjugend* (Hitler Youth) and a profile of "Hitler's paymaster," Hjalmar Schacht.

Schultz's piece in *The Graphic* gave her room to take a broader look at life in Nazi Germany. It also gave her the opportunity to editorialize on the "Nazi stranglehold on what is left of independence" in a way that the daily pages of the *Tribune* did not allow. The piece is an interesting combination of reported feature and editorial, in which Schultz's disdain for the Nazis is clearly displayed. The first page featured dramatic photographs of young German athletes, but the article itself dealt with Nazi Germany as a country of "rules, regulation, regimentation, meager living, fines and dues" in contrast to the Nazi propaganda, which pictured it as a "glorious new Sparta of rugged strength and freedom."

Schultz argued that you would learn more about National Socialism from "the everyday life of Mr. and Mrs. Average Citizen" than you could from long treatises on Nazi theories. In the article, she described lives burdened by rules and regulations at every level, focusing on the Bormanns, a skilled carpenter and his wife, both in their sixties, who lived in a large apartment building in Berlin.

The first thing you saw when you walked into their building was a blackboard in the hall where the block warden posted instructions, appeals for "voluntary" donations, and orders for the buildings' residents. Residents conscientiously studied the board, because failure to comply with the instructions could mean trouble. "Trouble in this case means more than getting in difficulties with the neighbors," Schultz explained, "—it may mean jail, confiscation of property or concentration camp if one incurs the wrath of the Nazi party through his warden, to cite only a few examples."

Moving from building-wide issues to the Bormann family, she described first the impact of the Great War and Germany's subsequent economic crises on their lives and dreams, the changes in their lives under the Nazi state, and the differences between their experience of Nazi Germany and that of their children. She looked at how "voluntary" and mandatory contributions deducted from "Pa Bormann's" paycheck affected his take-home pay, and the role of Nazi-sponsored organizations in their lives. Pa Bormann was "a great joiner by nature" and liked wearing a uniform and marching in parades. Ma Bormann was unhappy about the number of organizations he belonged to. In the end, most Germans adapted to the regimentation, as much from fear as from agreement. Those who grumbled did so quietly, Schultz told her readers: "too many have been punished for careless remarks."

Reading the German papers, which printed daily reports of arrests, property seizures, and defamation gave a partial picture of what happened to those who resisted such regimentation. And yet, Schultz concluded, it was hard even for a foreigner who lived in Germany to understand the role fear played in everyday life: "only people who have known you for years will speak frankly with you as a foreigner or a visitor." The casual traveler would see little or nothing of the terror, which, Schultz said bluntly, "explains the discrepancy sometimes noticed between straight news reports about facts and happenings and roseate reports of a few tourists."[2]

Over the coming year, the number of tourists issuing rosy reports would grow as crowds of foreigners came to Berlin for the 1936 Olympics.

⚬⚬⚬

At five o'clock, on March 16, 1935, more than a hundred foreign correspondents, including Schultz, crowded the conference room at the Ministry for Public Enlightenment and Propaganda. Two hours earlier the ministry had summoned them to a press conference at which Joseph Goebbels would make an important announcement. It was the first time foreign correspondents had been "invited" to a press conference since the ministry issued official statements about the Nazi Party purge the previous June. No one knew why they had been called together.

Finally Goebbels limped in, his face set in the self-important expression of a man with serious news to impart. His voice shook with emotion as he read the text of a proclamation Hitler had made to the Reichstag several hours earlier. In a single speech, Hitler had thrown out the Versailles treaty, resurrected the old German system of universal conscription, and announced that he would quadruple the size of Germany's army. Goebbels spoke too quickly for correspondents to take down the text of the speech, but it didn't matter. The gist was clear. Reporters from the big wire services—Louis Lochner of the Associated Press, Ed Beattie of the United Press, and Gordon Young of Reuters—ran for the bank of telephones in the hall without waiting to hear what else Goebbels had to say. The wire services lived and died on the immediacy of their reporting.

Other correspondents, who still had several hours before they needed to file their stories, waited until the end when a few officials remained to answer questions. Once it became obvious that they weren't going to learn anything that hadn't been included in the official statement, they drifted out by twos and threes, heading toward their offices to make a few calls and compose a story that would interest the "milkman in Iowa."

When *Tribune* readers opened their Sunday papers the next day, an article by Sigrid Schultz explaining the importance of Hitler's decree greeted them on the front page. Hitler claimed his proclamation was an impulsive response to a French decree earlier that day, which increased the term of an army conscript's service from one year to two. He was forced to act because other nations had refused to disarm, as called for in the peace treaty. Germany needed to take measures for its own protection.

Schultz questioned just how impulsive Hitler's action actually was. The previous Sunday Hermann Göring had announced that the civilian sports air club, which he had founded, had been incorporated into the Reichswehr. The world had not objected to the idea of a newly created German military air force, which was forbidden under the Versailles treaty. Expanding the size of the German army was the obvious next step.

Two days after Hitler's decree, Germany invited all the foreign military attachés stationed in Berlin to observe the city's first air-raid defense and blackout drill, a carefully staged event using Germany's new air force. In the afternoon, thirty pursuit planes and twenty tri-motored planes thundered over the capital in a mock air raid, "peacefully" demonstrating their ability to bomb a city. That evening, the center of the city was shrouded in darkness. Threatened with arrest or fines of $60 (roughly $1,180 in 2022 dollars) for any light visible from the outside, Berlin residents had covered their windows with black paper. (Hefty as the fines were, the possibility of arrest was probably a greater deterrent. Fear of the Gestapo was a powerful motivator.) Most of the area's streetlights were out. The 1,500 still lit were draped in thick black mourning crepe to cut their light down to a ghostly glimmer. "Enemy" planes dropped imitation bombs on the shadowy city, while residents practiced first aid and retreated to cellars and air-raid dugouts.

Foreign observers were well aware that they had just witnessed a practical demonstration of Germany's return as a military power.

───✦───

Working hard to separate nuggets of truth from the dross of German press releases, and to couch her stories in ways that would not endanger her sources or herself, Schultz reported on Germany's rapid rearmament and its growing shortages of butter, lard, other fats, and meat—two parts of the same story. As Joseph Goebbels told a huge audience in January 1936, "We had a choice between butter and cannon. We chose cannon."[3] She informed her readers about attacks on Christian churches, new restrictions and attacks on Jews, and eugenics-based policies aimed at strengthening Germany's gene pool. In her private reports to McCormick, Schultz warned that "Hitler wants to swallow Lithuania, the main part of Poland, and Austria. The fight against the communistic scourge is an excellent alibi to cover up Germany's activities in the East."[4]

A few months later, the story shifted as Germany concentrated its efforts on the coming 1936 Olympics, which Schultz described as "a general campaign to impress foreign visitors with the 'quiet harmony pervading Germany' for the sake of which agitation against church, reactionaries and Jews is to be relegated to the background."[5] Careful plans were underway for everything from public art to arrangements for the foreign press. Schultz watched the preparations with a cynical eye, reporting on the political underpinnings and overt propaganda angles of Germany's Olympic preparations. She was particularly bothered by the construction of new buildings in the Olympic village, which she informed her readers were intended for the use of the German army when the Olympics were over. They were built by compulsory labor—unemployed men, threatened with losing their dole if they did not work on the project. She described the stadium and other public facilities to McCormick, in a coded letter sent by way of her friend Janet Fairbank, as "megalomania frozen into cement" and compared them to the Egyptian pyramids built by slaves. An aspect of the Nazis' "superlative organization" for the Olympics that she was sure most of the impressed foreign visitors would miss.

Germany broadcast the huge bell pealing from the tower above the Olympic stadium to radio stations around the world on July 5, 1936, signaling that everything was ready for the competitors. In a story that appeared on the sports page, Schultz reported that Germany was also prepared for foreign visitors, right down to providing a cheap currency for tourists, the travel mark. The German government expected its people to cooperate in the effort. Schultz informed her readers that the headline in the German paper *Der Angriff*, owned by

Joseph Goebbels, made no attempt to hide Germany's intentions. "The Olympic games are a chance to make propaganda as never before," it read. The paper urged Berlin's citizens to be "more charming than the Parisian, more pleasant than the Viennese, more vivacious than the Roman, more worldly wise than the Londoner, more practical than the New Yorker." Drivers, bicyclists, and especially truck drivers were warned to drive carefully.[6]

In the weeks that followed, the Nazis transformed Berlin into a theme-park version of itself. They removed Roma families from their homes and marched them to a detention camp, where they would be kept away from the foreigners arriving in Berlin, along with 1,400 homeless people. Workers whitewashed run-down buildings by the railroad track, where foreigners would arrive, and decorated them with window boxes filled with red geraniums. Restaurants, hotels, and other public places removed the signs that declared "*Juden unerwünscht*" (Jews not welcome) from their windows. Newsstands did not display the popular and fiercely antisemitic *Der Stürmer*, which was pornographic in its hatred, though it may have been available under the counter for those who knew to ask.

The Nazi press office made special preparations for the convenience of foreign journalists, courting them with special viewing stands, free secretarial services, and the finest broadcasting equipment for transmitting their stories. The European manager of Press Wireless, an international telecommunications facility run by a consortium of American newspapers for its members' benefit, informed Schultz that the Reichspost had set aside high-powered, high-speed radio transmitters for the exclusive use of the American press.[7] The Germans expected the facilities to pay for themselves in the form of favorable news articles about Germany's modern efficiency and athletic prowess.

By June, Schultz complained to friends back home that "tourists who dutifully admire everything Nazi" were "turning up in droves" in anticipation of the Olympics.[8] She may not have intentionally evoked the image of a herd of not-very-bright animals, but that certainly summed up her opinion of American tourists who arrived and looked at all things German with an uncritical eye. Many would leave impressed with the experience of Germany the Nazis had created for them, with a renewed skepticism about the objectivity of those newspaper reporters who told a different story.

The most prominent Americans to visit Germany that summer were Charles and Anne Lindbergh, who arrived on July 23 as honored guests of the German military. It was the first of five visits the aviator would make to Germany between 1936 and the beginning of war in 1939. The Germans welcomed Lindbergh with open doors and ulterior motives. They allowed him to inspect otherwise off-limit air force bases, airplane factories, and aviation research facilities, accompanied by American military attachés who would otherwise not have been welcome. He met with military and civilian aviators. German engineers proudly showed him designs for new airplane engines and other aircraft improvements.

The visit was everything the German propaganda office could have hoped for. Both Lindberghs were impressed by what Charles described as "the organized vitality of Germany" under Hitler. Charles was even more impressed with what he believed was the overwhelming strength of the German air force. The accuracy of Lindbergh's conclusions is a matter of historical debate, but there is no doubt that they influenced prewar policy in both the United States and Britain.

Schultz was horrified when she learned that American attachés were not only involved in what she correctly saw as a blatant attempt to influence Lindbergh but were determined to keep him away from American reporters in Berlin. She went to one of the attachés with whom she was friendly and told him, "Look, we've got to sit on Mr. Lindbergh. I want to write a story about his being dined and wined by the Nazis the way he is." The attaché convinced her that Lindbergh's visits to German factories provided them with crucial information about Germany's air power that they wouldn't get any other way. She later claimed it was the only time she cheated the *Tribune*'s readers out of a story from a sense of patriotism.[9]

The final day of the Lindberghs' visit coincided with the opening of the Olympics, which they attended as the guests of Hermann Göring.

The 1936 Olympic Games began on August 1. A tall blond runner, the final participant in a twelve-day relay from Greece to Berlin, appeared at the eastern gate of the stadium, holding a silver torch with the Olympic flame above his head—a piece of imagery dreamed up by Goebbels's propaganda ministry to underscore a mythical relationship with classical Greece as fellow Aryans that has outlived its Nazi roots. The crowd of 120,000 spectators fell silent. He held the pose for a moment, then he ran around the red-clay track. When he reached the other end of the track, he dipped the flame for a moment before the führer, then ran up the stairs to the Olympic altar. He paused again. The Olympic bell tolled. He turned and touched the torch to a huge bronze cauldron mounted on a tripod. Flames burst from the cauldron. As the sun set, a white-robed choir rose and sang Handel's "Hallelujah Chorus." After a moment, the crowd joined in.

Like other foreign journalists who watched the opening ceremony, Schultz began her report of the first day of the Olympic Games with a description of the runner with the torch. But she was more interested in Germans' response to the event than she was in its pageantry. Germans, she told her readers, were basking in the belief that athletes from most of the participating nations had extended their arms straight in front of them in the Nazi salute as they passed the führer. Blissfully unaware of the distinction, Germans in the audience cheered athletes who raised their right arms in the very similar Olympic salute, introduced in Paris in 1924 and abandoned after 1936, in which the right arm was held slightly to the side at an upright angle. Unlikely as it seems, Germans even gave their old adversaries, the French, a standing ovation.

The American athletes did not leave any room for confusion. A last-minute decision called for the men to hold their straw hats over their hearts as they passed Hitler and for all American athletes to turn their heads in Hitler's direction. Instead of cheering, Germans greeted the Americans with shrill whistling, which Schultz informed her readers was the European equivalent of the Bronx cheer.[10]

Over the course of the games, Schultz reported on American athletes' triumphs and defeats, but she never forgot that the Nazis' "political olympics" continued behind the scenes while the world's attention was diverted by the drama of the games.[11] She was not the only correspondent to report on Germany's use of the games for propaganda purposes and Germany's demonstration of its military might to Olympic spectators. Paul Gallico, sportswriter for the *Washington Post*, for example, reported that "the anxious Germans are rehearsing for the next war right next door to where the athletes are . . . practicing to win the great peace games of 1936."[12] But for the most part, spectators and reporters alike were vocal in their praise of German organization and sportsmanship.

Before the Olympic Games began, Schultz had flirted with the idea of going home in October, but she told friends that she feared the Nazis would be up to new tricks by then: "the Olympic Games good behavior will have worn thin and I believe that Austrian situation is getting under Adolf's skin."[13]

Schultz noted that Germany's Olympic mask was already slipping in her report on the event's final moments on August 16. The ceremony was dramatic. At ten minutes past nine, the Olympic torch was extinguished and the Olympic flag was hauled down from the pole where it had presided over the games. On the dais, three top-hatted white-haired old men called to the world's youth to preserve the ideals of peace that had failed so many times during their own lifetimes. Then, echoing the relay with which the Olympics began, International Olympic Committee members William May Garland of Los Angeles and Count Henri de Baillet-Latour of Belgium passed the Olympic flag to Julius Lippert, the Nazi mayor of Berlin. Lippert in turn passed the flag to the wizened Count Michimasa Soyeshima of Japan, who accepted it in the name of peace and as a token for the 1940 Olympics to be held in Tokyo.

And yet, Schultz noted, despite the official emphasis on peace, more guards were on view in the stadium than at any time in the two weeks of the games. Heavy cordons of storm troopers (SA) and Schutzstaffel (SS) filled the streets leading to the stadium. Hitler's steel-helmeted bodyguards were out in full force. The number of gray-uniformed police officers had doubled, making sure no one stepped near the balcony where the German leaders sat.[14]

The Olympic Games were not quite over, but Germany was once again flexing its muscles for the world to view.

CHAPTER FIFTEEN

AKA JOHN DICKSON

I am proclaiming most loudly that I know nothing of the story because I believe we are on the eve of very interesting developments of vital importance for the future of Europe. I would prefer not to make it too easy for our Nazi friends to oust the Tribune Correspondent, just on the eve of big stories for which I've been making careful "strategic" preparations for months.

—SIGRID SCHULTZ to
Colonel Robert McCormick, October 3, 1936[1]

The Berlin Olympic Games were intended to dazzle the world. They were followed by a spectacle intended to dazzle the Nazis themselves: the eighth Nazi Party rally at Nuremberg.

On September 7, 1936, the day before the rally was to begin, hundreds of airplanes roared above the city in nine-plane formations. Hundreds of thousands of brown-shirted storm troopers, black-shirted SS men, and Nazis of all descriptions poured into Nuremberg, swelling the city's population with a million attendees.

The rally itself was a weeklong combination of political message, pageantry, folk festival, and hatred. Goose-stepping military parades and storm troopers demonstrating martial skills celebrated the Reich's military strength. Marching contingents of National Socialist organizations and memorial events for those lost in the Great War and the so-called Nazi martyrs who died in street battles during the party's rise to power were designed to enforce the idea of *Volksgemeinschaft* (the community of the German Volk). That sense of community was reinforced by the celebration of German Kultur—a common element of pan-Germanism in all its variations—in the form of folk dancing, opera performances, and concerts. In addition, attendees were treated to dramatic light shows and fireworks displays, which were unrelated to *Volksgemeinschaft* or Kultur but contributed to the overall spectacle.

At some level, the rally was an embodiment of the signs proclaiming "Jews Not Welcome" that reappeared in public places immediately after the closing ceremony of the Olympics. The persecution of Jews and other targeted groups, temporarily halted during the Olympic Games, resumed with increased savagery. The threat of what Hitler described as "our old opponent, the Jewish bolshevik" and Germany's readiness to respond to that threat was a recurring theme of the rally,[2] including a speech by Joseph Goebbels that Schultz described as one of the "fiercest anti-Jewish proclamations yet delivered in the Nazi drive against Jews."[3]

⁂

In late September, shortly after the Nuremberg rally, Schultz once again faced trouble with the Nazis, this time due to the Paris office, which apparently did not understand how dangerous reporting from Berlin had become. Colonel McCormick had sent Schultz a request through Paris asking her to write a new, expanded story on the June Blood Purge. Instead of forwarding the request in a secure form, an assistant in the Paris office called Schultz with the information, oblivious to the fact that the Nazis had tapped the Berlin office phone and routinely recorded its calls. David Darrah, then head of the Paris bureau, compounded the problem by sending a note about the assignment to her home. When she received it, the note had been opened without any attempt to disguise the fact. (She mailed the envelope to Chicago, with the censor control stamps still attached, as proof of "Nazi efficiency"— and possibly of the inefficiency of the *Tribune's* Paris office.)

Schultz was furious and frustrated. Unlike her colleagues in Paris, she was engaged in a dangerous balancing act—reporting as fully as possible on Nazi activities without angering the Nazis so much that they kicked her out, or worse. "Being kicked out always gives you a lot of possibly valuable publicity," she told George Scharschug, "but I would prefer to stick in Germany until the crucial months are over and be able to use the sources I have cultivated assiduously when the big story comes."[4]

Despite the potential danger the Paris office had created, Schultz was determined to write the story, not only because McCormick had requested it but because she wanted to counteract what seemed to be a growing feeling in the United States after the Olympics that "Naziism is not so bad after all."[5] Counting on the thoroughness of the Nazis who opened her mail, she sent the Chicago office a letter saying she didn't see how she could write the Blood Purge story because there was no new material available in Germany. She had said everything in the reports she filed as the news occurred.

With her tracks covered as best she could, she left for Paris to write the article.

When she mailed the story to Scharschug from Paris on October 1, she warned him the "yarn" would probably "get our Nazi friends tremendously mad" and suggested they not run the story under her byline. Perhaps they could credit it to someone whose byline was currently attached to stories about the election campaign in the United States and would be well out of the reach of Nazi retaliation. Or maybe they could create a name that would "sound pretty real to our dear Nazi snoopers." She was determined to give the *Tribune*'s readers "all the dope there is" even if it meant she had to "hide behind somebody's name or coat."[6]

She chose the name John Dickson.

Forty years after John Dickson made his appearance, Schultz told the *Tribune*'s archivist that the name was a whimsical tribute to her mentor and first employer at the *Tribune*, Richard (Dick) Little, whom she saw as her professional father, making her "Dick's son."[7] It might have been true, but the decision was probably not that simple.

Schultz could have made the same tribute as "Jane Dickson," but she chose a male name when circumstances made it wise for her to take cover behind a pseudonym. In practical terms, the gender swap put even greater distance between Schultz and her alter ego.

It also placed her in the long line of women who wrote under a male pseudonym or gender-ambiguous name, though it was relatively rare in the newspaper business. Historically, women have chosen to write under male names for a number of reasons: to encourage a male readership, to publish without prejudice in a male-dominated genre or field, or to enjoy the freedom of anonymity. At root, all of these boil down to a way for women to be heard.

Schultz already had a public voice and an audience. She seemingly didn't need the perceived authority of the male voice to be heard. And yet she chose to do much of her most important reporting from behind a male mask. Perhaps not surprising, given that Schultz always described herself as a newspaperman.

It was not the first time Schultz played with the idea of writing a "hot" story under a pseudonym. In the late spring of 1934, she reassured McCormick, and perhaps herself, that "if one is a little careful, I'm sure there is no need to be nervous." Then she mentioned a story one "Charlie Farmer" had filed from Luxembourg that had the German Foreign Office in an uproar. When they questioned her about the story, she told them she assumed Farmer was one of the special investigators McCormick sent to Germany occasionally "to handle matters which don't belong to our regular routine in a censored state"—it was much the same cover story the *Tribune* would later use for John Dickson. In what appears to be a sly aside, she then told McCormick, "Everything Farmer sent was investigated most carefully and from what I hear his figures are conservative."[8]

A few months later, Schultz told Scharschug she was sending several stories under separate cover and asked that he run them under any name that worked for him, except for hers. Further, "if someone could change the wording just enough so nobody could think the stories are from me—it might be wise. There is no use getting the tiger madder than he is—and is he mad!"[9]

Schultz's first article under the name John Dickson appeared in the *Tribune*'s Sunday illustrated magazine on November 1, 1936. It ran with a London dateline and the headline "Democracy Surrenders. Dictatorship Crushes Freedom in Germany. People Recall with Terror Hitler's Blood Purge." The magazine format provided "Dickson" with the room to give *Tribune* readers the background material, extensive detail, and editorial conjecture Schultz had previously reserved for her weekly reports to McCormick. She opened the piece dramatically, saying "Terror goes with dictatorship as the tide with the ocean." Terror, she said, now paralyzed the Germans and would continue to do so as long as the Gestapo had the power to arrest people with no appeal in public courts. "A few malcontents disappear," she told her readers. "Relatives and friends are silent, but the rumor of mysterious disappearances is enough to enforce the silence desired by the men in power."

In the case of the Blood Purge of June 1934, that terror had its roots in Hitler's insecurity and the competition between "the ruthless minor dictators basking in his favor." Schultz told the story of Roehm and Hitler's friendship in the early days of Hitler's political career, described the growing power of the brown-shirted storm troopers (SA) under Roehm's leadership, and outlined the political jealousies in Hitler's inner circle in 1933. With the stage set, she recounted the events of the Blood Purge in a narrative form that had not been possible in the rush of daily reporting as the story unfolded. Admitting "there is little mourning in Germany for stormtroopers who lost their lives in the June blood purge," she told the *Tribune's* readers about the murders of SA leaders, Hitler's political rivals, and their wives—and those of men who had nothing to do with the storm troopers, including one Willy Schmidt, a Munich music critic mistaken for a Nazi reporter of the same name who was a friend of Roehm's.

"The exact number of victims of the June blood purge is not known," Schultz told her readers at the end. She doubted if even the Nazi authorities knew exactly how many died. That uncertainty heightened the feelings of terror felt by the German people. "They realize unseen eyes are watching and things are happening in the dark that had better be left untouched by those who want to survive. Why arouse [the] powers that be?"[10]

Several months later, Schultz used the John Dickson name and London dateline a second time for an investigative piece. "Dickson" connected rumors in Germany about thousands of soldiers who went missing from their barracks and their jobs over Christmas with reports from outside the country that large groups of German soldiers had landed in Spain to support General Francisco Franco's Fascist rebels. Over the course of the article, Schultz established "Dickson" as a reporter from outside Germany, treating him as a character in the story he was reporting. At one point "Dickson" writes, "You will ask how I happened to have learned of this after spending only a few weeks in Germany." Later, he realizes he is under suspicion: "After I inquired about it I realized that the number of persons watching me was bigger than ever—and lest I compromise one of my friends I left Germany as fast as I could." An alert reader might have noticed that Dickson used one of Schultz's favorite reporting gambits. He took advantage of a mild case of the flu—"for which I would, in normal times take a good dose of whiskey"—to check into a hospital in order to interview a wounded soldier who had recently returned from Spain.[11]

Both Schultz and the *Tribune* made serious efforts to separate the person from the persona. The *Tribune* introduced an early Dickson article with the statement that because of Germany's tight censorship over the press, the paper "had sent one of its trained correspondents into Germany to obtain facts which its accredited correspondents in the *Tribune's* Berlin bureau have been unable to cable to America."[12] Schultz signed letters with Dickson's name and used it to approve other journalists' articles. Making use of the fact that her letters were under scrutiny by German censors, she referred to "Dickson" in letters to McCormick: "Did you get the message of John Dickson from Holland? He is firmly convinced that the Rintellen-von Papen policy of world war days is being carried out, but on a much bigger scale than before."[13] It was a clever way to reinforce Dickson's existence and pass along a piece of information in the process.

Schultz added a serendipitous extra layer of camouflage to her Dickson persona in September 1940, when she hired an actual John Paul Dickson, who continued to work at the Berlin office until Germany declared war on the United States.

⋘⋙

Schultz used the Dickson name well into 1940. Writing as John Dickson, with datelines in Copenhagen and Paris, she filed investigative reports on Nazi attacks on Germany's churches, the creation of concentration camps, and the growing persecution of Germany's Jews. "Dickson" gave the *Tribune's* readers an inside look at the Hitler Youth program, and a description of the way the Nazis card-indexed every German citizen—and every foreign correspondent. Under her own name, Schultz reported on more immediate news items, many of them equally inflammatory from the Nazi perspective, with headlines such as "Sterilize 20,000 Unfit Germans Under Nazi Law: Expect Work of Purging Race to Be Speeded."[14]

After the war ended, the *Tribune* revealed that John Dickson, author of some of the most hard-hitting reporting on Nazi Germany, was in fact Sigrid Schultz.[15]

CHAPTER SIXTEEN

NEVER ENTIRELY AT PEACE

We are much like people who have lived close to the rim of a rumbling volcano for years. I hear the rumblings, I see all the evidence that points toward an eruption, but I cannot quite believe that the volcano will erupt, that war will break out.

—SIGRID SCHULTZ, August 30, 1938[1]

As I read, I could get the very likeness and picture of the Berlin that you understood so well; I could see those various offices of yours in the Adlon and nearby points, with the clouds of war gathering all around and the darkness deepening, but never enough to chase the smile from your face and the ever-recurring words 'I want you to dine with mother and me' from your lips. You were something in the Berlin of those days—you and your mother—which kept us all human and hopeful in a world of blackness.

—THOMAS YBARRA to
Sigrid Schultz, February 2, 1944[2]

Europe was never entirely at peace in the almost twenty-one years between the two world wars. International wars, civil wars, and armed border disputes were a constant factor in European politics, beginning with the German revolutions that created the Weimar Republic. Some of the "wars between the wars" were small, like the conflict between the relatively new country of Italy (1861) and the even newer country of Yugoslavia (1918) over the Adriatic port of Fiume (now Rijeka). Some were large, like the Spanish Civil War, which was in many ways a German dress rehearsal for the Second World War. Other conflicts simmered for years, always ready to break into violence—most notably, the long-standing and complex conflict between Germany and Poland over borders and ethnic composition.

Many of the small-scale wars were attempts to solidify, expand, or negate the borders of the new states created by the peacemakers in Versailles. The theory behind the new states was that nations should be based on a shared language and history, unlike the multilingual, multiethnic empires which they had been part of before the war. Unfortunately, each of those states defined its "natural" boundaries as those held at its historical height. As a result, there were regions that several countries claimed as theirs by right, without reference to shared language or ethnicity. In addition, some of the new states had substantial populations of German speakers, a fact that would drive events in Czechoslovakia in 1938 and in Poland in 1939.

Over the course of 1936, the threat of war became more immediate. Germany continued to rebuild its military and to ship soldiers, pilots, and airplanes to Spain. At the end of the year, Hermann Göring would announce in a secret meeting of German industrialists and high Nazi officials, "We live in a time when the final battle is in sight. We are already on the threshold of mobilization, and we are already at war. All that is lacking is the actual shooting."[3]

By mid-May 1937, Schultz, writing as John Dickson, reported that the slogan "It is better to fight than to starve" was spreading through Germany. "The young and old daredevils of the Nazi party—those who did not know war, or those who enjoyed it—want action despite the risk involved," Dickson told readers, but they did not agree on what action Germany should take. Some called for open participation in the Spanish Civil War. Others wanted an expedition to retake former German colonies in Africa. A third group, ultimately the most important, spoke of the "necessity of rescuing the oppressed German brothers in Czechoslovakia, who are bound to rise against what the Nazis call 'their Czech oppressors.'" The army, according to Dickson, responded "not yet" rather than no: they did not have enough arms and ammunition to fight for longer than four months and the soldiers who came to them from the Hitler Youth, the SS, and the SA were not well trained.[4]

"Oppressed" ethnic Germans in Austria and Czechoslovakia became the triggers for German expansion.

By the winter of 1937–1938, rumors were flying through Berlin that a Nazi crisis in Austria was imminent. Schultz traced the rumors to an unlikely source, the Duke of Windsor, who had received warnings from German and Austrian friends not to go to Austria because of the danger of a Nazi uprising in the near future. German officials pooh-poohed the rumor, but the duke's friends continued to insist there would be a serious clash in March. April at the latest.[5]

The duke's personal news network proved to be remarkably accurate.

On February 12, Austrian chancellor Kurt Schuschnigg, met with Hitler in his mountain retreat at Berchtesgaden. They signed an agreement that would place Austria's foreign and military policy under German control and install Austrian Nazis in key positions in the cabinet. German Nazis predicted an Austrian Nazi would soon replace Schuschnigg as chancellor.

Germany's triumph was premature. On March 9, several days after publicly declaring that Austria would remain independent and would not tolerate illegal Nazi activity, Schuschnigg called for a plebiscite on the question of Austrian independence. Encouraged by Hitler, Austrian Nazis staged violent protests throughout the country.

On March 12, German troops marched into Austria.

Reporter Edmond Taylor was the *Tribune*'s "man on the spot" in Vienna, with front-page headlines detailing events in Austria. Schultz reported on the invasion and subsequent Anschluss from the German perspective. Early on March 11, truckloads of policemen and troops poured out of Berlin toward Vienna. The Nazi headquarters in Munich was staffed entirely by women, Schultz told her readers, replacing the usual "sturdy stormtroopers and Schutz Staffel men," who were themselves replacing the Berlin policemen mobilized to join their reserve units in the march toward Austria. German radio stations near the border broadcast propaganda to stir up the German-speaking population of Austria against Schuschnigg. Inside Germany, the Nazi propaganda office manufactured reports that the Czechs had invaded Austria and French Reds were hurrying to Vienna to fight the Austrian Germans. Schultz speculated these rumors were intended to make Germans more enthusiastic about their sons and brothers marching over the border.

Three days later, while Germany celebrated the new union of 75 million Germans, Schultz informed *Tribune* readers that Germany already had its eye on Czechoslovakia. While the Nazis assured British, French, and Czech diplomats that all they wanted to do was "safeguard the interests of a German minority," Schultz pointed out that they were already using tactics against Czechoslovakia that were similar to those they had used in Austria.[6]

———❀———

At the end of March, Schultz expanded her warnings in a long report to McCormick on Hitler's new Four-Year Plan for Germany's foreign policy, which he had formulated a few days after his triumphant return from Vienna. Austria was only the first step. The German people needed more space, food, and raw materials to make Germany strong enough to fulfill its destiny—a fundamental Nazi policy known as *Lebensraum* (living room). The next step would be to take the German-speaking districts of Czechoslovakia. The Czechs might try to resist, but Hitler believed France was tied up with its own internal difficulties and would not honor its treaty obligations to defend Czechoslovakia. If France didn't move to stop Germany, England would not act alone. Once Hitler controlled Czechoslovakia—which he estimated would occur within the year—the grain-rich region of Ukraine would be next, followed by the iron mines of Alsace Lorraine. As she wrote, Schultz told McCormick, large amounts of military equipment were being massed along the Czech borders with Austria and Silesia "to help make the Czechs more amenable to German wishes."[7]

Most of the three million Germans in Czechoslovakia lived in the Sudetenland, a strategically important and economically valuable region on the Czech border with Germany and Austria, which was part of the German Empire prior to the Great War. By the mid-1930s, the region was home to a strong German nationalist movement. In 1938, soon after Germany annexed Austria, the pro-Nazi Czech leader, Konrad Henlein, with Germany's support, began to demand regional autonomy, citing the right of self-determination that the framers of the Versailles treaty used to justify the creation of new nations, like Czechoslovakia itself. Edvard Benes, the leader of Czechoslovakia, refused, recognizing that giving the Sudetenland autonomy would be the first step in Germany's conquest of his country.

That May, reports of German troop concentrations near Czechoslovakia gave rise to fears of an imminent German attack. In response, Czechoslovakia mobilized its troops and strengthened its border defenses. France and Britain warned Germany they would come to Czechoslovakia's aid in case of an attack. No concentration of German troops was found, and the international fervor was short-lived. On May 23, Schultz informed McCormick that things had cooled off for the moment: "Friends of mine who usually have been very well informed are of the opinion that since it was averted this week it probably won't break out until the end of summer—if at all."[8]

By late summer, as Schultz's friends predicted, the Czech situation was again an international crisis. On August 7, reporting as John Dickson, she informed Chicago readers that Germany was preparing a "trial mobilization" of its 500,000 military reserves. With the reserves mobilized, Germany would have 1.5 million men under arms. At the same time, German workers were building a railroad to the Czech border and constructing emergency defense lines in the Hultschin district of Czechoslovakia, which Germany, Poland, and Czechoslovakia had all claimed at the end of the Great War. Dickson suggested the mobilization was intended as a reminder that Germany was ready to help Czechoslovakia's German nationalists if their demands for autonomy were not met. "If the Sudeten people do not get what they want," Dickson quoted the nationalists' supporters, "they will rise, and when the 3,000,000 Sudeten citizens of Czechoslovakia's 15,000,000 rise against Prague, they will find 75,000,000 Germans ready to stand by them."[9]

The Dickson story ran on the front page. A less dramatic version of the same story ran that day under Schultz's byline on page nine. It was an effective, though perhaps unintended, way to signal the separation between her two journalistic identities. In that article, Schultz focused on the German military's description of the extended maneuvers as a training exercise for their new reservists[10]—an idea many non-German veterans of the Great War may have found a disturbing reminder of the past.

Two days later, Schultz followed up with McCormick. The situation had become more tense since Dickson's article. "When all is said and done," she concluded, "Germany may not use her war-machine to kill, but she is certainly using it to bluff others into letting her have what she wants. Right now she wants the Sudeten German area of Czechoslovakia. England seems so scared of war that she may help Hitler get it."[11]

Throughout August and September, the world seemed once more on the edge of war. Germany and Czechoslovakia remained at a stand-off over the question of autonomy for the Sudetenland Germans. Britain and France, paralyzed by their memories of the Great War, first warned Germany that they would protect Czechoslovakia against German aggression and then wavered on whether they would honor their mutual defense treaties. After an uprising by the Sudeten Germans on September 12, Hitler increased his demands. Autonomy was no longer enough.

Hoping to broker a compromise, British prime minister Neville Chamberlain met with Hitler on September 19 at the German leader's retreat in Berchtesgaden and again on September 22 at Bad Godesberg. Each time they met, Hitler increased his demands, backed by the threat to invade Czechoslovakia if they didn't have an agreement by September 30.

Desperate to avoid war, Chamberlain suggested what Schultz called a "four-power parley" between Britain, France, Germany, and Italy to settle the dispute. Czechoslovakia was not invited to attend.

Hitler, Chamberlain, Mussolini, and Édouard Daladier, the French prime minister, met in Munich on September 29, 1938. The discussions lasted a little over twelve hours. The final agreement was signed at one thirty in the morning on September 30.

Hitler got everything he wanted from Chamberlain and Daladier in exchange for a promise that he would not demand any additional territory in Europe. Chamberlain believed that by sacrificing the Sudetenland, he had saved the rest of Czechoslovakia from invasion and kept Europe at peace. On his return to Britain, he told the waiting crowd that he came home bringing "peace with honor. I believe it is peace for our time."

Writing from Berlin on September 30, Schultz reported that the word on the street was "Never again will there be a war between Germany and England."[12]

On October 1, German troops marched into the Sudetenland.

CHAPTER SEVENTEEN

ON THE AIR FROM BERLIN

This is Sigrid Schultz, the Berlin correspondent
of the *Chicago Tribune*, broadcasting from Berlin.

—SIGRID SCHULTZ'S
signature radio opening, 1938–1941

I n 1938, radio was still relatively new.
The first national broadcast networks in the United States were
incorporated in 1926 (National Broadcasting Company, NBC) and
1928 (Columbia Broadcasting System, CBS). News broadcasts were
infrequent in the first days of radio, but by 1930, both NBC and CBS
offered regular news programs that consisted of a brief evening recap
of newspaper headlines, with "readers" instead of reporters. Interrupting
a program for breaking news was unheard of.

Shortwave broadcasts from Europe to America were feasible in 1930,
but there were only five shortwave transmitters powerful enough to send
a signal overseas. (By 1939, there were more than one hundred.) Moreover,
overseas broadcasts required cooperation from the local radio authorities,
many of which were government agencies. Because Germany, and other
European countries, had government-run national networks, their radio
officials signed exclusive contracts with NBC, assuming, incorrectly, that
the "national" in its name meant it was the official American network.
Consequently, when representatives of CBS and later the Mutual Broadcasting System (MBS) arrived in Europe, their program directors had
to talk hard and fast to get access to radio facilities.

Despite these difficulties, CBS aired eighty some international
broadcasts in 1930. (Most were talks by politicians or cultural figures.)

Sigrid Schultz; her mother, Hedwig; and their dog, Barry, in the yard of the house in Summerdale, ca. 1900.

Sigrid Schultz in the Kurhaus in Switzerland, the first of what would be many visits to health spas to recover from exhaustion and chronic illness. Her favorite treatment: hot mud baths.

Sigrid Schultz raised "bunnies" for meat and trade during World War I, when Berlin suffered from serious food shortages.

Sigrid Schultz, then the *Chicago Tribune*'s number-two Berlin correspondent, with her boss, George Seldes, in the *Tribune*'s office in the Hotel Adlon, ca. 1920–21.

The luxurious Hotel Adlon, which opened its doors in 1907 under the patronage of Kaiser Wilhelm II, was the unofficial "press club" for foreign correspondents in Berlin in the years between the world wars.

Sigrid Schultz with a bunch of "the boys" in front of the *Chicago Tribune* office in the Hotel Adlon, ca. 1927.

Sigrid Schultz at the 1933 Foreign Press Club Ball with Ambassador William Dodd and Martha von Papen, wife of right-wing German politician Franz von Papen. Known as the "Little Press Ball," in contrast to the ball given by the German domestic press, it was one of the most important and popular events of the German social season.

Sigrid Schultz striding out in Berlin. According to Gregor Ziemer, who worked part-time for her for eleven years, "She might have to stay up until long after midnight, covering a story, then be back early the next day, alert and quick in gesture, speech and decisions."

Sigrid Schultz, war correspondent for the *Chicago Tribune*, sits front and center at a group interview with Nazi leader Hermann Göring, three days after his capture by the US Army in May 1945.

Sigrid Schultz in her home in Westport, Connecticut, ca. 1977.

The networks saw the job of their European representatives as arranging special broadcasts, not reporting the news. They refused to allow their representatives, most of whom were originally reporters, on the air. If the network needed to cover the news, they hired a foreign correspondent to read it.

Foreign broadcast news changed completely when the German army marched into Austria. William Shirer, a former *Tribune* correspondent, was now a member of Edward Murrow's European broadcasting team for CBS in Vienna. He had a breaking story and no way to get it on the air. For four hours, Shirer argued with Nazi officials who had seized the Austrian state broadcasting facilities. They refused to give him access to a studio and finally removed him from the building at bayonet point at three in the morning. On Edward Murrow's suggestion, Shirer flew to London, by way of Berlin, where he broadcast the story.

The New York office was delighted with the broadcast and wanted more. CBS news director Paul White phoned Shirer and asked if he and Murrow could put together a thirty-minute program later that day, presenting reactions to Germany's annexation of Austria from major cities across Europe. Shirer said yes, though he had no idea how to arrange it. Then he called Murrow.

With only eight hours to arrange speakers and overcome serious technical challenges, Edward Murrow and William Shirer cobbled together a half hour of American foreign correspondents commenting on the Nazi invasion from London, Vienna, Berlin, Paris, and Rome. Nothing like it had ever been done before.

New York immediately asked them to do it again the next day. Shirer agreed without a moment's hesitation.

That half-hour news roundup created a new job description for CBS's overseas representatives: broadcast journalists.

Schultz's big chance at broadcasting the news came six months later, thanks to another CBS experiment in live radio.

On September 20, 1938, Shirer told Paul White they would need to cancel his usual 10:30 p.m. broadcast because that was when the train left for Bad Godesberg, where the second meeting between Hitler and

Chamberlain was scheduled to take place. White suggested he broadcast from the train. Perhaps he could interview other foreign correspondents who were traveling to report on the conference. Radio engineers from the German broadcasting company, Reichs-Rundfunk-Gesellschaft, commonly known as Rundfunk, quickly nixed the idea: no one had the technology to handle a broadcast from the train. Shirer asked whether they could manage a broadcast from Berlin's Friedrichstrasse railway station. They could. White loved the idea. Shirer scrambled to make it happen.

At ten that evening, using a microphone German engineers had set up on the railway platform, Shirer interviewed Schultz and several other American and British correspondents about the possibilities of war and peace as they waited to catch the train. Italian and French correspondents joined in as they strolled by, adding additional viewpoints to the broadcast. The interviews ended abruptly when the train began to leave the station and journalists had to sprint to catch it.

Schultz was the only woman included in Shirer's on-the-fly train-station broadcast—a testament to her reputation as a leading correspondent with two decades of experience covering German politics. Her brief appearance on the broadcast caught the attention of officials at the Mutual Broadcasting System (MBS), a cooperative network owned by member radio stations, including WGN in Chicago, which was a *Tribune* affiliate. (The station's call signal was a truncated version of the *Tribune*'s grandiose motto, World's Greatest Newspaper.) Founded in 1934, MBS was a relative new kid on the radio-broadcasting block and did not yet have a team of full-time correspondents based in Europe. The officials at MBS were impressed with Schultz's grasp of German politics. (As well they should have been.) The network immediately hired her to work as a stringer. Many newspapers did not allow their foreign correspondents to work on the side as radio broadcasters because they feared radio was a serious competitor in the news marketplace. Schultz didn't have that problem. Colonel McCormick saw her assignments with MBS as an extension of her work for the paper.

Schultz made her first broadcast for MBS on September 29 from the Munich conference. She arrived at the Munich Rundfunk station promptly at midnight for a show that would air during America's dinner hour. The storm troopers on guard waved her through when she showed them her journalist's pass, though they were surprised the scheduled broadcaster was a woman.

The announcer introduced the segment in a plummy voice, all exaggerated vowels and condescending tone: "The program originally scheduled for this time will not be heard. From Munich Germany the Mutual Network presents a commentary by the renowned woman correspondent 'Ziegried Schutz.' We take you now to Munich."

Listeners heard a long pause. The sound of rustling papers. Then Schultz began to speak, her clipped tones a sharp contrast to the announcer's mellifluous voice. She greeted her audience with what would become her standard opening: "This is Sigrid Schultz, the Berlin correspondent of the *Chicago Tribune*." She told listeners she had hoped to give them a clear-cut picture of the international situation, but that was impossible. The four representatives of the great powers were back in conference even as she spoke. The reporter in her may have worried a little since she had no hard news to share. Perhaps she dug deep for the spirit of the "trilingual child" who performed multilingual skits for her parents' guests back in Chicago's Summerdale neighborhood. In place of hard news, she editorialized in a way that would never have passed the cable editor's desk at the *Tribune*. She began with a satirical commentary on the four great men and their eight equally great aides who had "cast aside old iron-bound traditions and dropped much of the old-fashioned diplomatic routines" to fly to Munich "for a man-to-man" talk. Schultz told her listeners that she'd heard a lot about those man-to-man talks in her nineteen years as a "news-gatherer." It's easy to picture her leaning into the microphone as if sharing a confidence when she admitted, "I always get somewhat skeptical when that term [man-to-man talk] turns up but the big politicians like this term as well as the boys do and they talk a lot about it."

Unable to be in the room where that "man-to-man talk" happened, she tried to visit the hotels where representatives of the four great powers were headquartered, hoping to collect what she would have called "the dope." She admitted that it wasn't as simple as it sounded. After all, "foreign statesman must be protected from possible assassins or the merely curious." The black-uniformed SS officers who guarded the hotels were less accommodating than the brown-shirted storm troopers who manned the doors of the radio studio from which she was broadcasting. Her "perfectly good pink propaganda ministry license" meant nothing to them. They took their orders from the police, not the Propaganda Ministry. Unable to gain access, she imagined what the representatives of the four powers would tell her about the status of the negotiations, ending with the Italians, in swanky black outfits with black tassels on their shoes. The Italians, she said, were thrilled that "Mussolini's plan" was the blueprint for the negotiations. (It was revealed many years later that the German Foreign Office wrote the Mussolini Plan.)

With her mention of Il Duce's role in the negotiations, Schultz dropped playful editorializing in favor of political analysis. Czechoslovakia and its fate were vitally important, she explained, but they weren't the critical point of the conference. Czechoslovakia was a pawn in the hard game of European politics, in which the premiers of the western democracies faced for the first time, man-to-man, the leaders of the new authoritarian governments. The democratic leaders weren't holding up well, she told her listeners. "The weariness evident in the headquarters of the French and English were strongly contrasted by the alertness and energy displayed in German and Italian circles." Meanwhile, she concluded, "In Munich's breweries the population tonight is celebrating the historical conference, thoroughly convinced that when the statesmen get together tomorrow morning, possibly to sign the agreement, they will do everything in their power to avert war."[1]

Schultz was back on the radio at two thirty in the morning, Munich time, with a heavily censored script in hand. At one that morning, the four powers had signed an agreement ordering the Czechs to surrender the Sudetenland. It was an overwhelming victory for Germany.[2]

By January 1939, Schultz was a regular in the MBS lineup, with a fifteen-minute segment of news and analysis that ran on Sunday evenings live from Berlin and an occasional special program at the network's request.

MBS hired Schultz despite long-standing prejudices against female broadcasters reading the news. Network officials believed Americans had no objection to hearing women read ads or discuss "women's issues." (By which they meant recipes, housework, fashion, and childcare, not the barriers to entry that limited women's access to education, jobs, and political office.) Those same officials were sure audiences did not want to hear a female voice deliver the news.

Schultz did not escape the general network preference for a male voice altogether. In September 1940, MBS insisted she hire a man as its permanent representative in Berlin. Faced with the requirement of hiring someone to meet MBS's demands, she hired John Paul Dickson, even though he had no newspaper or radio experience. Dickson had spent eleven years in Germany studying engineering and teaching languages. The war left him unemployed. Schultz determined that despite his long residence in Germany, he was less corrupted by Nazi influence than any of the other unemployed Americans who had stayed in wartime Berlin.

⁂

Schultz was not a natural on-air. She read her copy too quickly, without pausing for emphasis. Sometimes she stumbled over her words or broke into giggles over a mistake.

She was aware of the flaws in her delivery and spent time trying to improve. She requested recordings of her broadcasts from the Rund-funk engineers so she could listen to herself. She even asked MBS net-work executives back home for advice: "I fully realize I am a 'greenhorn' in the field and am most grateful for whatever suggestion you make."[3] Unfortunately, sometimes the radio executives gave her contradictory advice. For example, when Fred Weber, the general manager of MBS, suggested she pitch her voice higher, she told him her normal voice was higher than the one she used on the air because she had been informed "that the boys preferred the lower pitch."[4] As far as women's voices and radio were concerned, it was impossible to win.

On one occasion, Schultz defended herself against criticisms. Writing to Fred Weber, she claimed, "My efforts to catch my breath . . . like a gasping fish are not always due to mike fright." She blamed the censors, who often didn't return scripts until two minutes before she went on. "Occasionally, they tried the little stunt of making a correction in the copy on top of deleting something—then as you read, you run up against something you dont [sic] quite recognize. . . . I will not read a correction smuggled into my copy. The censors can delete if they have to—there is nothing we can do about that but when in the midst of your copy you come up against one of the little traps you just gasp."[5]

Regardless of any problems with her delivery, the quality of Schul-tz's journalism was never in doubt. She gave her listeners in-depth analysis of the situation in Germany throughout 1939 and 1940. She sometimes broke exclusive stories on the air, scooping not only other journalists but also the *Tribune*. Long after her career on the air was over, Sigrid Schultz received fan letters from listeners who had looked forward to her Sunday evening broadcast and appreciated the expertise she brought to the subject.

CHAPTER EIGHTEEN

WAR SEEMED INEVITABLE

You'll no doubt like to hear the words with which Mr. Scharschug described you: "She's the best man we've got in Europe."

—CAREY LONGMORE, foreign correspondent, *New York Herald Tribune*, to Sigrid Schultz, February 20, 1939[1]

I am watching this war scare business as closely as I can, but refuse to overplay it, which to my mind would be a sign of poor nerves.

—SIGRID SCHULTZ to Robert McCormick, March 8, 1939[2]

Sigrid Schultz's dispatches from Berlin have given the most comprehensive accounts of Germany's moves and aims published anywhere.

—*CHICAGO TRIBUNE*, May 10, 1939[3]

A month after Germany marched into the Sudetenland, Schultz was at The Hague, enjoying a rare evening on her own, without family responsibilities or a story to track down.

Even before the Munich conference, Schultz had begun to think about sending her mother and dog to the United States. Now, with the Sudetenland under German occupation, and the threat of war more strongly in the air than before, she made up her mind. She didn't want her mother in Germany during another "Krisis." If something went wrong and she had to leave the country in a hurry, her mother might not be able to move quickly enough.

Schultz spent October 1938 watching her mother pack for a move to the United States. The process included sorting through years of what Schultz described as "family trash" that Hedwig had squirreled away in old trunks—"including the dog tags of Mother's favorite dog in Chicago, who died in 1901, and the last Chicago gas bill." While Hedwig packed, her friends poured into the house to say goodbye, wailing as if there had been multiple deaths in the family. The combination of packing and farewells upset Schultz's dog, a fat German boxer named Barbara, who repeatedly plunked herself down in the trunks, making the process even harder.

Getting Hedwig out of the country was not an easy matter. Her mother didn't want to go. She had not enjoyed her short time living alone in Paris in 1913. Living alone in the United States would be even worse. Hedwig had plenty of friends in America, thanks to keeping their house in Berlin open to expats and tourists, but the country was not home in any meaningful sense. After all, she had only lived in the United States from 1889 to 1901. Moreover, while Schultz claimed she had "mothered" her mother for as long as she could remember, it is possible Hedwig had a different opinion about who took care of whom and worried about leaving her daughter behind with no one to look after her.

In addition, Hedwig had passport problems that added a sense of urgency to the move. When Hermann became an American citizen, Hedwig, as his wife, automatically became a citizen, too. His death in 1924 muddied her citizenship status. She needed to have his naturalization papers verified before her passport could be reissued. Thinking back, Schultz realized she should have taken her mother to the United States immediately after Hermann's death to clear up her passport status. But she had been busy with the urgent task of untangling their apartment lease, which was in her father's name. In the intervening years, she had never resolved her mother's passport issue.

But even though Hedwig did not have a clearly valid American passport, she had a visa that was good for another four months. After her visa ran out, it would be difficult to get another one, with her citizenship status unresolved and the German visa quota filled.

Together, Schultz and her friend Janet Fairbank wore down Hedwig's objections. Fairbank wrote a long "very fierce" letter to Hedwig on the subject. She reminded Hedwig that "almost every Jew in Europe is trying to get to America—that all the Americans here are trying to get back—That you are terribly lucky to have a visa at all (considering the thousands of people who can't get them)." Fairbank pointed out that if Hedwig didn't go now, she might make it impossible for her daughter to leave when the time came. Then she made the sly suggestion that Schultz was under a great deal of extra strain because she was worrying about her mother. The best thing Hedwig could do to take care of Schultz now was go to America.[4]

Once the decision was made, Schultz bought a small car to ship to the United States and hired the brother of her former assistant, Percy Knauth, to drive Hedwig and Barbara the dog from Berlin to Holland.

The others had planned to join her at The Hague that evening, but the famous German roads did not live up to their reputation, and young Knauth had not made the kind of time he expected. So Hedwig, Barbara, and their frustrated driver were overnighting in Utrecht—and Schultz was sitting down to a solo feast of Dutch oysters and a "forbidden, very fattening" glass of Bass ale, enjoying her solitude. She had earned it. Writing to her friends the Deuels that night from The Hague, Schultz claimed the experience of getting Hedwig packed and moving was responsible for the streaks of white that had recently appeared in her thick blonde hair. On second thought, the events leading to the Munich Pact might have contributed a few streaks as well.[5]

⸎

The next "Krisis" came sooner than Schultz expected.

On November 6, 1938, seventeen-year-old Herschel Grynszpan shot Ernst vom Rath, an employee of the German embassy in Paris.

Several days earlier, the Nazis had arrested and deported thousands of Polish Jews, many of whom had lived in Germany for numerous years. The Germans transported them to Poland in cattle cars without food or water. Once there, the deportees found themselves stranded in a refugee camp in the border region between the two countries. Grynszpan's parents, who had lived in Germany since 1911, were among them.

November 9 was the fifteenth anniversary of Hitler's failed Beer Hall Putsch, now a holiday in the Nazi calendar. Celebrations were scheduled throughout Germany, with tributes planned to Nazis who died during the party's rise to power. Hitler and members of the Nazi old guard gathered in Munich to celebrate the occasion at a gala dinner. At nine o'clock, Hitler learned that vom Rath had died. He immediately left the hall. In his absence, Goebbels rose to his feet and announced that while the party should not organize demonstrations avenging vom Rath, such demonstrations should not be hampered if they erupted spontaneously.

Party members took Goebbels's speech as permission to unleash the antisemitic violence that would become known as *Kristallnacht,* or the Night of Broken Glass.

⸺◦◦◦⸺

Shortly before midnight, violent attacks on Jews erupted across Greater Germany.

Soon after the violence began, Pete House, a reporter for the International News Service, called Schultz, who was spending a rare evening at home, and told her the Fasanenstrasse Synagogue, the largest synagogue in Berlin, was under attack. When it opened in 1912, the synagogue was a visible statement of Jewish emancipation in the German Empire and as such was a major target for antisemitic violence even before Kristallnacht.

The synagogue was already in flames when Schultz arrived. Storm troopers ran in and out of the building, carrying Torah scrolls, stacks of prayer books, and bundles of prayer shawls to a nearby square. One of the storm troopers threw a torch on the pile, which burst into flame. Storm troopers jumped up and down with excitement and threw more objects from the synagogue into the flames as Schultz watched. She thought they looked like wild men, silhouetted against the fire in the dimly lit square.

A small pile of burned material was still glowing at five the next morning, she reported, and the inside of the synagogue had been smashed to pieces.

The vandals did not limit their destruction to the Fasanenstrasse Synagogue. Over the course of November 9 and 10, rioters destroyed hundreds of synagogues and desecrated Jewish cemeteries throughout Germany, Austria, and the Sudetenland. Storm troopers and members of the Hitler Youth smashed the windows of an estimated 7,500 Jewish-owned stores and looted their goods. The Gestapo arrested some 30,000 Jewish men and took them to concentration camps—the first time large numbers of Jews were arrested without any cause for arrest other than being Jewish. It was, Schultz told her readers, the largest antisemitic attack ever carried out in Berlin.

In the days after Kristallnacht, Schultz reported on the extent of the violence, the arrests, and the increasingly restrictive laws against Jews that followed. "The Nazi violence far outdid anything that happened along this line in Germany in the darkest days of the Red revolution," she told Chicago. "Then hungry mobs stormed food stores. Today the mobs gloated over the smashed stores of Jews. They helped themselves to clothes, furs, and toys, and scattered the goods in the streets for their friends to pick up."[6] She brought the bigger picture to life with stories of both violence against individuals and acts of individual bravery—easier for a reader to relate to than statistics.

As always, there were stories she couldn't share for publication, either for lack of evidence or because they would endanger her informants. For example, she told McCormick that the foreign correspondent community had been swamped by reports that rioters had hanged Jews from the lampposts in several small towns. But none of the reporters had seen it personally, and they could not find eyewitnesses willing to testify to its truth.[7]

The professional tone of her articles and her report to McCormick covered her very real distress and her need to help someone in a practical way, no matter how small. Her third and last great love, Peter Ilcus, made a suggestion. She needed a new coat. He directed her to a Jewish furrier he knew, from whom she bought a good sealskin coat—"much more expensive than I had a right to have" she said later—paying for part of it in valuable American dollars. Not a heroic action, but it was something she could do to help at least one person who had been hurt by the riots.[8]

<hr>

At the end of 1938, Schultz traveled back to the United States to buy "the tiny little shack Mother likes," taking with her books, paintings, and family furniture so Hedwig would be comfortable in her new home.[9]

There had been lots of discussion about where her mother should settle in the United States, with many well-meaning friends making suggestions. If it had been up to Schultz, they would have settled in Chicago, but she left the decision to her mother. Hedwig called on their extensive network of acquaintances to help her. She finally found what she was looking for in Westport, Connecticut, where old friends from Berlin, journalist Frazier Hunt and his wife, had built a house. They invited Hedwig to Westport to see "a crazy house in the center of town that had a studio." The studio may have been the deciding factor. They had always had a studio. Hedwig rented the house and moved in with borrowed furniture until Schultz could make more permanent arrangements.

For three and a half weeks, Schultz took care of business of one kind or another up and down the Eastern Seaboard. The most important stop was a visit to her "newspaper father" Dick Little at the old house in Virginia where he had retired with his wife. Schultz had always been afraid that he would die before she could see him again. At the end of her visit, on January 15, 1939, she purchased the crazy house in Westport for her mother. She left for Germany later that day on a Dutch liner, the *Volkendam*, which she described as "quite a sturdy little boat with a lot of old ladies on it [going] to France and England to 'see Europe before the war breaks out.'"

As the ship drew near to Europe, she felt more strongly than ever that it was "no place for elderly people or people who get excited easily."[10] Luckily, she was neither.

—∞—

On the *Volkendam*, Schultz befriended a brash young reporter named Sidney Kline. Twenty-six years old, with five years of journalism experience, Kline was taking his first trip abroad, with enough savings to support himself for several months, a nebulous job offer from the *Paris Herald-Tribune*, which evaporated on arrival, and a desire to be on the spot for the war that he believed "all thinking people knew was coming." Schultz was twenty years his senior and doubtless worried about the mother and dog she had left behind—and the challenges of what lay ahead.

After several days of shipboard camaraderie, in which Kline listened to Schultz share anecdotes about her life as a journalist and her insights on Hitler, Göring, and Goebbels, he asked her, "How is it that you never married, Sigrid?"

"Look at the men of my generation," she said after a moment. "In my youth, I worked with giants. Dick Little was my first bureau chief. Floyd Gibbons worked out of the bureau. Do you see men like that around?"

Kline had what he thought was a flash of understanding. Schultz was married to the newspaper business. No man could be a rival.[11]

In fact, it was an evasive answer from a woman who preferred to keep her private life private.

Petru (Peter) Ilcus first appears in Schultz's correspondence and daily logs in October 1936, almost exactly two years after the death of Carl Dennewitz. Little evidence exists about their time together in Berlin, but it is clear that their relationship had none of the drama of her relationship with Dennewitz. They were often apart. Work and family responsibilities meant that Ilcus—press attaché for the Romanian embassy in Berlin and brother of Lieutenant General Ion Ilcus, who was later Romania's minister of national defense and president of its Supreme Army Council during the war—had to travel back and forth to Bucharest. Schultz continued to "hop" out of the country on *Tribune* business and in search of health cures. Ilcus saw her off at the train station and met her on her return. (She returned the courtesy.) He made sure she didn't stay too long at official parties and scolded her for not taking care of herself when she was sick. ("Personally, I think it's the wrong technique," she wrote to Hedwig, "but I think it rather amusing."[12]) More than once, Ilcus drove Schultz into the country for a few hours of fresh air and sunshine. On occasion he brought her gifts from Romania that were unobtainable in Berlin: a soft wool blanket or a half pound of caviar.

Taken altogether, Schultz's notes about Ilcus at this period tell a story of tender care at a time when her life in Berlin was increasingly hard.

Back in Berlin, Schultz made plans for what to do if, or more likely when, Germany lit the flames of war. She informed McCormick that she intended to stay in Berlin until the American diplomatic staff left. They had promised to take her with them when the time came. As a backup, she buried a tank of gasoline in the garden in case she needed to leave by car. In the meantime, she was organizing couriers to send information out of Germany if it came to war.

Her immediate concern—and the one she wanted McCormick's opinion on—was where to relocate the office if she had to leave Germany. The choices, as she saw them, were the Netherlands, Denmark, or Switzerland. She could get both German and Italian news in Switzerland, but her military friends did not believe Germany would honor Swiss neutrality. McCormick did not need to consider language when making the choice, she explained: "I have a smattering of Dutch and Italian, my Norwegian (from my Father) can be turned into Danish—consequently from a language viewpoint it is all the same to me. I will not be eloquent but I will not be stranded."

All she needed was his instructions and she would set things in motion.[13]

———⊶⊷———

At the same time that Schultz was reporting on Europe's advance toward war, often on the front page of the *Tribune*, McCormick became one of the most powerful promoters of the isolationist movement in the United States. He used the *Tribune* as a platform from which he gave his approbation to the America First movement and lashed out against Franklin Roosevelt's support of Britain, East Coast fears of a German invasion, and the New Deal/Socialism/Communism, which he saw as all parts of the same movement.

McCormick's isolationism was fundamentally rooted in his experience as an artillery officer in France in the First World War. The thousands of casualties experienced by his own division still haunted him. "For twenty years," he wrote to William Allen White, the editor of the *Emporia* (Kansas) *Gazette* and a leading force in the movement in favor of American intervention in the war, "I have kept in touch with those whose existence has been a living death."[14] He did not want to see another generation of America's young men broken by a European war.

It is a measure of both Schultz's abilities as a journalist, and McCormick's integrity as a newsman, that his *Tribune* continued to publish her stories virtually without censorship, even though her views on Nazi Germany and the coming war were largely opposed to his. Her own experience of the Great War had taught her how important America's intervention had been. Fifty years later, she told an interviewer that she was still grateful to "our wonderful doughboys" who had "helped to lick the Germans."[15]

———⊶⊷———

Over the course of the summer, the threat of war never entirely went away. Tensions rose, then fell, then rose again in Berlin, and in Europe as a whole.

Anyone paying attention knew that Poland was Germany's next target. Hitler demanded that the ethnically German port city of Danzig, known as Gdansk in Poland, which had been part of the German Empire from the 1800s to the end of the Great War, be returned to Germany. Poland was determined to defend Gdansk/Danzig and its outlet to the sea. Britain and France wavered between supporting Poland and once again appeasing Germany.

On June 30, 1939, writing as John Dickson with a dateline from Brussels, Schultz reported that the German war council was working on plans to invade Poland. A week later, writing to McCormick from Paris, Schultz reported the atmosphere had cooled so much that "the Schutz Staffel officers who were toasting war ten days ago, now ask 'who ever talked of war?'"[16]

In late July, Schultz reported to McCormick that they were expecting action in August, but the excitement might turn out to be "the hot air of bluff" and nothing more. She shared a list of reasons Germans had given her, explaining why they had not yet taken action to regain control of Danzig/Gdansk. Most were a variation on "things aren't going as well/quickly/easily as expected." But the final reason her sources provided was more unusual: "Quite a number of Hitler's friends say that Hitler finds his horoscope more favorable in September and wants to wait until then."[17]

⊶⊷

Schultz spent a great deal of time on the subject of Hitler and astrology in the summer of 1939.

With the help of her favorite source, Dr. Johannes Ludwig Schmidt, Schultz managed to identify and schedule appointments with two of Hitler's favorite astrologers and a palm reader whom he often consulted. One astrologer, whom she met in a small apartment in Munich, told her he was not allowed to talk about politics. (He had already told her, "Old enemies will become close friends and the Führer will be at the zenith of his power in a very few weeks. Before winter sets in the world will know it." He must have thought that didn't count as politics.) A little prodding on her part produced predictions that startling developments would occur in mid-September and that Soviet Russia and Germany would cooperate. The palm reader, a small old man who lived in a small old house, placed Schultz's hands on a black velvet cushion to read her character and then predicted that "Russia and Germany together will settle the Polish problem." (He also predicted that the British Empire would fall apart as soon as Russia and Germany cooperated.) Schultz later speculated that the "seers" picked up impressions from Hitler, who could have tipped them off without knowing it.

The results of her investigations into Hitler's obsession with astrology appeared in a front-page article on July 14, titled "Hitler Gazes at Stars to Guide His Decisions." She described her visits with Hitler's favored seers, commenting that their predictions aligned with what Nazi officials had told her in private conversations. In recent months, Schultz wrote, Hitler had taken up the study of astrology. He had assembled a large library on the subject of the occult, conferred with astrologers at length, and learned to cast horoscopes himself. He made his own analysis of the constellations and compared his interpretations with those of the experts. Just how far his study of the stars had affected his decisions was hard to establish, Schultz told her readers, but a number of his friends admitted he would never take a decisive step when the stars were not favorable.[18]

Writing as Dickson, Schultz again considered the role of astrology in Hitler's life in a three-page feature titled "Europe's Man of Mystery! His Daily Life Revealed," which appeared in the *Tribune's Graphic* magazine on August 6. The body of the piece tracked Hitler through his day, using details drawn from Schultz's own observations as well as from people in his entourage, such as the barber who had shaved him at the Hotel Kaiserhof before he became chancellor and now made daily house calls to the chancellery to barber the führer. She ended the piece by again asking how deeply his study of the stars affected his decisions.

<hr />

Schultz's visits to Hitler's astrologers were more than a quirky human-interest story. They were part of a series of leads she was following for what would be the most important scoop of her career: Germany's nonaggression pact with the Soviet Union.

Schultz gave her first hint of the story in May, buried in the final section of an article comprised of small news items: "The Germans are attempting to establish closer relations with Russia in an apparent effort to isolate Poland."[19]

In July, writing as John Dickson, she forecast the German-Soviet nonaggression pact, which would be signed five weeks later, in a front-page article in the *Tribune*. According to sources in Hitler and Baron von Ribbentrop's inner circles (in addition to Hitler's astrologer), she reported, England had replaced Russia as Germany's number one enemy. As a result, plans for Soviet-German cooperation were under discussion in Moscow. "Dickson" concluded "the newest toast in high

Hitler Guard circles is 'To our new ally, Russia!'"[20] (Schultz once again buried the scoop, this time in the middle of a long meandering article about Hitler's current aims and aspirations. Perhaps it was the safest way to get the story out.)

Finally, on August 22, Schultz reported that Baron von Ribbentrop had flown to Moscow with a team of negotiators to finalize the details of the nonaggression pact and explained what such an alliance would mean for Poland, and by extension for Britain and France.[21] Two days later, she announced that the Molotov-Ribbentrop Pact had been signed, both in a front-page article in the *Tribune* and in a broadcast for MBS. In the broadcast, she gave what the *Tribune* described the next day as "a word picture of war preparations in the German capital" and shared the reactions of everyday Germans to the news. The article focused on political analysis, including the news that all forms of transport out of Germany were jammed as foreigners fled the country for fear of war.[22]

That fear was well-founded. In addition to the official nonaggression pact, the treaty included secret protocols that divided eastern Europe into German and Soviet spheres of influence. As had happened so often in the past, Poland was to be partitioned between its more powerful neighbors. With Russia's promise not to resist Germany's eastward expansion in place, Poland's fate was sealed.

⸎

By August 31, all efforts by Britain and France to keep Germany from invading Poland had failed. Hour by hour, Schultz and the other *Tribune* correspondents stationed across Europe filed bulletins suggesting tensions were rising. Peace between Poland and German could not last much longer.

In a dispatch that arrived in Chicago an hour before Germany marched into Poland, Schultz reported the mood was somber in Berlin. Faced with the possibility of war, women wept. Men squared their shoulders and declared, "You will see that we will manage to avoid war." Worried crowds gathered across from Hitler's chancellery on Wilhelmstrasse, where a broadcasting truck blared the latest news about the political standoff.[23]

At four thirty in the morning, on September 1, Schultz sat in the Kroll Opera House, which stood across the plaza from the burned-out remains of the Reichstag building and served as a temporary home to the German parliament on those rare occasions when Hitler called it into session, and watched as Hitler announced to a hastily called session of the Reichstag that the fighting with Poland had begun.

At six, she called William Shirer and told him. "It's happened."

After all the waiting, the war was on.

CHAPTER NINETEEN

THE BERLIN BLUES

Thanks again for your fine work. Believe
me when you are not in Berlin we know it.

—PAT MALONEY, managing editor,
Chicago Tribune, April 1, 1940[1]

Schultz sent the news that the war had begun in an early morning
cable that reached Chicago in time for the 7:18 edition—one of
eleven editions the *Tribune* published between midnight and nine that
morning as new dispatches arrived from Europe.

German reactions to the announcement were very different from
those Schultz saw at the beginning of the Great War. In 1914, Berlin's
streets had a carnival atmosphere. Church bells pealed and crowds
threw roses to the soldiers as they marched through the city to the
martial sound of brass bands. Now, in 1939, the mood in Germany
was grim and purposeful. The crowd did not cheer the troops when
transport trains pulled out of Berlin's railroad stations. No one threw
flowers. Instead of excited crowds, Berlin policemen and SS men
lined the streets leading to the Kroll Opera House, where Hitler was
expected to speak. Schultz reported that many of the women who
stood in line to buy the one egg per family member allowed under the
new rationing regulations were red-eyed with weeping because their
husbands or brothers or sons had been sent to the front. Policemen
remonstrated with them for crying, saying they should be proud their
men had the chance to do their duty for the fatherland. "You're not at
the front," a woman lashed out. "We'll see how your women behave
when you have to go."[2]

That evening, around seven, unscheduled air-raid sirens wailed in Berlin for the first time. A seventeen-minute blast cleared panicked citizens off the streets within minutes. Blackout regulations went into effect at the same time. The unfamiliar darkness added to the disorienting effect of the sirens. The city was pitch-black, except for the small pale blue lights that marked gas stations and fire alarms, giving the capital an eerie appearance. Schultz reported that it was difficult to make your way through Berlin that night and many people got lost in the darkness.

For the first two weeks of September, the front section of the *Tribune* was totally devoted to the war. Each day the paper ran eight to twelve pages of war-related articles by the *Tribune's* foreign correspondents and their colleagues at the wire services, analysis by *Tribune* commentators back home, maps, diagrams, and photographs.

Schultz produced forty-one bylined articles in thirty days, seventeen of which ran on the front page, and an unknown number of short news items attributed only to the *Chicago Tribune* Foreign News Service. She reported on the continued diplomatic maneuverings in the brief time before Britain and France entered the war on the side of Poland on September 3, on the arrival of a Soviet mission in Berlin, and on Germany's hopes for an active alliance with Russia. She shared official German statements about troop movements, carefully couching her reports to make it clear that she had not been able to verify the information through independent sources and indirectly casting doubt on the accuracy of German reports.

Throughout this period of the war, the *Tribune* was careful to note when Schultz's reports from Germany differed from those received from Paris or Poland. Sometimes they ran her articles side by side under a shared headline with those of David Darrah in France or Larry Rue in London, offering a different perspective on events. On other occasions, they would insert an italicized block of contradictory information from the viewpoint of one of Germany's opponents at a relevant spot in her article. Both were effective techniques that made it clear the information as reported was true to the best of the reporters' ability but not necessarily The Truth.

In addition to political and military news, Schultz wrote articles on life in wartime Germany, many of them focusing on food shortages and rationing—subjects that Chicagoans seemed to find as fascinating as Schultz did. In one article, in which she detailed Germany's complex seven-card ration system, she reported that foreign correspondents were classified as hard laborers for ration purposes, which allowed them slightly more than two pounds of meat a week—double the ration for most other adults. "This announcement did not make the foreign correspondents a bit mad," she added.[3]

<hr />

Americans could find Schultz on the air as well as on the front page of the *Tribune*. The *Chicago Tribune*'s radio station, WGN, in conjunction with MBS, broadcast continuously for the first seventy-two hours of the war. They and their competitors abandoned existing conventions and interrupted scheduled programs to announce breaking news, averaging more than twenty-five such interruptions a day. They also aired five scheduled newscasts each day, including a half-hour report from London, Warsaw, and Berlin each night at 7:31, Chicago time. On September 3, WGN announced its commitment to producing twenty-four-hour coverage as long as interest in the war remained high.

In an article describing WGN's war coverage, the *Tribune* shared the complexities of arranging radio programming from Europe with its readers. For the London-Warsaw-Berlin segment, each half-hour broadcast required many hours of coordination between MBS officials in Chicago, New York, and London; the BBC; Germany's Rundfunk; Press Wireless; AT&T; and RCA Communications.

The article didn't describe what the broadcast involved at Schultz's end. A program that aired live at 7:31 p.m. in Chicago required her to be in front of the microphone at the Rundfunk studios at 2:31 a.m., with her script approved by the censors—adding hours to workdays that already stretched into early morning.

Broadcasters submitted their scripts to a trio of censors for review two hours before they went on the air: one from the military, one from the Foreign Office, and one from the Propaganda Ministry. Once the script was approved, a censor would read along as the reporter broadcast, noting inflections and pauses.

The original censors did not speak idiomatic English, which allowed broadcasters to add shades of meaning to their scripts by using innuendo, slang, or Americanisms—the later more difficult for Schultz than for the other broadcasters due to her expatriate youth. With time, the Germans found censors who were fluent enough in English to recognize and remove the idioms and irony that subtly changed the intention of a script.

⎯⎯ ⚬⚬⚬ ⎯⎯

After the conquest of Poland, active hostilities slowed on the Western Front—a period of relative inactivity that became known as the Phony War in the United States, the Bore War in Britain, and the *Sitzkrieg* in Germany. Germany consolidated its hold on Poland. Britain and France built up their forces, took defensive positions along the Franco-Belgian border, and waited. As Schultz reported to George Scharschug, "War is gradually becoming a matter of routine with us."[4]

War was becoming routine at the *Tribune* as well. European war news, including articles by Schultz, continued to dominate the front page, but the paper no longer devoted an entire section to it. WGN and MBS also moved out of crisis mode, though all the networks retained the new habit of interrupting scheduled programs to announce breaking news. Schultz returned to her single broadcasting slot on Sunday night, though she remained on call for special broadcasts as needed.

⎯⎯ ⚬⚬⚬ ⎯⎯

Reporting on the war from Berlin required Schultz to be even more inventive than before.

The German military refused to allow Schultz to go to the front, though a number of her male counterparts were shepherded by the German army on what Louis Lochner of the Associated Press called a "route of victory," in which the Germans made sure the correspondents witnessed the final stages of a successful military action.[5] Schultz was barred even from these carefully organized press junkets, though it is unclear whether it was because she was a woman or because she was in the Nazis' bad graces.

Unable to travel to the front herself, even under the serious limitations of an official press tour, Schultz hired a young man named John Raleigh, the nephew of celebrated *Tribune* cartoonist John T. McCutcheon, to be her eyes and ears at the front. He had bicycled across Germany with his brother, so she assumed his German would be good enough to get by. For about six months, he traveled on press junkets to Poland and Czechoslovakia in her place. His scanty German proved to be more of a handicap than either of them expected, but he successfully produced several bylined articles using information from these junkets. During that same period, the *Tribune* published 150 articles with Sigrid Schultz's byline, 62 of them on the front page. Not being able to travel to the front was a handicap, but it didn't stop her.

By the end of the year, Germany no longer allowed any foreign correspondents at the front. "We keep asking for permission to go to the front," she wrote to McCormick, "but we are always told 'trips will be allowed later. For the moment they are utterly impossible'."[6]

At the same time, Schultz was having even more problems than before getting her dispatches out of Germany on a reliable basis. Three times in one week, she reported to Scharschug in frustration, messages failed to go through after the Berlin Press Wireless agent confirmed that they had gone out in a timely manner. She sent two stories a second time using the more expensive and slower Trans-Radio Press service. She killed the third one—its news window had passed.

Schultz also continued to tangle with the censors over her radio scripts. Sometimes the censors' decisions seemed arbitrary, at other times, silly. She shared one example with McCormick that she believed gave "a perfect illustration of the censor mind." In a broadcast about Christmas in Berlin, she described a toy antiaircraft gun that was one of the most popular gifts of the season. The censor cut it from the story because it might contain a military secret. The toy, she told McCormick "can be bought for four dollars in all Berlin toy stores."[7]

Occasionally, Schultz won a battle with the censors. Soon after the war started, Hitler responded to a case of labor unrest by addressing the workers involved. They gave him a cool reception until he made an impassioned promise that profits from the war would not enrich profiteers. Standing in the audience, Schultz realized that restrictions on war profits was the big story of the day, not the labor unrest. She made it the center of her script for that night's broadcast.

When she turned in her script, the censors on duty insisted she delete all references to profit restrictions.

"I heard Hitler make those statements," she said.

They handed her the late evening papers, which had published the official text of Hitler's speech. "There is no reference to any cut in profits, as you will see."

They were right. The papers had no such reference. Schultz handed the censors a copy of the full text of the speech, which she had purchased from one of the Berlin stenographers who took notes on important speeches and sold clean copies to correspondents so they did not have to take notes themselves. (A service that became increasingly dangerous to provide under the Nazis.) Hitler's comments about restricting war profits were clearly there.

By then it was after 2 a.m. Schultz was due to go on the air in a few minutes. The censors were frantic. Did they dare wake their bosses for instructions? They decided they did not and allowed Schultz to go on the air with her original script.

A small, rare victory against Nazi propaganda.[8]

Despite her difficulties with getting the news out, the Chicago office was more than pleased with her work. When asked by Colonel Mc-Cormick to report on the foreign staff situation, managing editor Pat Maloney's assessment of Schultz was brief: "SCHULTZ—Berlin. 1000%."[9]

The Phony War ended when the Nazis invaded neutral Denmark and Norway on April 9, 1940.

Germany's invasion of Norway must have been a blow to Schultz. She identified herself as Norwegian. Family members who she adored lived there. But almost nothing in her surviving personal documents says explicitly how she felt about it. The most direct statement of her feelings about the invasion comes from a discussion many years later in which she stated how much she hated the Swedes during the war because they allowed Germany to ship war materials across Sweden and into the mountains, where Norwegians fought to maintain their freedom.

Schultz's articles describing the invasion of Norway are similar to those she wrote about the earlier invasion of Poland: descriptions of the war from the perspective of Berlin and its people. She did not include her personal feelings about the war in Norway.

Schultz was more open about her opinions in her broadcast scripts at the time of the invasion, which led her to butt heads with the censors. In the lead-up to the invasion, she heard comments from people on the street, who were gloating about the booty they expected from the invasion of Denmark and Norway: "Oh, just think of all the beautiful

Norwegian furs we're going to get"..."All that butter... we're going to get a lot of that"..."The Norwegians make a wonderful... fish preserves ... oh this is going to be wonderful in our storage."[10] When she tried to include such comments in the script that she submitted on the day of the invasion, the censors hacked it up so badly that she refused to go on the air, leaving MBS with "dead air," a cardinal sin in radio. The program service manager at Mutual reassured Schultz, in response to what was probably a "hot" cable on her part, that the network agreed that she had been right to walk away from the microphone.

The next day she tried again. Once again, the censor took out all the comments about Germans' glee over getting food from Denmark and Norway. Schultz had to rewrite the entire script very carefully in order to keep at least part of the point in her broadcast that evening.

A few days later, she was once more at the Rundfunk. Writing to her mother as she waited to go on the air, she found it hard to believe that MBS would want her to continue broadcasting. What's more, she wasn't sure she wanted to: "I wrote so colorlessly about things I feel so strongly about today that I suffer."[11]

On May 10, a month after invading Denmark and Norway, Germany invaded three more neutral countries, the Netherlands, Belgium, and Luxembourg. In a few days the German army had swept through the Low Countries and moved on toward France.

Unable to visit the front and with little access to news outside Germany, Schultz continued to report on the progress of the war from the German perspective, using official German communiqués and her own observations drawn from life in wartime Germany. As time went on, she added commentary about the unreliability of German sources. For example, after reporting that "Jubilant Nazis asserted the Germans were within 76 miles of Paris," she added, "The assertion, however, lacked both confirmation and details."[12]

In July 1940, Schultz found herself in trouble as a result of another *Tribune* reporter's actions.

Early in the morning of July 26, Captain Maxwell Corpening arrived in Berlin from Switzerland. He was a longtime crony of McCormick's, a polo-playing West Point graduate who McCormick kept on the payroll the same way other businessmen employed ne'er-do-well nephews.

Corpening had a hot story to report, from a source he trusted. He was sure it would be an international scoop. But the Swiss censors kept tight control on everything going through their office. Almost every story he tried to file had resulted in a long conversation with the Swiss censor. Some stories had been cut all together. In other cases, the censors had removed so many details from the story that it was not worth printing.

As Corpening saw it, Berlin was his first opportunity to file his story on secret German attempts to negotiate peace with Britain, which stood alone against Germany following the collapse of France. Without waiting to talk with Schultz, he telephoned the story from her office in the Hotel Esplanade to the Press Wireless transmitting station in Amsterdam. The clerk in Amsterdam promised Corpening that he would give the story a Basel dateline. When the Swiss censor called the American consulate in Basel that night to tell Corpening the story could not be sent, the consulate told him there had to be a mistake. Corpening was in Berlin. The censor "corrected" the dateline, and the piece went through.

When Schultz arrived in the office late that afternoon, she found Corpening in possession. Pleased with himself, he told her the details of the interesting peace terms he had learned about in Switzerland but did not mention that he had already wired the story to Chicago. Schultz replied they had heard a lot about those same peace terms in Berlin recently but had been warned the subject was taboo and anyone who wrote about it would be tossed out of Germany. She assumed the matter was over.

She learned differently the next morning, when she received a summons to report to the Propaganda Ministry immediately on a serious matter.

When Schultz arrived at the Propaganda Ministry, the official on duty read her a story about proposed peace terms that had appeared in the *New York Times* that morning, with a *Chicago Tribune* Foreign Press Service credit and a Berlin dateline. The headline read "Reich Terms Reported Offered via Sweden; Alleged Peace Plan an 'Ultimatum' to British."[13]

According to William Shirer, the Propaganda Ministry was eager to kick Schultz out of Germany "because of her independence and knowledge of things behind the scenes."[14] She had already received three warnings from the ministry about stories that came close to the line of being unacceptable. The fact that the offensive story had been filed from her office seemed to provide their chance.

Schultz must have realized that Corpening filed the story. She may have cursed him in her heart. But she told the Nazi censors she knew nothing about it. They insisted the story had come from her office. She held her ground.

Once they let her go, she looked for Corpening, eventually finding him at the embassy. Schultz may well have treated him to one of her rare displays of temper, "flinging biting words into the blue" in all the languages she knew.[15] Corpening admitted he telephoned the story in before she got to the office. He did not cancel it after talking to her because he assumed she was being overly cautious when she told him the story could not be touched—because of course a man who had been in Berlin a few hours knew more about the political climate than a woman who had reported on the Nazis from the beginning.

Corpening rightly took the blame. He was placed under house arrest in the Hotel Adlon and left Germany as soon as he could get an exit visa. Schultz gave him credit: "He did everything he could to try to convince the Germans of the truth, which was that I really did not know about his filing of the story."[16] But it felt like another close call.

⸺∞⸺

On August 25, Schultz traveled on the subway through the blacked-out city to the Rundfunk studios in Berlin's Westend district with William Shirer, who was broadcasting nightly for CBS. Their broadcasts were timed to air live on the evening news. Shirer was scheduled at one in the morning, Berlin time; Schultz followed him at one thirty.

An air-raid siren began at twelve thirty, the sound rising and falling in a continuous wave. Schultz assumed it was a false alarm, as usual. Central Berlin had not been bombed before. Then, to her surprise, she heard the hum of airplanes overhead and the distinctive bark from the station's roof, which held a battery of the antiaircraft guns known as flak, a contraction of their German name, *Fliegerabwehrkanone*. The British Royal Air Force (RAF) was attacking the city.

The Battle of Britain had begun six weeks before. In the first weeks of the German air offensive, the Luftwaffe attacked shipping convoys in the English Channel, coastal radar stations, aircraft factories, and airfields, but left civilian targets untouched. On August 24, a lost German bomber formation dropped bombs on London by mistake. Churchill ordered the RAF to attack Berlin in retaliation. The following evening, the RAF sent ninety-five planes to bomb Tempelhof Airport, near the center of Berlin.

The flak was heavy near the Rundfunk office. The building's windows rattled in their frames every time an antiaircraft battery fired or a shell exploded. The air-raid wardens, dressed in firefighting overalls, raced through the building, ordering everyone into the air-raid shelter.

Neither Schultz nor Shirer were willing to take shelter until they had completed their broadcasts.

In order to get to the radio studio from the building where the censors approved their scripts, they had to walk two hundred yards across an empty blacked-out courtyard. As Shirer stepped into the open at five minutes to one, the antiaircraft guns on the building fired. Shrapnel fell around him. He dashed across the courtyard and made it safely into the studio, with the help of a flashlight that Schultz had loaned him, a pinhole of light shining through a cardboard filter taped over the lens. He made his broadcast without incident, though the German engineer insisted he lean into the microphone to minimize the sound of the raid.

When it was time for Schultz to broadcast, the shrapnel was heavier than before, sounding like hail on a tin roof as it fell through the trees into the courtyard. Shirer and others, including an SS guard, tried to dissuade her from leaving the safety of the building. She insisted on running to the studio. As she crossed the courtyard, a piece of shrapnel the size of an egg hit her in the knee and she fell to the ground. Once she was on her feet again, she discovered that her flashlight had failed, but she was able to pick her way down the steps to the broadcasting studio, with light from the flash of the antiaircraft guns.

Schultz staunched blood from the ugly gash in her leg and proceeded with the broadcast, even though she was in considerable pain. The transmitter, which had worked perfectly for Shirer, failed during her broadcast, though she did not know it at the time and continued to read her script into a dead microphone. The transmitter began to work again shortly after she spoke. In a short piece about the experience that appeared in the *Tribune* two days later, she reported, without commentary, that "authorities said the interruption had not been due to the air raid."[17]

Afterward, Schultz and Shirer watched the air raid from a balcony until almost dawn, as if the combined effect of bursting bombs, German searchlights flashing back and forth across the clouds, and exploding flak shells were a magnificent, terrible light show.

———— ∞ ————

When Schultz went out the next day to investigate the damage, she found the Berlin papers carried a nine-line statement that British planes had dropped incendiary bombs on the outskirts of the city, but had not done any damage. Rumor on the streets said the police had roped off areas in the center of the city "to prevent the curious from seeing what a bomb can do to a house."

The bombing on August 25, 1940, was the first serious air raid on Berlin. There would be a total of 363 air raids on central Berlin during the remaining years of the war. At first, Schultz and other correspondents were allowed to report on visible damage to the city. Schultz described bomb craters and fires caused by the raiders, streets cordoned off by the police, efforts to repair damage and restore services, rubbernecking Berliners scurrying around the city to see the wreckage—and Nazi attempts to limit how much damage correspondents saw by conducting in-city press tours of carefully chosen areas. She reported how the city's residents dealt with near nightly air raids and shared bits of idiotic advice from officials. For instance, General von Schroeder, president of Germany's Antiairraid [sic] Association, urged housewives to use their imagination to make their buildings' air-raid shelters more comfortable and recommended deck chairs as an ideal addition to shelters.[18]

Not content with reporting how Berlin's human residents were coping, Schultz—always an animal lover—made a trip to the zoo to learn how the animals were reacting to the air raids. Not surprisingly, most were distressed, though the zoo wardens reported the rhinoceros, living up to its reputation for thick skin, was seemingly unconcerned.

On December 16, that small amount of journalistic freedom came to an end. Correspondents who wanted to report descriptions of the damage caused by two British air raids the night before were told "emphatically" that they could send only what appeared in the German official statement.[19]

The only surprise was that it had taken so long for Germany to slam that door shut.

———— ∞ ————

Several days after being caught in the first British air raid in Berlin, on August 28, Schultz received a call at noon from the Nazi Propaganda Ministry inviting her on a press trip to witness the signing of the Second Vienna Award, the resolution of one of two territorial disputes between Hungary and its neighbors arbitrated by Germany and Italy. It was the first time she had been invited to go on a Nazi-sponsored junket, and she didn't feel she could turn down the offer since she had expressed her displeasure at being left out. In order to be in Vienna in time for the event, she had to leave that night. The timing was heartbreaking. Peter Ilcus had received orders to return to Romania permanently and was leaving Berlin the next day. Her plans for saying goodbye at the station were wrecked.

Once in Vienna, she made another plan. Ilcus was passing through the Austrian capital on his way to Bucharest. They would have an hour together before his train left the station. In fact, they managed more than an hour. Schultz met him at the station and rode with him to the next stop, getting back in time to file into the Empress Maria Theresa's "golden cabinet" in the Albertina Palace with the other foreign correspondents.

Writing from Vienna the next day, Schultz told her mother, "When I get back to Berlin, I'm going to feel like a widow for the third time in my life."[20] But for now, she had a story to file.

A year after the war began, Schultz was suffering from the "Berlin blues"—the name foreign correspondents gave to the wearing experience of life in Nazi Germany. She was beginning to wonder whether she could continue to report from Berlin. She might even do a better job from the United States, using her deep background knowledge about Germany and picking up German radio broadcasts.

On October 8, 1940, Schultz wrote to McCormick about her concerns. She told him that she went as far as she dared in her stories, trying to share what she knew without getting shipped out of Germany. Corpening, after all, was expelled for writing about something everyone in the know was talking about. She assured him, "I don't plan to pull an Edgar Mowrer or a Dorothy Thompson and say things that would make it impossible for me to come back." But censorship was getting worse, and the possibility of internment hung over every correspondent's head. "It is true it is not officially proclaimed censorship," she admitted, "but this kind of self-imposed censorship is exceedingly hard to cope with, especially when every few days we are told we must remember the high treason and treason legislation." A journalist convicted of treason would be lucky if she was expelled. The ultimate penalty for treason, provided in the laws passed immediately after the Reichstag fire, was death by hanging.

In addition, for the first time she seriously feared for her safety. "I don't mind air raids," she told McCormick. "On the contrary, I am sorry to confess, that the kind we have been having give me quite an enjoyable thrill. But the mysterious stalking, coupled with the permanent wearing of a muzzle have been hard to take."[21]

It had been a difficult few months. The Nazis had investigated her on every possible pretext, from the money she sent to her mother each month to her legal status in the country. "I have violated no laws," she told McCormick, "but this constant attempt to trap me at times seemed more than I could cope with. I was even denounced as being Jewish, which may seem funny at a distance, but all the accompanying incidents were thoroughly unpleasant."

In fact, the Gestapo questioned her about her "racial background" more than once. In one version of the story, Schultz claimed it was her great uncle Isaac on the Norwegian side who caught the Gestapo's attention: "I had a number of tough encounters with them in Grand Uncle Isaac's honor. I never had any trouble with the Nazis about mother, née Hedwig Jaskewitz, who was as cosmopolitan as they come."[22] (Once again, Schultz uses that code word "cosmopolitan," suggesting that Hedwig might, in fact, have been Jewish.) In another version, she told Alexander von Schimpff that my Great Grandfather, on Mother's side . . . he was a famous baritone and opera director; whose name "Jaschkewitz" [sic] used to get the Gestapo quite excited."[23] It was dangerous either way.

She was beginning to think she should go home for the winter and take some time to recover.[24]

CHAPTER TWENTY

GOING HOME

Back in Berlin, after I had hidden two old Jewish women
for a few nights, I discovered fear for the first and only
time in my life. I decided it was time to go home on leave.

—SIGRID SCHULTZ, 1951[1]

I found a letter of my Mothers awaiting me here and I
know that I am doing my duty by going home to look after
her. I do hope I'll be able to get her back into a physical
and mental shape that will allow me to go back to Europe,
because I do want to continue my work.

—SIGRID SCHULTZ, 1941[2]

In the weeks that followed, Schultz waited for a response from Mc-
Cormick and watched as the war entered a new phase. The Luftwaffe
continued to bomb Britain but shifted its focus from military sites to
civilian targets in London and other British cities. Germany signed the
Tripartite Pact with Italy and Japan, promising to support one another
if they were attacked by a country with which they were not already at
war, i.e., the United States. At the same time that Hitler had formalized
relations with new allies, Schultz heard rumors from her sources in the
Nazi ranks that he was preparing to move eastward, with the ultimate
goal of invading his ally, Russia.

On November 1, 1940, after visits to health spas in Baden and Bern,
indulging in the mud baths that were her preferred treatment for ailments of all sorts, Schultz set out on an eight-day, three-thousand-mile

tour of continental Europe, traveling from the North Sea to the Mediterranean, the Adriatic, and, finally, the Black Sea, then back north to Berlin, with the intention of reporting on conditions and attitudes in those countries that still "cling to their independence or what is left of it." In a long article that ran on the front page of the *Tribune* on November 11, she told her readers that, unlike Germany, which was buoyed by the conquests made by its armies and the hope of future victories, the countries she traveled through worried about living through a second wartime winter. She found two things that were consistent everywhere she went, even in countries not actively involved in the war, such as Switzerland and Romania: rationing and the "physical and mental gloom" from blackout regulations.

She reported that neutral Switzerland, fearful of food and fuel shortages, had made business concessions to the Axis powers. Hoarding had become such a problem that the government even issued warnings reminding people about what happens to cheese if kept too long.

In Italy, she was struck by the contrast between its air-raid warnings, which were so musical that she did not immediately recognize what they were, and those she had grown accustomed to in Berlin, which woke her up with a jerk. She also learned the hard way at the Swiss-Italian border that bringing a radio into Italy was strictly forbidden because of Italian controls on radio ownership and prohibitions on listening to foreign broadcasts. When the Italian customs officials found her travel radio in her suitcase, she refused to leave it behind and frantically scrambled to seal it in one of her suitcases, which she then shipped across Italy. She barely caught her train, lost her receipt for the sealed suitcase, recovered the receipt at a later stop, thanks to a helpful Italian customs official, and scrambled again to pick up the suitcase at the Italian border with Yugoslavia just in time to catch the next train. When she tried to use the radio, she found it had broken in the process.

In Yugoslavia, she heard bitter complaints about rising food prices as a result of the mandatory "export" of food to the Axis powers. (She wrote to her mother that the coffee was horrible. Quite an indictment given that coffee was scarce in Germany and coffee substitutes there were less than palatable.) Yugoslavs feared that the fighting in Greece, which Italy had invaded a few days before, would spill into Yugoslavia. Bulgarians, by contrast, though also dealing with rationing, were hopeful that they would acquire new territory at the expense of Turkey, with the help of their German and Russian allies.

Schultz gave special attention to conditions in Romania, where she found "neutral Romania" no longer looked so neutral. German troops and businessmen filled the cities and gathered at strategically sensitive points. German troop trains, oil tank cars, and freight trains jammed the railroads. The German army was training its Romanian counterparts. Perhaps most troubling, she reported, was the belief that the United States was in its own way part of Greater Germany. According to an editorial in the *Bucharester Tageblatt*, "Twenty million who speak German in the United States are at least as strong as the English there."[3]

It is possible that the chance to see Peter Ilcus, who was still unable to return to Berlin from Bucharest due to passport and visa problems, inspired the entire trip. Schultz's visit with Ilcus did not go the way either of them had hoped. Her train was two hours late. When she arrived, she found Ilcus, who had waited at the station through the delay, was nursing a horrible cold. They spent her first day in Bucharest together, but on the second day he was so sick that she ordered him to bed until the doctor confirmed that he was not in danger of catching pneumonia. While he rested, she visited with American diplomats and newspapermen stationed in Bucharest and interviewed the Romanian propaganda minister. Despite the fact that they had to abandon Ilcus's plans for entertaining her, she wrote to her mother that they were able to discuss most of the things that mattered to them, including the possibility that Schultz might be leaving soon for the United States.

On November 12, three days after she returned to Berlin, Schultz finally got a response from McCormick. "Dear Sigrid: You have had a pretty tough siege," he wrote. "Any time you want to come home for a vacation you are welcome to."[4]

It was time to go home.

It took Schultz several months to prepare for the trip.

Arranging a substitute when one of the bureau chiefs went home for a month or two to rest, to take care of family business, and to touch base with America was always complicated. With Europe at war, it was even harder.

After much discussion, the final choice for her replacement was Alex Small, whom Schultz had once rejected as her assistant and sent back to the Paris Edition because, though he wrote like an angel when he was sober, "he simply could not cope with German beer."[5] Small had redeemed himself as a reporter in her eyes during the Nazi invasion of Poland. The last foreign correspondent to leave Poland, he escaped cross-country after the Germans reached Warsaw. The three-week trek left him ragged and exhausted. When he finally reached Berlin, she later reported, he didn't "fully realize that he had the best story of all the correspondents in Poland." She helped him pull himself together and got him on the road to Holland, where he could safely write the story, as quickly as possible. The resulting series of sixteen articles, which ran in the *Tribune* in October, is an extraordinary firsthand account of Poland's collapse.

Once the *Tribune* arrangements were made, Schultz faced difficulties with the authorities in Berlin. Foreigners now needed German approval to leave the country as well as to enter it. The Foreign Office, the police, and the Gestapo all had to approve her exit visa. The Germans delayed her departure over and over until the American embassy exerted pressure on her behalf—an odd state of affairs since Nazi officials had threatened her with expulsion more than once.

They may have feared what she would write once she was out of the reach of their censors. Or it may not have had anything to do with Schultz herself. The correspondents who tried to leave after she did found it even more difficult to obtain exit visas. Eventually, the Germans refused to provide a journalist with an exit visa until his replacement had arrived. At that point it was clear to everyone that the Germans were collecting hostages to exchange for their own people when the time came.

Documents finally in hand, Schultz left Berlin on a night train to Basel on January 31, 1941. She expected to be back in two months. Three at the most.

Under other circumstances, the trip could have been enjoyable.

"This trip would be so much fun for me, if it wasn't for the fact that my dearest friend is staying in Europe," she wrote to Peter Ilcus from Bern, four days into the trip. "Without the one and only it is not quite as much fun."[6]

Before she left, she had asked him to make the trip with her, but he had turned her down with regrets, unable to get a passport or permission to travel abroad. "Keep hoping," he wrote, saying that he already realized it was a missed opportunity. "And even more, keep confident that we will meet again in a better time that is not too far away."[7]

———

Schultz met with difficulties at every stage of the three-week trip.

She couldn't get a sleeper compartment on the train out of Berlin and had to ride in a car with half-drunk Nazis. She worried all the way about what they might do.

After a brief stay in Bern, she traveled with four other American correspondents on a sleeper train from Switzerland through unoccupied France to Spain. At the Spanish border, they missed their connection while the French customs officers argued among themselves about how to handle the Americans' luggage. Then, on the Spanish side of the border, they watched unhappily as the train left on time for Barcelona, several hours before the Spanish border guards completed their lengthy baggage inspection—and determined how much money the passengers were bringing into the country. Each border crossing was complicated by the fact that Schultz carried two large bags filled with pictures, china, and silver.

They spent the night in a miserable railroad hotel in Portbou that no longer had running water. Before the Spanish Civil War, the town must have been a thriving place. But now, Schultz wrote to Ilcus, Portbou was "a dead little town, shot to pieces"—there were entire streets with nothing left but burned-out buildings destroyed in air raids during the civil war. In the main church, the statues of the saints were headless—she speculated they had been knocked off by a combatant's "artistic" shooting.[8]

From Portbou, once again on trains without sleeper cars, they continued to Barcelona and Madrid, enjoying a few hours in luxury hotels in each city, though Schultz was distressed by the beggars and starving dogs that haunted the hotels' doorways, returning immediately each time the porters chased them off. The countryside was "incredibly beautiful and romantic," but the Spanish trains were filthy and flea-ridden.[9] At each station, children fought over cigarette stubs and crusts of bread that passengers tossed from the window.

Schultz's impressions of the trip, written a few days after she arrived in the United States, added new insights to her observations from her trip through the Balkans four months earlier. The trip "from war to peace, through countries trembling in fear of what the next day will bring" was arduous, she told her readers, but it gave her a clear picture of the impact of the war on the peoples of continental Europe.

"In Switzerland," she told her readers, "the national strength is being mustered to preserve what is left of the country's independence," even if that meant producing goods for Germany to insure access to coal and other raw materials. In unoccupied France, which was "dazed by defeat and suffering from a shortage of food," the new Vichy regime under Marshal Philippe Pétain was frantically trying to organize itself. In Spain, bombed-out buildings stood everywhere as grim reminders of the civil war, and "misery stares at you out of the eyes of mothers clutching their emaciated youngsters and begging for food."

It was a relief when she reached Portugal, which was "clean, friendly, full of life and energy." And yet, she told her readers, Portugal, too, lived in fear of what might come.[10]

Lisbon, which had been an economically depressed backwater before the war, was now a major transportation hub. Americans poured into the country from across Europe, eager to return to the United States. Refugees of every nationality filled Lisbon's hotels and crowded Lisbon's cafés, drowning out the fluid musicality of Portuguese with a babel of foreign tongues.

Hotels in Lisbon proper were not just fully booked, they were overbooked. With the help of one of her many connections, Schultz got a room in the luxurious Hotel Palacio on the Portuguese Riviera in nearby Estoril.

"I would enjoy this city if you were here with me," she wrote to Ilcus.[11] Even without his company, she wished she could stay in Lisbon for a time and rest up. The hotel was comfortable and Portugal's spring sun was warming after the chill of Berlin in winter. But unlike the unfortunate souls who waited for days, weeks, or even months as they tried to arrange passage across the Atlantic to the Americas or Africa, Sigrid had her passage booked already on what she described as "the non-appetizing *Siboney*."[12]

It proved to be a rough Atlantic passage.

The SS *Siboney* sailed from Lisbon on Friday, February 14, two weeks after Schultz left Berlin. With three hundred passengers, the ship was overcrowded, with four people assigned to a cabin. Once on board, Schultz may well have regretfully compared her accommodations to those she had enjoyed on that "sturdy little boat," the *Volkendam*, on which she had made her previous Atlantic crossing.

The *Tribune* reporter who met Schultz at the docks when she landed in Jersey City accurately described the *Siboney* as a "small liner of ancient vintage."[13] It had served as a transport ship in World War I. Between the wars, the ship operated first as a transatlantic liner between New York, Cuba, and Spain and later, after serious damage and extensive repairs, on shorter runs between New York, Cuba, and Mexico. In late 1940, the patched and elderly *Siboney* returned to transatlantic service in response to the growing and often desperate demand for transport from Lisbon to the United States created by the war.

Schultz's voyage on the *Siboney* tested its seaworthiness. One day out of Lisbon, the ship was caught in a major storm, the worst to hit the Portuguese coast in almost a hundred years. The storm lasted three days, reaching its greatest strength on Saturday night, when the *Siboney* was three hundred miles out to sea. Several times, the ship listed forty-eight degrees, several degrees past the angle considered safe, flooding the forecastle and leaving the cooks up to their waists in water in the galley. Sixty-mile-per-hour winds smashed twenty windows on the promenade deck. Water poured through a broken porthole into Schultz's cabin. A third of the passengers were treated for concussions and bruises in one day. The ship suffered heavy storms for the rest of its thirteen-day voyage.

Writing to McCormick from Bermuda, the ship's first scheduled port of call, Schultz was already thinking about her next story. "I shall attempt to avoid making statements that could jeopardize my chances of returning to my post," she told him, again. And yet, there were stories that needed to be told, particularly what she called the "euthanasia story." Her informants told her eighty thousand people who had been identified as crippled or insane were systematically killed in German hospitals because caring for them was considered a waste of national resources. She looked forward to seeing McCormick soon, so that she could tell him about this and other stories "without having to think about how this or that word or item would strike the Germans."[14] McCormick rejected the euthanasia story: no one would believe it and publishing it would jeopardize her return to Germany. Schultz might have managed to change his mind, as she had occasionally in the past, but she was soon too ill to try.

⸙

The ship arrived at its final destination on February 28, three days late. William Fulton, a *Tribune* staff writer stationed in New York, met Schultz at the docks. This time she was the story, not the storyteller.

Recognizing that "Miss Schultz, short of stature, full of energy, with blonde hair and a cheery smile" had weathered one of the worst crossings in recent maritime history, he gave her room to tell stories about the experience. Everything that was loose careened about the boat, she told him, including people. She pointed out a small boy in a blue school suit, the youngest passenger on the ship. Eight-year-old Hermann Gottschalk was traveling alone from his grandparents' home in Berlin to rejoin his parents in Detroit. "He was slithering back and forth in a sitting down position during the storm and remembered very forlornly that his grandmother had told him to be careful of the seat of his pants, that they were already thin."

It was a good human-interest story and Fulton gave it full play, including a photograph of a photogenic young Gottschalk looking out of a porthole. But he was more interested in hearing what Miss Schultz, "dean of the press corps in the German capital," thought about the current atmosphere in Germany.

Germans, she told Fulton, were "waiting today in a tense, bated-breath atmosphere like that which preceded the offensive into Norway." No one was sure what Hitler's next move would be, but Germans were betting ten to one that the war would be over by May. August at the latest.[15]

Schultz explained. The people who thought the war would be over by May expected Britain, which—together with the Commonwealth nations—had stood virtually alone against Germany since the fall of France the previous summer, would soon succumb to the Luftwaffe's blitzes. Those who expected victory to come a few months later also believed Britain was the primary target, whether that meant a submarine blockade to starve the British into submission or clearing the British fleet from the Mediterranean. With Britain defeated, Germany could expand eastward unchallenged in pursuit of Hitler's long dreamed-of *Lebensraum*.

Several days later, speaking to an audience of two thousand intellectuals, politicians, and businessmen in Chicago, Schultz made her own prediction about the progress of the war. According to her sources, if the Nazis could not bring Britain to its knees within the next three months, they were prepared to dig in for a long war of at least three years. Either way, it was bad news for the world.

CHAPTER TWENTY-ONE

SICK AND TIRED

I don't relish the thought of returning to Nazi infested
Europe, but when asking for leave wrote to the chief that
I would not refuse to return after my vacation and I've
never yet broken my word and so I am getting ready to go.

—SIGRID SCHULTZ, early summer 1941[1]

I suppose things are so slow because I worked too hard in
these last 20 years and now I must pay the price.

—SIGRID SCHULTZ, 1941[2]

One thousand members of the Chicago Council on Foreign Relations sat down to lunch in the Grand Ballroom of Chicago's
Stevens Hotel. The day's program, "Report on Germany," featured
Chicago's own Sigrid Schultz. Another thousand, there only for the
program, filled the balcony and overflowed into every available corner
of the room well before the hotel staff served the first course. The event
had been delayed for several days to accommodate the late arrival of
the ship bearing Schultz back to America. The council had been more
than willing to reschedule.

Schultz was the most recent in a long line of prominent speakers
the council had hosted since 1922, when the independent, nonpartisan
organization was established in response to the isolationism dominat-
ing political discussion in the American Midwest after the Great War.
By the 1930s, the council had become a key player in the debate about
American participation in the war everyone was sure was on its way.

Its members were eager to hear what Miss Schultz had to say about conditions in Germany.

Schultz spoke to another four hundred avid listeners at the Chicago Woman's Club that evening. She gave five more talks the following week to audiences large and small. In between her public appearances, she met with various departments of the *Tribune*, which took up whatever time and energy she had left. (She did make time to visit the portrait her father painted of his friend, former mayor Carter Henry Harrison Sr., which hung in the current mayor's office.)

Schultz wrote to her mother that the crowd in Milwaukee was hostile and a storm kept people away from the event at the high school, but "the big ones which were important went fine." The Executive Club had to turn five hundred people away. She thought she had done well: "I can make 2000 people sit still and listen to me and that's a new experience."[3]

Noel B. Gerson, publicity and talent director of *Tribune* radio auxiliary WGN, informed Colonel McCormick that Schultz received the second largest fee the Council on Foreign Relations had ever paid a speaker. He added, with some frustration, that he could have arranged twenty or thirty engagements for her during her first month back if she had been willing. "From the responses I have had," Gerson wrote, "Miss Schultz is unquestionably one of the greatest individual names—as a personality—in this part of the country."[4]

But much as she loved Chicago, Schultz was adamant that Gerson not schedule any more events for her until she saw how they went. She feared her talks would be a flop. She was determined not to do or say anything that would prevent her return to Germany as the *Tribune*'s correspondent. (Among other things, she refused to accept speaking engagements from Jewish organizations, fearing the Nazis would use such speeches as a reason to refuse to grant her a visa.) As a result, she didn't think she could compete with other correspondents who were not returning to their posts in Europe and thus felt free to "be sensational" in their talks.[5]

Schultz had another reason to limit the number of speeches she gave. Though she didn't tell anyone other than her mother, she was in pain. She had an agonizing abscess—the location of which she left unnamed—that had grown to the size of a half dollar.

<hr>

That abscess was just the beginning.

Schultz had suffered from a high fever and a rash over her face and body while at sea, but both were gone by the time the ship landed. She assumed, incorrectly, that whatever ailed her had run its course.

During her lecture tour in Chicago, Schultz developed a high fever in addition to the abscess. As soon as her last speaking engagement was over on March 14, she was admitted to Passavant Memorial Hospital in downtown Chicago. The abscess was cut open and drained, which eased her immediate suffering, but the underlying problem remained undiagnosed. She had a second, worse, bout after she reached Connecticut, with two abscesses the size of her fist. She was operated on a second time in Norwalk and hospitalized for more than a week.

In Norwalk, after considerable testing, she was diagnosed as having "spotted war typhus," which could have been any one of several typhus fevers carried by lice, fleas, or ticks that are historically associated with wartime troop and refugee movements. It was not clear where she contracted the disease. In her correspondence with the *Tribune*'s insurance department, she noted war typhus was raging in Poland when she left Berlin, and that she had been exposed to plenty of recently returned German soldiers who might have been carrying "a few extra fleas." However, she believed it was more likely that "enemy fleas" attacked her in Spain, where the disease reached epidemic proportions shortly after she traveled through the region.[6]

On March 24, she wrote to Alex Small that she was beginning to sit up but not yet allowed out of her hospital bed. She told him she expected to sail for Europe in mid-May, which would bring her back to Berlin sometime in June. Unless, she added, she suffered a relapse—which she did almost immediately, to the dismay of both. Small was as eager to leave Berlin as she was to return.

She reported to the *Tribune*'s managing editor, Pat Maloney, on April 8, that she was recovering from a third relapse. This time it was caused by an adverse reaction to the drugs they were treating her with. "I can be up for an hour," she told him, "but then bed seems quite the right place." She was shocked to learn she was suffering from malnutrition, which contributed to how hard the disease had hit her. "This illness is rather a joke on me," she wrote, "since I felt so sure I had spent enough money to get the food I needed. . . . Looking back I realize that I did use a good part of my extra food reserves for entertaining purposes, to worm background stuff out of people instead of eating them myself."

Even though she was still unable to sit up for more than an hour, Schultz was already pondering ways to find new leads for the war news and thinking about getting back to work. She told Maloney that as soon as the doctors cleared her to travel, she would head to Washington to apply for a new passport and the necessary visas to travel to and in Europe. In the meantime, she wondered whether it might be worth going to San Francisco while she waited for her visas. One of her old sources, General Fritz Wiedemann, was Germany's consul general there and might be good for some leads.[7]

Schultz was less optimistic a few days later. Responding to a question from George Scharschug about a "mailer" she sent him before she left Berlin, she admitted she was still "too groggy for any kind of sustained effort." She was trapped in a four-day cycle of disease and discomfort: two days of fever, one day getting over the fever, and the beginning of a new abscess on the fourth day. She continued to react poorly to the available drugs. The only hope the doctors could give her was their expectation that each attack would be less violent than the ones that preceded it.[8]

By May, the fever was lower and she was able to sit up for a couple of hours each day. The doctors told her she would recuperate quickly, once the fever was gone. "I should," she told Maloney, with a touch of impatience. "I have never been such a model patient in my life, as I am now. I must confess this is not pure goodness—I am just too weak to cheat."[9]

Schultz's idea of being a good patient may not have matched that of her doctors. Even during her months of enforced quiet, she continued to run the business end of the Berlin office from her hospital bed, responding to anxious letters from the *Tribune* auditor in Europe and staff members in Berlin about vacation pay, business accounts, reimbursement policies, storage of the *Tribune* archives that she kept in the basement of her Berlin apartment, problems related to her personal business, and instructions about what to do in case the worst occurred and they had to close the Berlin office.

Schultz also kept watch on events in Germany, thanks to reports from her friends and informants. And she managed to write occasional background pieces for the paper's use, whether they wanted them or not. As she admitted to Scharschug, she was getting restless: "Life is certainly no fun without work."[10]

In June, Schultz, once again optimistic, began the process of reinstating her passport and acquiring the necessary visas and travel permits.

She wrote to Scharschug asking for a letter, required by the State Department, stating that the *Tribune* wanted her to return to Europe, including Germany. She told him that she had not taken the next step and inquired about available passage on ships, information also required by the State Department, "for the simple reason that I am not quite sure when I shall have shed the last trace of fever." She had accepted two dinner invitations the week before and learned that being with four or five people at a time was more than she could handle. Her fever was very low, but it was enough to leave her weak.[11]

Her *Tribune* colleagues had reservations about how realistic her travel hopes were. Maloney sent her the letter the State Department requested but informed her that Colonel McCormick's instructions were clear: "It is his wish that you return to Berlin but only—as he has stated—'But only when she is entirely recovered.' You realize that it might be tragic for you and difficult for us were you to return to Berlin and be overtaken by ill health. Indeed, it seems to me your health should be even stronger than usual, in view of the conditions which you will face. Therefore, be careful."[12] A week later, Scharschug echoed Maloney's sentiments: "Take it easy, get lots of rest and do not worry about hurrying back to Berlin. The Colonel wants to see your health fully restored, and so do the rest of us, before you tackle any new tough jobs."[13] John Steele weighed in from London, with the realistic assessment that "all the correspondents who have not already gone will have to go pretty soon."[14]

By late July, Schultz had visas and travel permits in hand, but she wasn't happy about the details on them. The German consulate had "pulled a little stunt" with her visa: they specified that she could only enter Germany by plane from Lisbon. She suspected they didn't want her to see conditions in Spain and Southern France. Whatever their reason, she told Scharschug, she needed to be able to stop in Switzerland and make arrangements for sending news to Chicago.

The State Department hadn't done much better. Her permits to return to Germany only allowed her to travel through France, Spain, Portugal, and Switzerland. She needed to get those reissued. If the Germans had closed the border when she got to Portugal or Switzerland, she would have trouble making alternative travel arrangements without more flexible permits. She realized this probably seemed like red tape to Scharschug, but the European police would take it seriously.

Problems with paperwork weren't her only concern. She had gone to Washington in part because she wondered whether she was babying herself too much. She quickly learned she was not. "I am fine if I see people for about one hour—or two at the maximum," she told Scharschug. "And that means being together with people who are friendly and not with people whose every move has to be watched and in front of whom one must be suspicious to the very depths of ones [sic] soul or mind"—a statement that reveals a great deal about what dinner parties were like in Nazi Berlin. She thought she would be over the hurdle in another four weeks or so, but in the meantime, she was taking vitamins, getting injections, turning down invitations (always a hard choice for Schultz), and trying to count her blessings: "Since people generally die of this disease which I brought home, I suppose I must be grateful to be alive and trust that I'll continue in this gradual climbing back to health."[15]

A few days later, Schultz learned that her plans were moot. She had a passport. She had visas and travel permits, even if they weren't quite right. But she didn't have an assignment.

On August 2, she received a letter from Pat Maloney, with explicit directions from Colonel McCormick: "We will not send Sigrid Schultz back to Germany unless the tension should lessen. When she is well enough we can send her to some country that she can get out of." Maloney hoped she would think it was good news.[16]

Schultz's answer was a long sigh of relief. "I'll certainly go wherever ordered but it would be hypocrisy to try to deny that I am deeply grateful to relax and not to have to steel myself for possible heroism. I don't mind war and bombs and inferior food, but Gestapo atmosphere is harder to take." She now felt that her chances to survive the war had increased tremendously. She had not shared her fears with her colleagues at the *Tribune* and certainly not with her mother, but "I never was confident that the Gestapo would let me leave if tension increased much more," she told Maloney.[17]

The next day, while Schultz was heading to Grand Central Station to catch the train to Westport, a taxi backed into her while she was crossing the street.

She might well have been distracted.

A few hours before the accident, she had telegraphed Peter Ilcus that she would not be returning to Berlin in the near future. It was a blow. As she would write to him several weeks later, she could not help but wonder "if one can feel completely alive until one is reunited with one's partner?"[18]

After twenty-two years of working for the *Tribune*'s Berlin bureau, she had cabled the office to cancel her lease and arrange to store her things, including the *Tribune* records stored in her basement, a suitcase filled with bottles of high-quality alcohol, and a "collection of carefully curated shoes from Paris" that she had left in February when she thought she was coming back. (Of all her belongings, she particularly mourned the loss of the shoes.)[19] Where she would be stationed next was an unknown: her life was in limbo until her health was restored.

Distracted or not, the taxi's rear fender caught her right knee, the one that had been damaged by shrapnel in Berlin, and threw her to the ground "while hundreds of cars flew past or rather should have been flying past, but had to stop while I was moved out of the road."[20] An X-ray of the knee showed that nothing was broken, but ligaments were torn. Ever an optimist, she expected the knee would be fine by the following week. She was almost as aggravated by the loss of a good pair of silk stockings as by the injury itself.

The damage to her knee proved to be worse than she initially understood: a combination of torn ligaments and torn cartilage required a steel brace and another period of inactivity. At the same time, she was suffering from a new bout of war typhus. In an astonishing act of positive thinking, she told Scharschug, "It would be hard to go thru this new enforced period of quiet if my war typhus did not keep coming back, despite all the injections. The spots are smaller than they used to be and the fever is lower than last spring, but it is all enough to keep me in the vegetating state. The doctor says that I get two more weeks of injections and then he hopes the war typhus waves will finally stop. I certainly hope so too."[21]

CHAPTER TWENTY-TWO

"A MILD LITTLE WAR MONGERING TOUR"

Peace has charm but I'll certainly be happy when I am
strong enough to cover a good hot story. The noise of
bombs would sound like music.

—SIGRID SCHULTZ, December 3, 1941[1]

I do hope and trust that when the situation changes and
my knowledge of Europe can be of use, you'll reactivate
me. I covered the story of Hitler's rise and I certainly
would like to be in on the kill—when the time comes.

—SIGRID SCHULTZ, May 7, 1942[2]

The *Tribune's* pro-isolationism policy ended with Japan's surprise
attack on Pearl Harbor on December 7, 1941, and the United States'
subsequent entry into the war. Under Pat Maloney's direction, the Foreign News Service was transformed into a war correspondent corps,
and its members dispatched to hot spots around the world.

Though she may not have felt like it when she first heard the news
of the attack, Schultz was lucky that she wasn't in Berlin at the time.

Two days after the attack, the American government arrested hundreds of German, Italian, and Japanese citizens who were residents in
the United States as enemy aliens. Among those arrested were German
diplomats and journalists. In retaliation, the Nazis put American correspondents who were still in Germany under house arrest, including
"Tribuners" Alex Small and John Paul Dickson. A few days later, they
were sent by train to the resort town of Bad Nauheim, along with

American embassy and consular personnel and their families. The Americans were interned in the Grand Hotel, a summer resort hotel that had been vacant since the beginning of the war and was by that time not so grand. Dubbed the Grand Refrigerator by the internees, the building was cold, and the food was inadequate—in all fairness, the conditions weren't that different from those suffered by the average German at the time. The Americans were held there for five months while the American and German governments negotiated details for a personnel exchange.

There is reason to doubt whether Schultz would have been among those exchanged. At least two of her colleagues, Joe Harsch and William Shirer, were sure the Germans would never have let her get out alive, she wrote to a young Norwegian woman who had traveled with her on the *Siboney*—"and I have a hunch they may have been right."[3]

Schultz had mixed emotions about being safely in the United States. On her good days, two a week on average at that point, she chafed at not being an active member of the *Tribune* team. On those days, she told D. M. Deininger, the *Tribune's* business manager in Chicago, "I am well enough to be champing at the bit and to notice that my vanity is suffering because I cannot air my knowledge about Europe and the war in print, in speeches, or over the radio." But when she suffered from a few bad days, Schultz told Deininger, "I turn around and thank my stars that I am not at the mercy of the Germans in Nauheim or somewhere else in Germany."[4]

—⦂⦂⦂—

Her feelings of well-being were short-lived.

On January 3, Schultz got the unhappy news from Pat Maloney that her benefits with the *Tribune* were coming to an end. She had received vacation pay for March and April of 1941, and full-time sick leave benefits for the months of May to December. According to the rules of the benefit plan, she would go on half-pay through the end of April.[5]

She responded that she appreciated the *Tribune's* patience with her. The money had been important, not only because of doctor and hospital bills, but because for many months she had continued to pay rent on her Berlin apartment pending her return. However, she expected she would be back on her feet before the end of April.

Her supervisors in Chicago, her staff in Berlin, and all her friends had heard many variations of this over the previous eight months: she would be fine in another two weeks, another four weeks, by the end of July. Her optimism doubtless helped her keep going through her illness and the accident, but Maloney had no reason to believe she was right this time.

She then raised the possibility of working part-time for the *Tribune* until she could resume full-time reporting. She was currently working two hours a day—another claim Maloney had heard before—in part dealing with a stream of letters regarding *Tribune* business in Berlin. Beyond what she was already doing, she suggested, "I could write a story a week on the German background or would I be more useful if I spoke over the radio or gave a lecture or two a week." In previous speaking events, she had done "a tightrope dance for the sake of the Nazis," but now, she told Maloney, she could "go to town."

She recognized Maloney might think it would be better for her to wait until she was fully restored to health. Schultz disagreed: "I believe if I started working very slowly, . . . it would help me get rid of the feeling that I am not doing my bit to help fight the invidious Nazi poison."[6]

In February 1942, while she was still on half-pay, Schultz received a letter from Douglas Miller, previously the American commercial attaché in the Berlin embassy. He asked her to join the American propaganda effort as part of William ("Wild Bill") Donovan's Office of the Coordinator of Information (COI), renamed the Office of Strategic Services (OSS) four months later. Miller wanted her to work at the German news desk in Washington as part of the COI's Foreign Information Service. The news desk currently produced sixteen hours of news a day for radio stations throughout the United States and were lining up time on British stations. "We could particularly use you here," he told her, "on account of your wide background, your intimate knowledge of personalities in Germany, and your undoubted ability to work up special stories on the basis of small items which we pick up here."[7]

Instead of feeling relief at the prospect of a job that would use her skills, Schultz was unenthusiastic about the offer. Writing to Pat Maloney the next day for advice, she described it as a "new problem that has just blown in by Special Delivery." It is clear that she hoped the *Tribune* would give her a resounding "no!" "I would certainly like to do my share to fight the dictator menace," she told Maloney. But she wondered if this was the right way to serve. "I feel strongly that my real field is the foreign news field as it has been the last 22 years—when I am fully restored."

What's more, she doubted whether she would fit into a civil service job, even if only for the duration of the war. It was a reasonable concern from a woman who had run the Berlin bureau for seventeen years with only long-distance supervision. She saw herself as a team player, but only for a specific team. "I am a Tribuner, more than anything else," she told Maloney.

That comment about being a "Tribuner, more than anything else," is telling. In a later letter to Maloney, she asked whether she could continue to pay her dues into the *Tribune* benefits program if she took a temporary assignment with the government. There was more behind her question than protecting her pension and other benefits, though she never lost track of the issue of financial security. She had "paid her dues" with the *Tribune* in more than one way for a long time. Continuing to contribute to the benefit program would make her "feel less like the orphan that is out on its own in a new world."[8]

The reality was that she still could not put in a full day's work. Only a few days earlier she told the *Tribune*'s insurance representative, "I can work about two hours a day now, but when I do, I feel as if I had done my customary 12 hour stint in Berlin."[9]

Instead of telling Maloney that she was still not physically up to the work, she proposed several possibilities that would not involve taking the job. Perhaps she could go to DC for a couple of weeks, working part-time in a temporary advisory capacity. That way no one could say she had refused to offer her country her expert advice. Better yet, she suggested, the *Tribune* could send her on a lecture tour designed to develop patriotic spirit—"it would be a kind of warwork that could be useful all around." She ended with a request for direction: "I shall do whatever you advise me to do because from my retreat here I am unable to see clearly what the *Tribune* would want me to answer in this case."[10]

Maloney's answer was clear: the *Tribune* wanted her to take the job. "That is the record of the *Tribune* and *Tribune* employees in wartime," he told her. "In the long run—regardless of whether you are happy or not in the work—I am sure your conscience will be easier if you do what you can."[11]

Schultz began to sabotage her chances for the COI job as soon as Maloney gave it his support.

She met with Miller in New York in early March. Then he called her to Washington for a second meeting, this time with Irving Pflaum, the foreign editor for the *Chicago Sun-Times* before the war began and now a key player at the COI. In that meeting she told them she wanted her "own special nook with some kind of definite title." Otherwise, she would have no influence. "I don't want to be one of the little mutts," she told Maloney. "You may call it vanity. I call it realism, which makes me feel better."[12]

Although she doesn't seem to have realized it, Miller and Pflaum immediately began to back away. The agency dragged its heels over Schultz's appointment. In late March, Doug Miller asked her to be patient: everyone he talked to wanted her there, but they had not been able to figure out the correct civil service designation for her job. Moreover, they wouldn't have room for new employees in the Washington office until they completed a move into a new building in New York. Schultz was baffled by the plea for patience. Miller had bombarded her with phone calls about the job until she told them the *Tribune* had approved her taking it. By May, she wrote to Maloney, it was clear: "The gentlemen who just could not wait until I brought my 'expert knowledge' into the Donovan organization don't want me now—at least not as a regular member of the staff."[13]

Even though Schultz did not end up with a full-time job in intelligence or propaganda, she agreed to write a series of biographical reports on influential Germans for what was now the OSS, not that different from the background reports she wrote for McCormick over the years. Donovan wrote to her in September 1942, saying, "I have had you in mind from the first as the best-qualified person I know of for this project." He wanted more than simple biographical data. He was looking for character profiles and information on the subjects' relationships with others, anything that could help the OSS determine how individuals might act under various circumstances, and thus influence policy.[14] Schultz accepted with pleasure. In some ways, it was just what she had asked for: a job of her own that acknowledged the depth of her specialized knowledge about the players in Germany. In fact, she was so enthusiastic and productive that Donovan wrote to her again six months later and gently put the project on indefinite hold until his staff had a chance to process the character profiles she had already written. He would be in touch, if and when they needed further material from her.

⸎

At the end of April, although her sick leave benefits had been exhausted, it was clear to Schultz and everyone else that she was not yet well enough to return to work full-time, and it was not obvious when that might change. At forty-nine, she was not old enough to qualify for a pension under the *Tribune's* Pension Board rules. Nonetheless, Maloney recommended that she be given the standard pension until she could return to work. The Pension Board agreed; her monthly pension of $100, roughly $1,800 in today's dollars, went into effect on May 1.

Despite the fact that Maloney had clearly bent the rules on her behalf, Schultz was sure the *Tribune* moved her from salary to pension because she was "flirting with the administration" in the form of the COI/OSS.[15] (McCormick may have put his isolationism on hold after Pearl Harbor, but he still was anti-Roosevelt.) On the other hand, she later blamed not getting the COI job on McCormick being unpopular in Roosevelt's administration.

⸎

In the meantime, Schultz set out to do the only thing she knew how to do: report on current events in Germany, whether that was in the form of magazine articles, radio broadcasts, or lectures.

The timing was bad. Schultz had not appeared on the front page of the *Tribune* or been heard over the airwaves for a year. Paid speaking jobs in particular were hard to come by. Organizations that had paid speakers a year ago were now donating most of their funds to the war effort. Government agencies provided speakers free of charge to any group who would listen.

Her primary challenge in selling articles to publications other than the *Tribune* was that she had been away from Germany for a year. Her contacts were broad and her information was deep, but a great deal had happened since her return to the United States. One editor summed up the problem, kindly but clearly: "I got a lot of fun out of reading the story of your adventures with German bureaucracy and the Gestapo, but I cannot see any possibility of using it in *The News.* We are so crowded with the story of what's going on today that I am afraid there is no chance of telling what happened before the war."[16] Schultz's news had turned to history while she was recovering.

Nonetheless she managed to sell enough articles and appear on enough radio programs and public forums to maintain her reputation as an authority on Germany. As a result of that reputation, in late 1942, Schultz set out on what she described to her literary agent, George Bye, as "a mild little war mongering tour"[17]—a chance to earn some money, see the country, and warn her countrymen about the dangers of Nazism. She spoke to volunteers in the War Bond Savings program, educators, businessmen's associations, and a great number of women's groups, and served as the keynote speaker at the New York Newspaper Women's Club's town hall forum, the wartime replacement for their annual ball.

Despite still not being completely well, Schultz enjoyed lecturing. Moreover, she wrote to McCormick, the tour "helped me get the feel of the country again, which is excellent when you have been away for long years. I feel so sorry for some of the exiles who are back home but have lost their own roots."[18] An astonishing statement from a woman who had lived away from the United States for most of her life.

⸺ ⬥ ⬥ ⬥ ⸺

Now that she was no longer in the *Tribune's* direct employment, Schultz began to explore the possibility of writing a book.

In the spring of 1942, Schultz wrote to a young friend, "All my colleagues have been writing books but my paper forbade me writing one—which was pretty good because I was too sick to do it. Now it would like me to do one—but the crucial moment seems past and where a year ago publishers ran after me now if I did settle down to do the book, I have to run after them.[19]

Editors had begun asking her about the possibility of a book as early as 1937. Schultz's reply to an expression of interest from Houghton Mifflin summed up her thoughts at the time: "I certainly would love to sit down and write a book—but—I don't see where I could find the time. The daily show is brimming with excitement and when it is over, I am all primed for the next act and I must be." She went on to discuss some of her concerns about taking on a book, which would recur in her future discussions with editors. She feared the things that were worth discussing couldn't be written yet. She worried the market would be flooded since a new newspaper book appeared every time a correspondent returned to the United States. And she couldn't quite see what her book would look like. "Did you have any special angle in mind?" she asked, as she would many times in the future.[20]

Over the course of 1941, when Sigrid was fighting typhus, inquiries from publishers rolled in. Even Maxwell Perkins, legendary editor of Ernest Hemingway and F. Scott Fitzgerald, reached out to her, saying: "I have often listened to your broadcasts from Berlin with very great interest indeed, . . . and I have long thought that you were perhaps better equipped than any other correspondent to write a book about the Germans." He felt she could make an important contribution to understanding the situation in Germany and how it came about.[21]

For months, Schultz did not have the strength to consider writing a book, even if the *Tribune* would allow it. She told editors who contacted her that if she was too sick to write for her paper, she could not think of writing a book.

Finally, she threw the question into Maloney's lap, just as she had with Douglas Miller's job proposal. "Publishers cannot kid me—I know I am just a reporter and what is more, I love being a reporter," she wrote. But maybe things were changing. Shirer's success with *Berlin Diary*, which sold more than three hundred thousand copies in the first two months, showed that the public was hungry for books related to the current crisis—"maybe it would take to the reports of the Tribune girl on duty in Europe." What did the *Tribune* want her to do, she wondered. "Should I, when the Schultz mind clears, write a series for the Sunday edition and expand it for book purposes? Or has this been done to death? Or should I let them publish all my broadcasts together and just add annotations and comments? Or do you say 'hands off'?"[22]

Schultz had hoped for a "no" about the intelligence job and received unmitigated approval. Now, when she appears to have hoped for a "yes," she received an unambiguous, and self-interested, "no" from McCormick, via Maloney: "He hopes you will not find the time to write a book. He thinks you should just rest and when you are able to do anything you should let us know and go back on the job in Switzerland or Portugal, or whatever country it seems best to send you."[23]

Six months later, when her sick leave benefits ran out, Schultz told George Bye that she was finally free to write a book.[24] The first rejection came in six weeks, from Perkins. For some inexplicable reason, Schultz sent him the outline for a novel rather than an account of her experiences in Germany. Based on what she had sent him, he did not think she had the skills to write fiction, but he believed "she might do a very fine book out of her very deep and wide experience of life in Germany. But I do not think it should be a quick, journalistic book, but a very thoughtful one. There have been too many of the other kind."[25]

It is clear from Schultz's letters that a "quick, journalistic book about her experiences in Germany might have been readable and fun, if inherently ephemeral, as were those of most of the returning correspondents. Instead, she followed Perkins's advice and aimed for a deeply wonky, argument-based book.

Other rejections followed: Scribner's; Little, Brown; Houghton Mifflin; Viking; E. P. Dutton. Many of the rejections said the same thing. The material was interesting. She had the background to write it. But it wasn't new. When she tried to write about her experiences, editors told her "Shirer, Flannery and a few others have covered the field too thoroughly already."[26] When she tried to write a book that explained how Germany got to where it was today, publishers rejected her on the grounds that "we doubt that this is the time for another book on why Germany has been and is an aggressor nation."[27]

Schultz had missed her window of opportunity, but a crowded market was not her only problem. She struggled to identify what she wanted to write and worried about differentiating her book from other journalists' books already on the market. She changed agents twice during the process. At one point, she took a two-week retreat to "labor on this book project all by myself until I have found which of the three angles that have presented themselves will be the one with which I click best and do the most satisfactory job."[28] More than once she sent writing samples to editors and asked for advice on the general approach she should take.

Working on the book brought other troubles as well. Schultz told one interested editor that "after concentrating on that old Nazi period I'm indulging in nice nightmares about the Gestapo catching me just as I [am] slicing up Hitler's liver."[29]

———

In June 1943, Schultz landed a book deal with Reynal and Hitchcock, the firm that published the first American translation of *Mein Kampf* in 1941 in conjunction with Houghton Mifflin. With a contract in hand, she struggled to write the book. She was correct in her assessment that she was a reporter first and last. The longer format was not a natural one for her: she claimed to have difficulty with "the technical art of ending or starting a chapter, the way chapters are supposed to start and end according to the ideas of publishers."[30] Eventually she had to hire a ghost writer to help her finish the book.

The anxiety Schultz suffered did not end when the book was finished. In the months between turning it in to her editor and its publication, Schultz sent her current agent, Mary Abbott, a stream of letters, worrying about the physical book, the publishing schedule, and publicity ideas. The book was so important to her, and so many things were out of her hands. Would her picture be on the cover? Who was responsible for pitching the book to the book clubs? Could the *Tribune* run it as a serial? She was thrilled by the ad for the book in *Publishers Weekly*, and crestfallen when it was not a Book of the Month Club selection, though it did make the recommended list. Abbott responded with soothing letters and information about how the process worked—and tried with varying success to keep Schultz from stepping on the publisher's toes.

<hr />

Germany Will Try It Again was published on January 20, 1944.

The book was an opinionated blend of memoir and analysis in which Schultz argued that Germany began preparing for a second world war as soon as it was clear they had lost the first one, and that they were already setting the stage for a third world war in the event they lost the current war. Much of it is the written equivalent of Schultz pounding her fist on the table as she makes her argument, interspersed with personal anecdotes chosen to illustrate her points.

Germany Will Try It Again is not very readable for a modern audience, but it was a modest success. It went into a second printing four days after publication. A third edition was out by April 1944. Reviews were good, even discounting those written by her friends and the *Tribune's* in-house reviewer.

Reader responses—positive and negative—were often impassioned. Schultz was surprised to report to Mary Abbott that "a number of insulting letters are trickling my way from irate Germans and their friends."[31] But the hate mail was balanced out by letters from her boosters, many of whom felt her book should be required reading for Americans who wanted to understand Germany and the war.

On July 7, a month after D-Day, the Westport Bond Rally auctioned off the manuscript of *Germany Will Try It Again*, which Schultz had donated as an incentive to bond sales. She reported to her agent that it sold for $10,000, roughly $154,000 in today's dollars, which she felt was "quite a nice round figure."[32]

Sigrid Schultz was pleased with the success of her donation, but her focus wasn't on bond sales or lecture tours. She was eager to go back to Europe as a reporter.

CHAPTER TWENTY-THREE

FROM FOREIGN CORRESPONDENT
TO WAR CORRESPONDENT

Sigrid Schultz, for twenty years *Chicago Tribune* correspondent in Berlin, is sitting in Westport, Connecticut.
She has uncountable German and other European connections, speaks German, French and Swedish, and why
she is not in Sweden collecting data on Germany from
the Germans who come and go from there is beyond me.

—DOROTHY THOMPSON, "Why Not Use
Our Women," *Ladies' Home Journal*, March 1944[1]

I thought I would be philosophical about D-Day, but I
discovered that life is barely worth living when you can't
help cover the big story.

—SIGRID SCHULTZ, July 5, 1944[2]

In December 1943, Schultz had nothing left to do for her book but
wait for its publication.

Restless, she reached out to Pat Maloney, who was running the
Tribune's team of war correspondents. "Now that I have rid myself of
the German preoccupations which have been simmering in my mind
ever since I came home," she wrote. "I am ready to resume interest in
the active world. I would like to return on duty abroad in the course
of the late spring or summer."[3]

Maloney was delighted that she was finally well, but he didn't have
anywhere to use her at the moment. The only possible spot was Lisbon,

but with war-related white paper rationing, they had to make every column inch count. "I would not know what we would do with propaganda pieces or rumor pieces out of Lisbon," he told her. But he had her in mind and would let her know if he thought of a way to use her.[4]

If Schultz was disappointed, she didn't let it show in her answer—though she made a small plug for the Lisbon assignment when the time came. She was in no hurry, she told him. In fact, she wanted to be in the United States when her book came out so she could "cash in on decent lecture fees."[5]

By late March, Maloney had thought of a way to use Schultz: send her to Sweden, which was officially neutral, with what he described as "a view to wiggling your way into Russia in the hope that you might be the first one into Germany." He had a list of practical questions, ending with "Have you any reason in the world to believe that you could go to Moscow, to say nothing of going to Germany?"[6]

"I have no concrete reason to assume that I could get into Moscow," Schultz answered, "but I figure it would be interesting, if unpleasant, and there might be a good story." As for his questions about safety, she reminded him, a bit flippantly, "I managed to get run over on Madison Avenue in 1941, suffering worse injuries than when shrapnel hit me in Berlin." Given that the *Tribune*, and every other newspaper, had to keep paper rationing in mind when choosing what stories to run, Schultz didn't think there was any point in leaving until after the presidential election in November: "Unless developments move so swiftly and promise to become so spectacular that they could claim some of the presidential battle space! In that case I would be willing to move immediately."[7]

Maloney was intrigued by the possibilities and started inquiries about how to get Schultz to Stockholm even before he heard back from her. The word came back that Swedish ships and planes were now only allowed to carry Swedish passengers so she would have to fly on a British airline from either London or Lisbon. Either route would require British travel priority approval. He believed it would be possible to get the priority approval from the British embassy in Washington.[8] By April 13, Maloney was excited enough about the possibilities that he urged Schultz to go as soon as possible rather than waiting until after the election.

A few days later, all flights between Britain and Sweden were suspended indefinitely as a result of the approaching invasion of Europe at a time and place as yet undisclosed.

Schultz had no interest in going to Britain, where she would be one more correspondent competing with other correspondents to land stories when there wasn't enough news to go around. Instead, encouraged by Ruth Shipley, a longtime friend and head of the State Department's Passport Division, Schultz approached the Russian embassy for a visa.

The process hit a snag. The Russian embassy required a letter from the *Tribune* requesting the visa—a familiar and routine request for foreign correspondents. McCormick, who was virulently anti-Communist, refused to give her the letter, apparently because he didn't want to kowtow to the Soviets. He suggested to Schultz (via Maloney) that since the *Tribune* was not popular in Russia, she should try to get a visa on her own.

Neither side was likely to budge, but it turned out not to matter. After the invasion of Normandy began on June 6, the idea of getting to Berlin by way of Moscow had lost its relevance.

By late July, Maloney had another idea. It looked like the end of the war was near. (Even assuming that Maloney was referring only to the war in Europe, the end of the war wasn't quite as near as he hoped. Allied troops liberated Paris on August 25, 1944, and Germany surrendered on May 7, 1945. The war in the Pacific went on until September 2, 1945.) Would she be interested in covering the German end of the peace?[9] His plan was to send her into territory already "well-occupied" by the army, first to Paris and then into Germany, where she would focus on stories with a German angle.

While Schultz and Mahoney were trying to work out when and where the *Tribune* would send her back to Europe, she was offered an assignment from an unexpected source.

On September 16, 1944, Schultz received an intriguing telegram from Otis L. Wiese, the innovative editor of *McCall's Magazine*: "HAVE SPECIFIC PROPOSAL TO OFFER YOU. PLEASE CALL ME IMMEDIATELY UPON ARRIVAL NEW YORK FRIDAY SEPTEMBER TWENTY SECOND TO ARRANGE CONVENIENT APPOINTMENT. IF IMPOSSIBLE, PLEASE WIRE OR CALL MEANTIME."[10]

When the United States entered the war in 1941, American women's magazines looked for ways to make their content relevant for their readers in a time of national emergency. They went beyond their core subjects of fashion, homemaking, and romantic fiction to produce stories about topics such as dealing with wartime scarcity and rationing and the importance of women taking war jobs outside the home.[11]

McCall's led the pack. When the United States declared war, Wiese scrapped the planned cover for the February 1942 issue. Because print magazines work months in advance, it was the equivalent of a newspaper stopping the presses to insert a new headline in its morning edition. Instead of a frilly valentine, the February cover featured a young woman wearing a button that boasted "I've enlisted"—a powerful word choice implicitly comparing women on the home front to the thousands of men who rushed to enlist in the weeks after the attack on Pearl Harbor. The button referred to *McCall's* new consumer defense campaign. The magazine urged readers to do the same. More than 150,000 *McCall's* readers "enlisted" in the first three weeks by signing the pledge and returning the printed coupon included in the magazine.[12]

The *McCall's* campaign later became part of the government's Consumer's Pledge for Total Defense campaign. The government's goal was to enlist (that word again) thirty million homes to sign a consumer pledge that read, "I will buy carefully. I will take good care of the things I have. I will waste nothing." The campaign kicked off with a photograph of Eleanor Roosevelt and White House housekeeper Henrietta Nesbitt signing the pledge.

The war became a dominant theme in *McCall's*. Ads for US savings bonds and stamps appeared throughout each issue. The magazine ran a section titled "On the Homefront," which interviewed women about their solutions to the challenges of running their homes during the war and another called "Washington Newsletter," which shared information drawn from *The Magazine War Guide*, an Office of War Information publication designed to give magazines ideas on how to spread the war message. But despite the focus on how the war affected its readers' daily lives, *McCall's* had few articles on the war itself outside of the "National Defense" section, which became a feature in 1940.

Wiese wanted to change that.

The magazine had a history of commissioning well-known women reporters to write pieces on international politics. Wiese sent muckraking journalist Ida Tarbell to interview Mussolini in 1927 and to report on conditions in Germany in the early 1930s. At much the same time, he sent journalist, novelist, and labor activist Mary Heaton Vorse to report on the Soviet Union.[13] Now he wanted Schultz to spend several months at the front, writing stories for *McCall's* from the "women's angle"—a traditional way of allowing women to report on war. Schultz and her contemporaries expanded the "women's angle" beyond articles on rations, food shortages, and women's war jobs to include topics such as rape, civilian experiences of the war, sanitation, and field hospitals. All of which were important war issues even if editors, most of them men, classified such stories as soft news.

It was an experiment for both of them. Sponsoring a war correspondent was a new venture for *McCall's*. And Schultz had no experience writing for women's magazines.

⚭

Whether Schultz went to Europe as a correspondent for *McCall's* or for the *Tribune*, the United States military had to accredit her as a war correspondent. Reporters seeking accreditation applied to the Overseas Liaison Branch of the War Department's Bureau of Public Relations. Applicants submitted a security questionnaire signed by their sponsoring news organization, and a letter from that organization requesting a specific theater of operations and transportation. They also signed a contract agreeing to follow military rules and to submit their work to military censors before sending it to their editors. Once the Liaison Branch approved a correspondent, whether they would be accredited for a specific theater or unit depended on the approval of the commanding officer, some of whom, according to Edmund Stevens, war correspondent for the *Christian Science Monitor*, thought a correspondent was "at best a busy body and at worst a potential spy."[14]

Prior to 1944, the regulations surrounding war correspondents did not explicitly distinguish between men and women. Nonetheless, as the pioneering photojournalist Margaret Bourke-White observed, there always were limitations in place that were "written in invisible ink."[15] The process was never woman-friendly, even after the military officially acknowledged the value of reporting on "the woman's angle" in 1944. That was particularly true when that woman was (just barely) in her fifties. Despite the hurdles, more than 180 women succeeded in getting their correspondent credentials.[16]

In Schultz's case, the accreditation process was complicated by the fact that two publications wanted to send her overseas. (She had also contacted MBS about broadcasting for them as she moved with the army but clearly intended that to be a side job once she was accredited for another organization—the same arrangement she had with them in Berlin.)

After applications for Schultz from both the *Tribune* and *McCall's* reached his desk, Colonel Richard Powell, the overseas liaison of the War Department's Bureau of Public Relations, informed *McCall's* Washington office that "only one sponsor is needed or would show on our records. The writing Miss Schultz does on the side for anyone else is her own business."[17] As far as he was concerned, *McCall's* and the *Tribune* needed to work it out between them. Ellen Hess, *McCall's* managing editor, didn't think it was appropriate for the magazine to negotiate with the *Tribune* and turned the problem over to Schultz to resolve when she got to Washington.

Schultz's accreditation status became still more complicated two months later, in December 1944, as a result of developments on the Western Front. Hitler made a final attempt to halt the Allies' advance on Germany, launching the major counteroffensive in the Ardennes, Belgium, Luxembourg, and northeastern France that became known as the Battle of the Bulge, after the shape created when the Germans pushed through the Allied front line. Walter Trohan, "number two man" at the *Tribune's* Washington office, informed Maloney that due to the pressure of the German offensive, the army would now accredit only correspondents who would work with combat troops on the front lines and stay with troops in the trenches. In light of that policy, the army refused to accredit Schultz for occupied Germany at that time but invited the newspaper to reapply when the situation looked better. Trohan did not think she should be considered for combat work, even if the army would consider it, given the recent problems with her health. He recommended the *Tribune* let the question of her accreditation ride for the moment. (In all fairness to Trohan, Schultz wrote to more than one friend wondering how she would hold up to the rigors of the experience: "because I know it is going to be very hard."[18])

Maloney pushed back by cable to Trohan's boss, Arthur Henning, that same day. He confirmed that he had never planned to place Schultz with combat troops. However, he saw no reason why the army couldn't approve her now for entry into Germany once it was occupied so that she was already on the *Tribune's* accredited list when the time came.

The next day, Henning informed Maloney that the army had agreed to get the red tape out of the way for Schultz's accreditation so there would be a minimum of delay when the time came for her to go into Germany.

That didn't help Schultz with the *McCall's* assignment.

Schultz continued to push the War Department about getting immediate credentials, dealing directly with the chief of the public relations department, Colonel Warner. Schultz told Ellen Hess that Warner said her best chance for accreditation was to go as a combat correspondent, if she was willing to risk it. "I naturally said yes," she told Hess. Warner then suggested Schultz go back to Westport and wait until he figured things out. She declined. Instead, she planned to stay in DC for a few days, to "survey the field," and see if any of her friends would cooperate with him in his efforts to help her.

"Surveying the field" meant investigating other options for getting to Europe in case Colonel Warner didn't come through. Ruth Shipley told Schultz if the army would not accredit her, she could get a permit for the civil district in France. Once there, Schultz told Hess, "I could watch out for my first chance to get to the Front." Switzerland was also an option: she might well be able to get "dope about Germany" there, the kind of information she could use to write "factual, meaty stories without pro-German bias." She would apply for civilian credentials for France or Switzerland if Hess thought it was a good idea. Left to her own devices, she would press to be a full-fledged war correspondent on *McCall's* behalf.[19]

Once things began to pull together, they happened quickly.

By January 18, Colonel Powell's office had approved Schultz as a war correspondent for *McCall's Magazine* and requested an assignment for her in Europe.

On January 26, 1945, Schultz received her official travel orders. Her departure, flying from New York to an unnamed destination, was scheduled for February 3—almost four years to the day since she had left Berlin.

CHAPTER TWENTY-FOUR

BEARING WITNESS

Sigrid Schultz, for 16 years chief of the Berlin bureau of The Chicago Tribune, has returned to Germany. She is attached to Gen. Eisenhower's armies. Miss Schultz has been assigned to compare present day Germany with the reich [sic] as she knew it in peace time.

—*CHICAGO TRIBUNE*, April 15, 1945[1]

Under the provisions of War Department Cable WARX 29101, 30 January 1945, the European-African-Middle-East Campaign ribbon is awarded, for outstanding and conspicuous service with the armed forces under difficult and hazardous combat conditions to these American War Correspondents: Sigrid L. Schultz
By command of General Patton

—Extract from order awarding Schultz the European-African-Middle Eastern Campaign Ribbon[2]

Sigrid Schultz arrived in Paris in early February 1945. It was not the city she remembered: "Everyone looked blue and green with cold—everyone was hungry and shabby—the stores were empty after five years of German rule and looting."[3]

Like other war correspondents, she stayed briefly at the Hotel Scribe, which the Allies had commandeered as a permanent press camp when they liberated Paris. Once a luxury hotel, the Scribe now housed as many as five hundred correspondents at a time, providing them with meals, limited hours of heat and warm baths, electricity, official news briefings, easy access to the censors who cleared their work, and facilities for transmission. Schultz wrote to her mother that the atmosphere at the hotel was "simply grand, charged with excitement and I sure would feel sorry for myself if I had missed it."[4]

Nonetheless, Schultz did not intend to stay at the Scribe for very long. Correspondents who made their headquarters in its relative comfort reported on the war from the rear. Schultz was eager to get to the reality of the front.

Or at least as close to the front as the United States military allowed women correspondents. The Supreme Headquarters Allied Expeditionary Force (SHAEF) did not permit women journalists to travel closer to the front than women service members, which effectively meant field hospitals with nursing detachments. SHAEF justified the policy in terms of providing housing and latrine facilities. (Some things don't change.) This was not always as much of a limitation as the rule-makers intended. Women journalists interpreted the ruling liberally, stretching it to include surgical teams, which allowed them to go as far as battalion headquarters, as long as no one objected. According to Colonel Barney Oldfield, the officer responsible for organizing and overseeing official military press camps and tasked with enforcing SHAEF rules governing women journalists, "Nobody in his [sic!] right mind wanted to get any closer than that."[5]

It was a cold day when Schultz left Paris via army jeep for Spa, Belgium, the current headquarters for the First Army, to which she was attached as a correspondent for *McCall's*.

The trip started out on a positive note, with the help of a small bottle of French cognac. Having shared the cognac with her driver, Schultz further endeared herself to him after they stopped at a restaurant to eat and she used her French language skills to convince the restaurant staff to warm up their American military rations, which were always better warm than cold because heat melted the grease in the cans.

Making friends with the jeep drivers was as useful as making friends with waiters and telephone operators had been in Berlin. Correspondents needed the drivers' help to do their jobs. Each day, as the Allied troops moved closer and closer to the Rhine River, Schultz, in company with one or two other correspondents, went by jeep from Spa to investigate news stories in Germany. It was sometimes difficult to get a jeep and driver, but Schultz's friends among the drivers did their best to take care of her.

⸺⸺

As a war correspondent for *McCall's*, no matter how temporary the assignment, Schultz was part of a new development in journalism. Magazines were providing real competition to newspapers in reporting on the war. Weekly magazines, like *Time*, kept up with the news. Monthly magazines, like *McCall's*, specialized in the longer-form pieces newspapers referred to as "specials."

Schultz was used to the two-part rhythm of newspaper reporting, balancing the immediate demands of the daily deadline with the slower pace of the reported mailers and "specials," in which she had the time to do as much background reporting as she thought the story needed. The pace of the magazine format, which combined a longer but strict deadline with content similar to a special story confounded her. Working on a story on women in Germany, she cabled Hess in April that she needed to delay the story because it required more research. *McCall's* cabled back that the deadline was June 1. Period. She met the deadline, and *McCall's* loved the piece. But she found it difficult to make the transition to magazine reporting, perhaps because she had spent so many years focused on reporting the news as it occurred. Over and over, she received frustrated cables from Ellen Hess and Otto Wiese, reminding her to concentrate on the story angles they had discussed before she left, not the news of the day. They didn't need traditional news stories. People had already seen the newsreels showing the destruction of German cities. They wanted the stories that didn't make it into daily newspapers and that the newsreels couldn't capture.

⸺⸺

In early April, Schultz switched her accreditation from *McCall's* to the *Tribune*, earlier than she had intended, because the army would approve only a two-week trip to the front for magazine correspondents. As a correspondent for a daily newspaper, she had unlimited time at the front. She was relieved to resume reporting for the *Tribune*, doing work she thoroughly understood, though she continued to pitch article ideas to *McCall's* and other publications. Her assignment was to focus on stories with a German angle and not "interfere with" military stories, which were already covered by other *Tribune* correspondents. Barring other instructions from the *Tribune*, she planned to hook up with the Eighth Air Force, which had a press camp in Frankfurt and sent expeditions deeper into Germany. She intended to start filing stories between April 15 and 20, "Unless I run into stories that seem to me to be of such interest that it would be a shame for the *Tribune* to miss them."[6]

Schultz reached the Eighth Air Force's "Air Power Press Camp" at Frankfurt on April 6, shortly after the city was liberated. Captain William Robert Laidlaw, a freelance journalist before the war and now a correspondent for *Air Force Magazine*, organized the press camp with the approval and support of Major General Frederick Anderson, deputy commander of operations for the US Strategic Air Forces in Europe. As Laidlaw later described it, they believed that an Air Power Press Camp did not need a "scampering group" of brash young correspondents like Walter Cronkite and Maggie Higgins. Instead, they needed "a nucleus of mature correspondents who, with intellectual instead of merely Reader's Digest chromosomes, had known Europe and especially Hitler's Germany, and the Germanies before it, . . . and thus could evaluate what they saw now." According to Laidlaw, "Sig" Schultz was exactly what they wanted.[7]

Schultz kept her promise to Maloney not to report on military stories, even though she was much closer to the front than anyone had expected and the temptation must have been great. Her first story for the *Tribune* appeared on April 15, the background to the execution in August 1944 of Dr. Otto Kiep, a former German consul general in New York suspected of inciting the German army to sign an independent peace treaty with the Allies. The story was a prime example of Schultz doing exactly what the *Tribune* hoped she would do, working her contacts to provide a behind-the-scenes story from Germany and making herself a small part of the story in the process.[8]

<hr />

Several days before the story on Dr. Kiep appeared, Schultz was in place to report on a story that demanded to be told.

On April 11, word reached the press camp in Frankfurt that American troops under General Patton had taken Weimar and liberated a death camp at nearby Buchenwald—the first major death camp freed by American soldiers.

The Eighth Air Force flew its correspondents from Frankfurt to Weimar. Schultz and photographer Margaret Bourke-White sat in a jeep on the plane. Schultz later remembered that the flight had "some of the magic of an Arabian fairy tale." That sense of magic evaporated as soon as they landed. They were greeted by soldiers with horror-stricken faces, who had marched into Buchenwald only hours before. A young captain sent the reporters off to the camp, issuing orders automatically, as if he did not want to think.[9]

When they arrived at the camp, the correspondents went to the officer in charge to show their passes. What looked like pieces of parchment sat on his desk. The correspondents were shocked to learn they were made from human skin. Prisoners with tattoos had been taken to the wife of the camp's commander. If the design appealed to her, the prisoner was given a lethal shot. His skin was then tanned and given to Frau Koch, who would use it for craft projects.

Human parchment was the first of the horrors the correspondents saw that day. Arriving only hours after the American troops reached the camp, Schultz and the others had an unfiltered view of the camp's atrocities. The corpses of twenty men who had died within the last day were piled like logs along the crematorium wall when the American soldiers arrived. Over the course of the correspondents' tour, the number grew as survivors wheelbarrowed dead prisoners and added them to the pile. Soldiers showed the reporters the gallows hooks on which dying prisoners had hung for hours and the elevator on which their bodies were transported to the rows of incinerator ovens. The correspondents found the remains of three half-charred corpses on one of the oven trays—the prisoners at Buchenwald were so emaciated that three of their bodies could be loaded on a tray designed to hold one corpse.

In addition to the shared horrors of the day, Schultz experienced Buchenwald at a more personal level because of her ability to speak to the former prisoners.

Before she left Paris for the front, a friend gave Schultz a list of accomplished young French scholars whom the Germans had sought out and arrested. They were sent to Germany as slave labor. Schultz looked for a French prisoner who seemed to be sturdier than the others. (Sturdy being a relative term.) Having identified one, she showed him her list. After he recovered from the surprise of hearing her speak French, he told her, "I think I knew two of them. They will not be coming home."

After Schultz left the Frenchman, she spoke to some Austrians and a German newspaperman. Then she heard someone behind her saying in Norwegian, "She can talk French, she can talk German, but nobody is talking to us."

Schultz turned around and asked in Norwegian, "What do you have to tell me?" She later said she had never seen a group of more surprised or happier young men. They roared with laughter at her rusty Norwegian and then tried to lift her in the air as if in a Norwegian folk dance. Their moment of joy was overtaken by sorrow when she asked their story. There were five of them, part of a group of eight hundred Norwegian Jews, including women and children, whom the Nazis had seized and originally taken to Auschwitz. They were among the prisoners who suffered through a forced march to Buchenwald as the Russians approached. As far as they knew, they were the only members of the original eight hundred to survive.

Before Schultz had a chance to recover from the emotion of speaking to the Norwegians, the Frenchman came up to her again. He had watched as she went from group to group. Now he pointed to a barracks set apart from the others. "If you have the courage, would you go to a hospital in the back there?" he asked. "There are mostly Frenchmen in there and a few Poles and they are dying." The American doctors were working hard in the main hospital, but these prisoners were beyond help. "It would be good if they heard someone speak French to them . . . and tell them that they are free."

Still shaken, Schultz went to the hospital. She later said it was the most gruesome thing she had ever seen. Three tiers of bunks held dying men. Blood and other fluids dripped from the men on the top bunks on to those below them. There was nothing she could do to make them more comfortable. All she could do was call out to them over and over again in French, "You are free." After a while, she added, "I have just come from Paris. The chestnuts are in bloom in Paris."

One man sat halfway up and reached a hand toward her. She went over and took it.

"Is it really true?" he asked.

"It's really true. You are free. American planes are coming."

"The chestnuts are in bloom?"

She nodded. And then he was gone.[10]

The *Tribune* ran a much-reduced version of Schultz's heartfelt description of that day. Larry Rue sent her a telegram from the *Tribune*'s overseas headquarters in Paris giving her the bad news: "TRIBUNE QUOTE COMPLIMENTS SCHULTZ PAINSTAKING REVELATION BUCHENWALD BUT WHITE PAPER RATIONING MAKES SPACE LIMITATIONS INFLEXIBLE STOP USED ONETHIRD [SIC] STOP BE BRIEF UNQUOTE."[11]

Pat Maloney made it clear how hard the decision was in a letter he wrote to all the war correspondents that same day, dealing with the paper's space restriction and the demands of the news:[12] "It grieved me no end last night to have to cut about two-thirds of Sigrid Schultz's wonderful story on Buchenwald prison camp. It was the most shocking story I have ever read. We had had a little on it from the AP the night before and so ran about 60% of a column of the Schultz story which ran nearly two columns in the original."[13]

We don't know how she felt about the news, but she can't have been happy.

A day after the liberation of Buchenwald, General Eisenhower visited Ohrdruf, a sub-camp of Buchenwald, which American troops had liberated on April 4. His purpose, as he cabled to General George C. Marshall, chairman of the Joint Chiefs of Staff, was "to be in a position to give firsthand evidence of these things if ever, in the future, there develops a tendency to charge these allegations merely to 'propaganda.'"[14]

A week later, Eisenhower instructed Marshall to bring members of Congress and newspaper owners and editors, including Colonel McCormick, to the newly liberated camps so they could witness the atrocities for themselves. McCormick declined the invitation, on the grounds that he did not question the reliability of his staff's firsthand reports of the atrocities—a position entirely in keeping with his deeply held belief that anyone who worked for him was, by definition, the best in their field until proven otherwise.

Schultz witnessed atrocities at other camps in addition to Buchenwald.

On April 18, American troops fought to gain control of Leipzig, the site of one of the last battles the Americans fought in Europe.

While the battle continued, the journalists of the Air Power Press Camp traveled into the city. They hoped to see the factories where Erla Maschinenwerk produced Messerschmidt fighter planes. When they reached the factory, they found there was nothing to see except a group of nervous German factory workers. (A few days later the correspondents learned why the Erla employees were so nervous: the basement was filled with German soldiers.) The correspondents moved on to Thekla, an industrial suburb of Leipzig that was home to several Erla factories and a concentration camp. Prisoners were transferred from Buchenwald to Leipzig-Thekla, where they worked as slave labor in Leipzig's Erla factories.

As they approached the Thekla camp, Schultz and the others noticed a sickening smell. When they were near enough to peer through what had been an electrically charged barbed-wire fence, they saw an enormous burned-out hole where a building had once stood. They had arrived at the camp a few hours after the Germans had tried to burn the remaining prisoners alive.

In the weeks before the attack on Leipzig, the Germans marched prisoners from Thekla further east by the thousands. Three hundred some prisoners remained when the American troops grew closer, most of them foreign engineers and airplane manufacturing specialists. When the Americans were close enough that the inhabitants of the camp could hear their gunfire, the SS decided to kill the remaining prisoners rather than allowing them to be liberated. They locked the prisoners into a wooden barracks that served as a mess hall, doused it with flammable chemicals, and set it on fire. Some prisoners escaped the burning building, but most of them were shot. A few managed to escape unharmed, using the dense smoke as cover.

Smoke still hung over the camp when the correspondents arrived. (One of them—not Schultz—threw up.) Corpses of men who were shot as they tried to escape over the fence hung on the barbed wire. A few charred skeletons remained in the pit caused by the fire; one man's hands were clawed at the ground as if he had tried to dig his way out. A surviving prisoner pointed to a gold chain and religious medal around the dead man's neck and told her he had been one of Poland's best-known airplane engineers. When she heard his name, Schultz realized she had met him at a reception at the Polish embassy before the war.

What Schultz saw in the concentration camps cemented her hatred of the Nazis. An event several days after the liberation of Buchenwald gave her a new distaste for the German population at large. On April 17, Patton ordered one thousand residents of Weimar to view the remains of Buchenwald. Several surviving prisoners sat in their rags on a low stone fence and watched as soldiers showed the prosperous-looking burghers and their wives the equipment used to torture, kill, and burn the bodies of tens of thousands of prisoners and listened as an American officer described details of the camp's procedures.

Schultz noticed a group of "well-fed, tightly corseted" women looking at the sky and paying no attention to what was being said. She went over to them and told them to listen. Each of them claimed they hadn't known anything about what had happened there.

At that point, one of the former prisoners got off the fence and shook his fist at the women, shouting, "Ladies, we were often ordered to work in your houses to help as plumbers and carpenters, and if any of our fellow prisoners complained about what was happening to us, you reported them and you know that many of them were shot because of your reports. You jolly well knew what was going on in the camp. You knew."

Describing the event many years later, she asked the interviewer, "Do you know how a burning corpse stinks?" Weimar was close enough to the camp, she explained, that it was impossible for the city's residents not to smell the stench when the bodies were burned. They knew.[15]

While she continued to believe in the integrity of her old friends and sources, she was disturbed by the number of Germans who claimed to have had no knowledge of sufferings under the Nazis and by the threats against those sources who were willing to talk about their experiences. Increasingly, she divided the population into good Germans and bad Germans.

A third concentration camp had been on Schultz's mind ever since she had arrived in Europe. The first friends she called on after she landed in Paris told her the Germans had arrested their twenty-one-year-old daughter, Giselle, two days before D-Day, for her work helping downed American and British flyers. They learned through the underground that Giselle had been taken to a camp called Ravensbrück.

After that, wherever she went, Schultz asked people for news from Ravensbrück, hoping she would hear something about Giselle. In Leipzig, she learned that a number of women had come to a Buchenwald sub-camp at the Hasag armaments factory as slave labor from Ravensbrück. She interviewed thirty of them. None remembered Giselle, but they told her a great deal about conditions at Ravensbrück.

Those interviews led to a substantial article on Ravensbrück and the Hasag camp, which ran in the *Tribune* on April 27—part of a page devoted solely to the camps—as well as to a radio broadcast the same day. She told her readers, and listeners, about the women guards who reigned at Ravensbrück, the tortures suffered by the women as a group (including standing for "roll call" for twenty-four straight hours), and the women used as human guinea pigs in medical experiments. As at the Thekla camp, the guards sent most of their prisoners on "death marches" heading east in mid-April in the face of the Allied advances. Those left behind, 232 of the original 5,000, were liberated by the American forces on April 18.

Schultz ended the article with an estimate of how many women went through Ravensbrück: "A month ago the last women to arrive in Leipzig from Ravensbrueck had registration numbers above 110,000. Since the Germans always were methodical, it is clear that more than 110,000 women passed through Ravensbrueck or died there."[16] She was close. Scholarly estimates calculate 120,000 to 132,000 women were held in Ravensbrück between 1939 and 1945.

Speaking to an audience in Chicago eight months later about her search for information about Giselle and Ravensbrück, Schultz said, "There are hours when I wish I knew a little less about it and other concentration camps."[17]

———

On May 1, Schultz and the Air Power Press Camp arrived in Nuremberg, where she had covered Nazi Party rallies in previous years. There they heard the announcement on German radio that Hitler was dead. The following day, Berlin surrendered to the Soviets.

A week later, Schultz stood in the square in front of Munich's town hall, part of a crowd gathered to hear the official announcement of Germany's surrender. It seemed like everyone who could find their way to Munich was there or crowded into one of Munich's parks. American

soldiers and released concentration camp victims were equally eager
to hear the news.

Schultz stopped to talk to three girls who sat giggling in the sunshine. "We can't help laughing," they told her, "because we've just recovered our freedom since a few days. We were political prisoners and
it's wonderful to be alive."[18]

Schultz stayed in Munich for most of May and June, waiting for
the main event the *Tribune* had sent her to Germany to cover: America's
entry into Berlin.

While she waited, she wrote stories about the last days of the war
in Munich, focusing on plots by and against the Nazis, on German resistance movements, on smaller scale Nazi atrocities, and on individual
acts of heroism. She fed Americans' fascination with Hitler's daily life,
reporting on his "two love nests" in Munich, the elaborate furniture he
designed for his victory celebration, and rumors that he had gone insane
during the last months of the war. She explored reported food shortages, rations, and cases of hoarding. She shared stories about American
soldiers' interactions with Germans, both military and civilians. Many
of these revealed a combination of humor and aggression on the part of
the GIs that Schultz clearly relished. One example that amused her in
particular was the case of a German colonel who had been appointed
to command one of the camps for demobilized German soldiers. "He
arrived at American headquarters clad in underwear, shoes, and a rain-
coat someone had lent him," Schultz reported. "He had been deprived
of his uniform along the road but refused to state who had taken it.
There seemed little doubt that the job was done by GIs."[19]

<hr />

Schultz took part in a group interview with Hermann Göring, three
days after he surrendered to the Americans.

Göring sat in an upholstered armchair under a shade tree in the
garden outside the Bärenkeller School in Augsburg where he was held
for a brief time. American correspondents and photographers sat and
stood three and four deep around him. Schultz snared a prime seat in
the front row, directly across from Göring.

Once again, Schultz made herself part of the story. "Goering has
barely changed since I interviewed him last [in] November 1940," she
wrote. "Only then he was bedecked with decorations, sported costly

rings, and oozed self-confidence. This time he wore only platinum wedding bands and adopted an air of sweet reasonableness."

In his days as Hitler's right hand, Göring was a dandy who changed his uniform five times a day and flaunted his military decorations and jewelry. Now, "all that was left of his fancy medals were long rows of eyelets crisscrossing the left side of his chest, which he tapped occasionally as if wanting to feel them. Blood red shoes provided a touch of color for the field marshal who formerly was so deeply concerned with sartorial matters."

When the Nazis were in power, Göring had described himself as the "most loyal paladin of the fuehrer." Now he attempted to spin the interview as best he could, throwing as much responsibility as possible on Hitler and emphasizing his own attempts to distance himself from Hitler's policies as the war came to an end. As he spoke, he pulled nervously at his dove gray gloves.

When faced with difficult questions, Göring displayed obvious discomfort. William Laidlaw of the Air Power Press Camp, there as a correspondent for *Air Force Magazine*, asked about Göring's statement early in the war that "if the allies ever bomb Berlin my name is Meyer." Instead of answering, Göring blushed, wiped the sweat from his forehead, and waited for the next question. Schultz asked him an equally pointed question: "What about the concentration camps?" In 1934, he had told her more than once that the camps were "merely education camps to improve German discipline and unity." Now, like the plump ladies of Weimar, he claimed he knew nothing about the camps until the American officers to whom he surrendered told him.

Schultz reported his statements, and highlighted his lies, in her account of the interview, which ran on the front page the next day.[20] A telegram from the *Tribune*, sent through the press center in Paris, read "EXCELLENT GOERING STO [sic] SCHULTZ BE CAREFUL NOT EDITORIALIZE."[21] It must have felt like old times: a front-page story and a telegram of congratulations.

Schultz was on the list of correspondents approved to go to Berlin with the army, but she began to get nervous as other correspondents received their notices to travel to Weimar to join the official convoy to Berlin and she did not. What if someone decided they didn't want a woman along for the triumphal entry into Berlin? After all, no women journalists were included in the D-Day landing. Her own experience was that men got the best press camp assignments, while women were assigned to camps that did not have adequate facilities for transmitting and broadcasting the news. Removing her from the accredited list would make no sense, she wrote to "the boys," presumably the *Tribune* staff at the Paris office, "since I was tough enough to take it when Berlin was being bombed and run by Gestapo." All she could do now was "entrust the Schultz fate" to their hands.[22]

Despite her worries, Schultz remained on the accredited list. The air force flew correspondents from the Air Power Press Camp to Weimar on July 1. From there, correspondents left the next morning in a military convoy to Halle, where they would stay until the actual move into Berlin. Schultz told her friends it would be a couple of days of "sleeping bags and cold rations and restricted activities," but it would be worth it if she could make contact with some of her old sources.[23]

On July 3, after the first American convoy reached the Berlin suburbs, Schultz and other correspondents who had covered Germany in the old days "jeeped at top speed through the Brandenburg Gate."[24]

The city had been reduced to rubble. Not a single building was undamaged for mile after mile in the center of the city. Unter den Linden was a ruin from one end to another. The buildings that had housed the *Tribune's* Berlin bureau at various times—the Hotel Adlon, the Esplanade, the little Hohenzollern palace, and Berlin's modernist landmark, the nine-story Columbus Haus on Potsdamer Platz—were all burned-out shells. The last building where Schultz and her mother had lived was completely destroyed, and it looked as if a battle had taken place in its courtyard, which was full of German helmets.

In the first article that she filed from this "new" Berlin, part of a multicolumn spread on the first page under the collective headline "Cheer U.S. Army in Berlin," Schultz focused on the wreckage of Hitler's chancellery and the destruction of the signs of power with which he had decorated it. The giant eagle that spread its wings over the entrance was now a twisted mass of metal. In the room where foreign leaders signed pacts with Hitler, the ten-foot crystal chandeliers were still attached to the ceiling, but their bottom crystals touched monumental piles of debris on the floor. The huge cupola that crowned the building took a direct hit from a heavy bomb that tore through the chancellery and the three stories of underground shelters below. Schultz did not say "how fallen are the mighty." She didn't have to—the details spoke for themselves.

In the days that followed, Schultz wrote a combination of human-interest stories about life in occupied Berlin and political pieces about the occupation. She tracked down details of how the Russians had identified Hitler's and Eva Braun's bodies with the help of a woman who worked as assistant to Hitler's dentist, as well as details about the subsequent disappearance of Hitler's body, the dental assistant, and the dental technician who made Eva Braun's distinctive bridgework. She compared the Berlin black market under the Nazis with the black market in Russian-controlled Berlin. She covered negotiations regarding the division of Berlin into zones of interest by the joint command of the four Allied powers and the practical impact of those negotiations in the American sector. She repeatedly emphasized the interest of German women in American soldiers, an interest she portrayed as both predatory and understandable, given the large number of German casualties.

She interviewed American soldiers, most of whom weren't keen on being part of the army of occupation. Schultz was deeply opposed to the idea of occupation. Not only did she object to American soldiers and resources being used to protect postwar Germany; she believed that "any army of occupation is apt to be fascist in its tendencies"[25]—a belief rooted perhaps in her experience of the occupation of the Ruhr and Rhineland regions by Allied forces after World War I. Given her opinions on the subject, she may have searched out the "right" soldiers to interview—something that would have been anathema to her during her Berlin days.

Schultz also spent time looking not only for her own friends but those of *Tribune* readers who had requested help in finding out what had happened to their loved ones. When she found someone, she wrote a note to their inquiring relatives, saying that while they had no doubt heard about how difficult things were in Berlin now, their brother/aunt/mother was alive and well.

A week after Schultz reached Berlin, Pat Maloney wrote to her about the status of her assignment. He thanked her for the good work she had done for them over the last few months, particularly for the stories she had written since her arrival in Berlin. But the sad fact was that readers were less and less interested in news from Europe now that American soldiers were coming home or being redeployed in the Pacific Theater. With the ongoing white paper restrictions, the *Tribune* needed to reduce its European staff at once. Since Schultz had told him from the beginning that she intended to come home in August or September, she was the obvious choice to be let go.[26]

Schultz was happy to leave Berlin.

As she waited in Weimar to join the convoy to Berlin, she had come to the conclusion that it would be a bad idea for the *Tribune* to reestablish a permanent Berlin bureau based on what she heard about living conditions there. After seeing Berlin, Schultz had not changed her mind. The level of destruction made daily life difficult, even for Americans with dollars to spend. There was so little work that the censors and copy-room boys hovered around the press club bar begging correspondents to file an occasional report. And the smell of the dead in the canals and the subway that Hitler had flooded when he feared the Russians were coming was even worse than had been reported. "Three weeks in Berlin has been enough for me," she wrote to journalist Bella Fromm, who had left Berlin in 1938, "—it is a tragic city and there is so little one can do about it."[27]

It was time to go back to the United States, with no doubt this time that it was truly home.

CHAPTER TWENTY-FIVE

WAR CRIMES

WILL REMAIN EUROPE TO COVER NURNBERG
TRIALS AS INSTRUCTED. Sigrid Schultz.

—Telegram to *Chicago Tribune*,
August 8, 1945[1]

Schultz was preparing to go home. She had research to complete—
work that might lead to future writing projects. She had personal
property to track down, in Paris, Munich, Berlin, and press camps
across Europe. She had travel arrangements in place.

Then she received a telegram from Chicago: Would she stay in
Europe to cover the Nuremberg trials? She agreed, even though accepting the assignment meant once again canceling or postponing
several lecture commitments. It was, after all, an important story. *The*
important story for someone who felt as she did about Nazi Germany.

Schultz wasn't entirely comfortable with her choice, particularly
once it began to look like the Nuremberg trials would be seriously
delayed. (Among other things, she was concerned about the cost of
canceling her lecture tours again.) She made her ambivalence about
staying clear from the start. On August 19, writing to Pat Maloney, she
wondered whether the public would be interested in the trials: "I have
a hunch that it will become quite dull after two or three weeks—my
hunch may be wrong. If it is not, I'll be perfectly willing to come home
before it ends."[2] A few days later, she warned *Tribune* reporter David
Darrah, who was still running the paper's headquarters in Paris, that
she might have to ask Maloney to release her from the assignment if

the trials continued to be delayed, no matter how much she wanted to cover them.[3]

⸻ ⸙ ⸻

With the start date for Nuremberg still uncertain, the *Tribune* asked Schultz to cover the trials that the US Third Army was running at Dachau.

The first Dachau case focused on an Austrian named Franz Strasser, a local Nazi Party leader, who was found guilty of killing two American flyers. Schultz's account of the trial is straight reporting, unlike the human-interest articles she wrote in Munich and Berlin in which she sometimes revealed her deep hatred for the Nazis and increasing distrust of German civilians. She explained how the trial was run, including the fact that Strasser was defended by two American lawyers, with a sergeant as an interpreter. She described the charges, the primary witness's testimony, and Strasser's defense. She put the case into the larger context of the war trials. Finally, she ended with one of the small, humanizing details at which she excelled: as the death sentence was read, "Strasser picked up some cigarette butts in an ash tray and slipped them into the pocket of his coat." Schultz left it to the reader to speculate why.[4]

The Strasser case was unique among those tried at Dachau in that a single individual was on trial. After it ended, the Dachau trials went into recess for several months as the army prepared for mass trials of war criminals captured in American-occupied portions of Germany and Austria, which would run through December 1947.

Schultz was once again at loose ends, but not for long.

⸻ ⸙ ⸻

Schultz received a telegram from Chicago shortly after she filed her Dachau story, instructing her to cover the Bergen-Belsen trials, which were held at the small city of Lüneberg, near the Belsen concentration camp. Forty-five Germans who worked at the Belsen and Auschwitz camps were charged with war crimes and crimes against citizens of the Allied nations. (Charges of crimes against humanity and genocide were reserved for the higher-level trials in Nuremberg.)

The most important defendants were Josef Kramer, known as the "Beast of Belsen"; his deputy Franz Hössler; the Belsen camp doctor

Fritz Klein; and Irma Grese, known as the "Hyena of Auschwitz," who oversaw women prisoners first at Auschwitz and then at Belsen. The trial was run by a British military tribunal, with British officers appointed as attorneys for both the prosecution and the defense. Although they were overshadowed by the later trials at Nuremburg, the international coverage of the Dachau trials gave the world its first in-depth look at the horrors of the death camps.

Schultz and other journalists left Wiesbaden for Lüneberg in an official convoy on September 13. She was one of more than a hundred journalists from around the world who reported on the proceedings, which ran from September 17 through November 17. The British army housed them in nearby barracks and shuttled them to and from the courtroom, which had previously been the town's gymnasium, using troop transport vehicles. Schultz was impressed with the facilities. She wrote to fellow journalist and old friend Thomas Ybarra, "The cigarette rations are superb and mess is best I've had in since Airpower folded up."[5]

The *Tribune* published twenty-five bylined articles by Schultz from Lüneberg between September 17 and November 14, with a sharp drop-off after the prosecution closed its case on October 7. It seemed Schultz was not as interested in the defense's case as she was in that of the prosecution.

Schultz's articles from the trials were not as impartial as her Dachau piece. As far as she was concerned, objectivity about the atrocities of the death camps was not possible. She said much later, "The British ran that trial with wonderful dignity and extreme fairness," but nothing they did could mitigate "the absolute ruthlessness of some of those guards on trial."[6]

She reported on the witnesses' testimony about the mass deaths at Belsen, the gas chambers at Auschwitz, and the violence suffered at the hands of the prison staff, with an emphasis on the treatment of women prisoners. That emphasis underlined her portrait of the female overseer Irma Grese, the only one of the defendants whom Schultz brings to life as a villain. Calling her the "Nazi Belle" and the "Belsen Blonde," Schultz devoted two articles to Grese's examination by the prosecution and gave her readers cameo views of Grese in several others, in which Grese smirks, giggles, and outright laughs at descriptions of atrocities committed in the camps. In one of the articles, Schultz describes her as "evidently relishing their former victim's [sic] emotions"—a piece of editorializing that she would not have allowed herself before 1941.[7] (It is perhaps not a surprise that Schultz chose Grese as her villain. She devoted an entire chapter of *Germany Will Try It Again* to the idea that German women were more ardent Nazis than their male counterparts.)

As a counterpoint to Grese, Schultz also gave her readers a heroic figure, Dr. Ada Bimko, a Jewish doctor forced to serve at Auschwitz. She survived twenty months in the concentration camps. Her six-year-old son, her husband, her parents, and her siblings died in the gas chambers there.

Bimko was unflinching in her testimony. Schultz describes her pacing down the middle of the courtroom, along the dock where the prisoners sat, floodlights turned on them so she could see them clearly. Fifteen times she leveled her finger and pointed, slowly and deliberately, at one of the accused as she identified them as having participated in the crimes at Auschwitz. "For the first time since the trial began some winced a little," Schultz told her readers. "Others, at whom she did not point, trembled in fear."[8]

Bimko was equally impressive during cross-examination by the defense attorneys. Over and over, she held her own. One attorney, noting the doctor was short and stout, asked whether she, too, was emaciated when the British liberated the camp. She informed him, calmly, that doctors were not subjected to the forced march from Auschwitz to the Belsen camp that most of the other prisoners had endured. Moreover, the doctors enjoyed better conditions than the other internees. "We had beds to sleep in and a chance to keep ourselves clean," she told him. Another asked her whether, as a doctor, she had felt she was part of the staff. Her answer was sharp: "I always knew I was a prisoner." At one point, an attorney suggested Bimko's statement that she saw Kramer kick and beat inmates was a fabrication. "I would like to point out that I was present . . . during those conditions which I described," she snapped, then reminded the defending counsel that he was not.[9]

Bimko wasn't the only witness to push back at the British defense attorneys. When one of them tried to rattle a woman named Dona Szafran by pointing out that the statements she made in court were not included in the affidavit she signed in May, Szafran answered, "If I and others were to write down the full story of what we saw it would take weeks. If I have erred at all during this testimony and others it is that I could say only part of what I know and had no chance to tell the full story."[10]

—∞—

By mid-October 1945, Schultz was restive. The trial was running on
and on, she complained to Scharschug. The court officials still hoped to
finish the proceedings by the end of October, but she had her doubts.
In the meantime, she worried she was filing too many stories. (No
one had complained.) She worried whether her stories were reaching
Chicago on time—rumor had it that stories were being held up in
London. (The *Tribune* had not reported problems.)

Mostly she worried about the schedule of the Nuremberg trials,
which continued to be delayed. For a few days it had looked as if
Nuremberg might start on November 5. Now there were rumors that
the trials wouldn't start until January. Or that they would be held off
until spring because of the coal shortage. "That would delight my heart,"
she told Scharschug. "It would enable me to fulfill my lecture pledges
and look after mother for a few weeks then return for the real fray, and
it would mean we won't be freezing while the trial goes on."[11]

—∞—

Schultz had begun working on reservations for her return home before the Dachau trials started—a complicated process that involved
multiple telegrams and notes between Schultz, the army officials who
had to approve her travel priorities, and David Darrah, who had to
organize her replacement. On November 7, she received her travel
orders from United States Forces, European Theater, relieving her
from duty effective November 15, with orders to proceed to Paris for
transportation home.

The last two articles Schultz wrote from Lüneberg appeared on
November 12 and 14, before the court began its deliberations. The first
warned the *Tribune*'s readers that anyone who believed the trials would
change Germans' minds about the Nazis would be disappointed. Nineteen out of twenty Germans she interviewed the day before believed the
people on trial were being punished because Germany lost the war, not
because they had participated in mass murder. The care with which the
British defense lawyers tried to disprove the charges against the jailers
of the Belsen and Auschwitz concentration camps did not convince the
Germans that the trials were fair, she told her readers: "They accepted
the claims of the defense as the only valid ones and wiped the charges

and evidence of the persecution out of their minds."[12] On November 14, she reported on the closing statements of both prosecution and defense.

For the balance of the trial, from November 15, when deliberations began, through November 19, when Kramer and Grese declared their intent to appeal their death sentences, the *Tribune* ran stories from the Associated Press.

Schultz was en route to Washington, DC, courtesy of the Army Air Force's Air Transport Command, on November 20, the day the Nuremberg trials started. She planned to return to cover the trials in late February or early March, when her speaking engagements were over, assuming the trials were still in session. Given that the relatively simple Belsen trial lasted for two months, she believed the court officials who claimed the Nuremberg trials could drag out for six months. In fact, the trials continued until October 1946.

⁂

In December 1945, Schultz was in Chicago as part of her lecture tour. While there she stopped by the *Tribune* offices to see her "family" and to talk to Colonel McCormick—something she did whenever she was in Chicago if their schedules allowed.

She was chatting with McCormick about conditions in Germany and the Nuremberg trials when the conversation took an unexpected turn. Perhaps thinking about what he termed "excesses" by American and British officers in the armies of occupation, a subject with which he was currently concerned, McCormick said, "We have officers who should be put on trial."

Schultz had disagreed with McCormick before, particularly on the topic of American isolationism. She had even done the unthinkable and contradicted him during one of the exclusive eleven o'clock staff meetings in his personal office in the Tribune building. (She was never invited back.) Despite their disagreements and despite McCormick's well-known habit of meddling in the work of the foreign press service, she had never received instructions from him on what position to take about the political news in Germany. For many years the *Tribune* published her stories even when they disagreed with the position the Colonel adopted in the editorial pages. But this was more than she could stomach, given everything she had seen and heard during her recent months in Germany. Perhaps, she thought later, he might have had a different opinion if he had accepted Eisenhower's invitation and seen Buchenwald with his own eyes.

As it was, she felt she had to speak up, as she always had: "Colonel, I'm sorry I can't go along with that."

They changed the subject and continued their conversation.

When Schultz left McCormick, she walked down the long stairs from his office, and went straight to Pat Maloney. By her own account, she was weeping her head off.

She told Maloney, "I think I'd better stop working."

Her twenty-six years with the *Tribune* were at an end.[13]

EPILOGUE

Most things, except lecturing have gone wrong since I got
back from Europe in 1947. I know that I'll get over the
hurdles, some time, but for the moment I can record only
failures. . . . If I were riding the crest of a big success at the
moment I probably could have a better chance at placing
stuff—but my line is not the popular one—or has not been
for the last year and a half.

—SIGRID SCHULTZ to Geoffrey Fraser, April 1949[1]

In January 1946, Sigrid Schultz turned fifty-three. Her career was
effectively over, though she did not realize it.

The speaking tour that led to her unhappy visit to McCormick's
office ended in April. Her intention had been to return to Nuremberg,
where Hal Foust was covering the trials for the *Tribune*. Prior to her
return to the United States, the *Tribune* had arranged for her to report
on the trials in tandem with Foust. Schultz was to write general stories
about the men on trial and the events of the trial itself. Foust, drawing
on his experience covering the Quisling trial in Oslo, was to focus on
the trial's legal aspects.

That plan didn't come to pass, but Schultz still hoped to return to
Nuremberg. Over the coming months, she tried without success to get
back to Germany to cover the final months of the trial, which ended
on October 1. She pitched more than one editor for the assignment,
leaning on her experience as an old Berlin hand. As she wrote to George
Scharschug, in a letter that was half *Tribune* business and half letter to
a friend, "I see lots of angles that newcomers can't really be expected
to see."[2] No one took her up on it, though her reports from Lüneberg
made it clear that she was uniquely well-qualified to explain the trials
to the American public. It was the job that she had trained for her

entire life, but she was too late. Any publication interested in covering the trials already had a correspondent in place.

Schultz scheduled a trip to Europe in May, which would no doubt have included Nuremberg, but she developed, as she described it to Scharschug, "one of those luxuries that I seem to allow myself every few years—acquiring a fancy illness"—a virus that settled primarily in the knee that had been wounded by shrapnel in Berlin and later by a taxi in New York. Recovery was slow, and as a result, she had to turn down two overseas assignments. By late September, she could once again walk two blocks. "Sitting up to type is still quite a thrill," she told Scharschug.[3]

◦◦◦

Having left the *Tribune*, Schultz needed employment. It was a hard time for women to find work as men returned from the war were reclaiming their prewar jobs. Nonetheless, her reputation as a reporter was such that she received offers from other newspapers. She didn't feel she could accept them without endangering her *Tribune* pension. At fifty-three, with an aging mother to support, she didn't feel that was a chance she could take.

Many of her male counterparts found work after the war, and a place in popular memory, as correspondents and pundits on television news programs. That was not a realistic option for Schultz. The discrimination against women newscasters common in radio was even more pronounced in the newly developing world of television. (And would remain so for decades.) A woman in her fifties, no matter how respected she was as a journalist, didn't stand a chance.[4]

In the years immediately after the war, Schultz got work based on her reputation as an expert on Germany. She continued to get speaking engagements. She was occasionally a guest on radio or television programs focused on current issues. And she still received hate mail from pro-German readers and listeners.

The *Tribune* asked her to write occasional background pieces about Germany, as well as a chapter for a proposed *Tribune* history of the war. She remained the newspaper's go-to reviewer for books on Germany through the late 1950s. "We shall be calling on you again," Alfred C. Ames, the editor of the *Tribune's* "Magazine of Books," wrote upon receiving her review of *Hitler's Secret Conversations* in 1953. "We really feel strengthened to know that you are available."[5]

Her reviews were detailed, thoughtful, and opinionated, and she was still known well enough for her praise to mean something through the 1950s. Other publications, such as the *Saturday Review*, occasionally contacted her for a review. Publishers used "pull quotes" from her reviews in print ads for books.

She pitched, and sometimes sold, articles to publications such as *Collier's* and the *Saturday Evening Post*. She encountered the same problems in selling articles that she had faced before 1945. She continued to pitch stories about her experiences with the Nazis, clinging to the past rather than reporting on the postwar world. Moreover, she required a degree of hand-holding that few magazine editors could afford to provide. "As you saw I am still groping for the right way to present the story that preoccupies me so deeply," she wrote to Martin Sommers of the *Saturday Evening Post* regarding a manuscript she had turned in. "I am doubly grateful to you for the criticism. . . . I think my best bet is to let the matter stew until I get back to Europe and liven things up with more local color."[6]

Some editors were willing to give her the chance to acquire more local color and new material. She returned to Europe for several months in 1947 as an accredited correspondent for *Collier's*, with no financial support but with an approved list of ideas for possible articles, including stories in Romania and Czechoslovakia, which might have pushed her beyond her obsession with a continuing Nazi threat. (In an in-house memo detailing the story ideas that he and Schultz agreed on, Joe Morris of *Collier's* noted, "We don't know whether there is a story in Rumania [sic] but both of us feel that there should be and that Miss Schultz can find it."[7])

From Schultz's perspective, the real story in Romania was a chance to see Peter Ilcus, who was still not able to leave the country, at least in part because his brother was both politically prominent and under suspicion in the postwar regime. She hadn't seen him since her trip across Europe in late 1940, though they continued to exchange letters despite the difficulties of sending mail through the Iron Curtain. Even with *Collier's* sponsorship and help from both Ruth Shipley of the Passport Division and the American military attaché in Bucharest, who was an old friend from Berlin, Romania denied her visa request. (According to her military contacts, Romania had not approved any visas for Americans for some months.)

Schultz was in Europe again in the summer and fall of 1949 as an accredited correspondent for *McCall's*. And yet again for an extended period beginning in May 1952, as a representative for MBS. Her accreditation for MBS was largely a courtesy to a former colleague. According to Milton Burgh, the MBS news director, "We do very little foreign broadcasting at the present time, relying in the main on AP, UP, INS and REUTERS. However, from time to time, there may be a feature or a news break which warrants direct radio coverage either by shortwave or tape recording."[8] Schultz underlined her relationship with MBS in her response, telling Burgh, "It is a real joy to feel that I 'belong' again in a small way to Mutual for which I worked with such satisfaction in Berlin in 1939 and 1940!"[9] She was still looking for an organization to call home.

Schultz made her last broadcast from Germany in 1952, reporting on the signing of the Bonn-Paris Convention, which ended the Allied occupation of West Germany. She pitched it as a "double eyewitness yarn, touching on the broadcast I did for Mutual from Berlin on October 1, 1939, when the trouble started and the supposed end of trouble on May xyz [sic] 1952."[10]

It was her last trip to Europe, though she never gave up hope of returning.

⚬⚬⚬

By the late 1950s, Schultz's value as an expert on Germany had faded. She continued to seek work as a freelance journalist, but the language skills and personal networks that served her so well in prewar Berlin had little value for a reporter in the United States. Worse, she became a political dinosaur due to her inability to accept that Soviet Russia had replaced Germany as the "Big Bad" in United States' politics.

She tried desperately to write and sell another book, with no success. Because she was no longer the "noted woman foreign correspondent of THE TRIBUNE,"[11] she had lost her built-in audience. Moreover, she never adapted to the structural requirements of the longer form, which had plagued her in her first book. She wrote draft after draft, looking for new angles on old ideas, in her constant search for the right format.

Another European trip was not a possibility. Hedwig was ill and could not be left for long stretches of time, and Schultz's own health was fragile. She settled into life in Westport, gardening, cooking, and taking care of her mother. She had a talent for friendship, maintaining a large and active correspondence with friends, old and new, around the world. Even though she could not entertain on the scale she had in Berlin, she usually had a bottle of champagne chilling in the refrigerator, ready to share with friends who dropped by.

Schultz nursed her mother for eight years until Hedwig's death from cancer in 1960. After her mother's death, she thought she would return to active life, but she had a heart attack in the summer of 1962. In 1965, she wrote to Alexander von Schimpff, who had worked for her for so many years and now was translating documents in Berlin: "I still have the illusion that I'll be able to go gadding about again—anyhow, even at a slower pace life remains exciting and interesting and thoroughly infuriating at times . . ."[12] She admitted to her friend Ernst Preuss, a German refugee during the war who was aging uncomfortably as an expatriate in England, that she sometimes felt lonely: "At least you are not alone you have Margaret at your side. The only moral support I get in the romantic line when things get rough is an occasional letter my poor, best guy manages to smuggle through the Iron Curtain—a somewhat slim diet—but a treasured one!"[13] By that point, neither Schultz nor Ilcus were in good enough health to travel, even if they had been able to get the required visas. She received her last letter from Peter Ilcus in 1978, signed "with deepest love, as always."

After Hedwig's death, Schultz found a refuge in the Overseas Press Club (OPC), traveling from Westport to attend meetings in New York as long as her health allowed it. It was a pale imitation of the Berlin press corps in its heyday, but it kept her in contact with old friends and newspaper gossip—and was occasionally the source of a stimulating exchange of angry letters over club politics. Among other things, Schultz edited the *Overseas Press Club Cookbook*, which came out in 1962. One of four books put out by the OPC that Schultz contributed to, the cookbook was a quirky combination of recipes and essays centering on memorable meals. She contributed two pieces to the cookbook: "'You Gorge Yourselves While the Masses Starve,' Said Göring" and "A Lunch for a Man's Freedom." Both recounted times when Schultz invited high-ranking Nazis to her home for a meal for political reasons, accompanied by recipes that were far cries from the soggy sandwich or "hot dog wrinkled with age" that she claimed foreign correspondents often survived on when working long hours, waiting for a big story to break.

In 1969, Schultz received a lifetime achievement award from the Overseas Press Club at a gala event in her honor. Her longtime friend Wally Deuel, one of the speakers at the event, summed up the group's sentiments: "She knew more about Germany than all of us put together."[14] The award was engraved: "To a tough competitor, staunch friend, honest reporter, she worked like a newspaperman."

Younger women who were members of the club objected to the word "newspaperman," but it remained Schultz's preferred description of herself. Like many female contemporaries who succeeded in male-dominated fields, she framed her success in terms of undoubted hard work and talent. Looking back on her career, her memory was selective. Instead of proudly claiming the challenges she had overcome, she denied facing any special barriers as a woman, although she acknowledged the importance of a male mentor, Dick Little, in opening doors for her. She positioned herself as "one of the boys." At the same time, also like many of her contemporaries, she did not hesitate to use being a small, attractive woman to manipulate the men she dealt with—whether sources, other journalists, or Nazi officials—when that was the easiest way to get the job done. Moreover, though the men she competed and cooperated with readily admitted that she was as good, if not better, at the job, they never quite forgot that she was, as William Shirer put it, "the only woman correspondent in our ranks, buoyant, cheerful, and always well informed." There was always an element of condescension in their praise, as there was in the names they used to describe women reporters: "front-page girls," "girl reporters," and, perhaps worst of all, "news hens," *Time*'s favorite appellation for successful women journalists. Even the seemingly neutral "newspaperwoman" had undertones of "less than" in the years when Schultz was a foreign correspondent—a distinction early second-wave feminists might not have been aware of. By choosing to describe herself as a newspaperman, Schultz claimed her position as an equal in the press room, the Adlon bar, and on the pages of the *Tribune*.

Schultz lived the last years of her life in Westport in the 240-year-old cottage she had purchased for her mother, surrounded by cats, stacks of unfiled documents, and half-written articles, memoirs, and histories. The cottage itself was surrounded by a municipal parking lot, a compromise she negotiated when the city tried to take the house by eminent domain.

Although she had disappeared for the most part from public view, some still recognized her importance. In the 1970s, she gave extended interviews to both the William E. Wiener Oral History Library and the Tribune Oral History Project—the last a "sudden and belated" afterthought by the *Tribune*'s archivist, Harold Hutchings, who had known her in the 1930s when he was on the cable desk and she "as Berlin correspondent, fearlessly and honestly chronicled the rise of Hitler and Naziism."[15] A younger generation of journalists and scholars, including Pulitzer Prize–winning historian John Toland, sought her out for information about her work with Colonel McCormick, her days in Berlin, the rise of the Nazis, or her experiences as a woman foreign correspondent. They found her living in reduced financial circumstances—the amount of her pension remained unchanged over the course of her life, steadily eroded by inflation. In her last years, she was so fragile that she was confined to a wheelchair. And yet, they were consistently able to look beyond the clutter, the cats, and the dirt to see the charm, the intelligence, and the force of her personality.

At the end of her interview with Westport resident Alan Green for the William E. Wiener Oral History Library, a few years before her death in 1980, Schultz said, "Talking to you really makes me a little bit more alive."

He responded, "I don't see how anybody could be more alive than you are Sigrid."[16]

⸺∞⸺

News reporting is an ephemeral art for all but the most notable.

Sigrid Schultz did not win any major awards for her writing, unlike several members of the Berlin foreign press corps who received Pulitzer Prizes for books about their experiences in Nazi Germany. (It's worth pointing out that they, too, lapsed into relatively obscurity; their books, like Schultz's, are rarely read except as sources for historians. Only William Shirer's *Berlin Diary* has survived as a literary work.) She is not recognized as an important media figure, unlike Edward R. Murrow, who effectively created broadcast journalism. She is not remembered by the news-consuming public, unlike slightly younger colleagues, such as Walter Cronkite and Eric Sevareid, who had long successful careers in television news. (Who knows if they will be remembered after the generation that grew up watching them is gone?)

Schultz summed up her own career in 1941 when she wrote to Pat Maloney, "I know I am just a reporter and what is more, I love being a reporter."[17] She stumbled into her career; she was in the right place at the right time with an unusual set of skills. For more than twenty years, she utilized her command of European languages and unparalleled network of contacts to write incisive and often powerful articles about German politics and society, both from Berlin and in the final months of World War II.

A combination of bad luck and questionable decisions meant that she was no longer able to use those skills effectively after the war ended. She struggled in her attempts to work outside the realm of daily newspaper reporting, whether she tried to write books, write for magazines, pitch radio programs (the problem was landing a sponsor), pitch film ideas, or create board games. Whenever she got a longer assignment, she became mired in the research. Every story she tried to write twisted into her fear that Germany would, in fact, "try it again." By the 1960s, she would write to friends, "I am, frankly, a has been."[18]

And yet, Schultz was never entirely forgotten. Her vivid letters and her crisp reporting are referenced in histories of the rise of the Nazis and early twentieth-century American journalism. Her career, not only as a pathfinding woman journalist but as a key member of the *Tribune* foreign press service, appears in encyclopedic accounts of twentieth century journalists. Her report on the violence of Kristallnacht is included in Library of America's *Reporting World War II* alongside pieces by Ernie Pyle, Edward Murrow, Margaret Bourke-White, and John Hershey.

⟨∞⟩

Sigrid Schultz died at home in her sleep on May 14, 1980, at the age of eighty-seven—a quieter death than she could ever have foreseen during her years as a correspondent in Nazi Berlin.

Her longtime home in Westport was bulldozed soon after her death and turned into a parking lot, the final stage of her hard-fought agreement with the city that allowed her to live out the remainder of her life in "the crazy house in the center of town" that her mother had chosen as their home.

The big house in the Chicago neighborhood of Summerdale that had remained the home of her heart throughout her long years as an expatriate in Europe, was razed in 2019, the last of the Schultz homes to survive. Prior to its demolition, the owner of an architectural salvage firm found seventy-five glass-plate photographic negatives of Hedwig, Sigrid, and Barry the St. Bernard hidden in its attic. Their discovery triggered a reappearance by Miss Schultz in the pages of the *Chicago Tribune*—a hundred years after she first became "the number two man" on the *Tribune*'s Berlin team.

ACKNOWLEDGMENTS

The Dragon from Chicago has been a long four years in the making. I had a lot of help along the way, but there are a handful of people to whom I owe a special debt of gratitude:

Agent extraordinaire, Leila Campoli, agreed that the Sigrid Schultz story was worth telling and provided a voice of sanity whenever one was needed, which happened more often than I would like to admit.

Amy Caldwell, my editor at Beacon Press, urged me to dig deeper, encouraged me to trust myself, and regularly reminded me that this book is frighteningly relevant. Her questions and suggestions made *The Dragon from Chicago* a better book.

Like everyone else I know who worked on serious, research-based nonfiction during and immediately after the pandemic, limited access to archives and research libraries made the task harder. I was luckier than most, thanks to help from the librarians and archivists at several institutions: the Wisconsin Historical Society, the Northwestern University Special Collections Library, the Westport Museum in Westport, Connecticut, and the Pritzker Military Library. The staff at all four institutions found ways for me to work around limited access and showed extreme patience with my difficulties in navigating reservation systems and finding aids. This book would have taken me even longer to write without their help.

My BFF from graduate school, Dr. Karin Wetmore, volunteered her considerable research skills on my behalf, talked me through many tough points, and repeatedly asked "Why?" until I could give her a good answer.

Anke Irmscher translated a set of important letters that were well beyond my language skills.

Morley Boyd, Wendy Crowther, and John Suggs, local historians in Westport, Connecticut, generously shared their research and knowledge about Sigrid Schultz.

My accountability buddies, Amy Sue Nathan, Evelyn Herwitz, Natalie Dykstra, and the members of my top-secret, permanent floating Facebook writing challenge group cheered me on, listened to me grumble, raged on my behalf, and occasionally kicked my behind, as and when appropriate.

The members of my daily Zoom write-ins, one hosted by Amy Sue Nathan and the other by Anne Hawley, were there every day for the last three years. Knowing I had someone to write with inspired me to get to my desk on the hard days.

And last but never least, my husband, Sandy Wilson. He read drafts, listened to me talk through problems, drove me back and forth to the Wisconsin Historical Society archives week after week during the pandemic when it didn't feel safe to take the bus, dragged me away from my desk, and was infinitely patient when the book threatened to take over my life. He is the reader in my head and in my heart. It's hard to imagine writing without him.

NOTES

PROLOGUE

1. Over the course of her career, Schultz wrote hundreds of pieces that ran without a byline. They were credited to the Chicago Tribune Press Service and did not include any direct references to the reporter.

2. William Shirer, "The People Behind Hitler, and Ahead of Him. Sigrid Schultz Distills a Quarter Century's Experience; Don't Trust Germans, She Says," *New York Herald Tribune*, Jan. 23, 1944.

3. "Sigrid Schultz, 87, Hitler's Enemy," *Overseas Press Club Bulletin*, June 1, 1980.

4. Schultz, "Hermann Göring's 'Dragon from Chicago,'" in *How I Got That Story: Top Reporters Give the Behind-the-Scenes Story of Covering Great News Events*, ed. David Brown and W. Richard Bruner (New York: E. P. Dutton, 1967), 75.

5. In many accounts, Schultz claimed to be barely five feet tall; official identification cards state she was five feet two.

6. Schultz, "Hermann Göring's 'Dragon from Chicago,'" 81.

CHAPTER 1: A TRILINGUAL CHILD

1. Alan Green interview, William E. Wiener Oral History Library, 1971, Sigrid Schultz Papers, Wisconsin Historical Society, Madison, box 2, folder 5.

2. Green interview, Madison, box 2, folder 5.

3. Schultz, unpublished memoir, 1959, chapter 1, p. 6, Madison, box 34, folder 1.

4. Morley Boyd, Wendy Crowther, and John F. Suggs, "Sigrid Schultz's Secret," *06880*, https://06880danwoog.com/2020/01/29/sigrid-schultzs-secret-an-06880-exclusive.

5. Green interview, Madison, box 2, folder 5.

6. Schultz, unpublished memoir, 1959, chapter 1, p. 31, Madison, box 34, folder 1.

7. To Barney Oldfield from Schultz, Mar. 10, 1951, Madison, box 10, folder 6.

8. Green interview, Madison, box 2, folder 5.

9. Women were first allowed to enroll at the Sorbonne in 1880. By 1914, they made up 10 percent of the student body.

10. Green interview, Madison, box 2, folder 5.

CHAPTER 2: STRANDED

1. Schultz, unpublished memoir, 1959, chapter 1, p. 15, Sigrid Schultz Papers, Wisconsin Historical Society, Madison, box 34, folder 1.

2. Alan Green interview, Madison, box 2, folder 5.

3. Green interview, Madison, box 2, folder 5.

4. Schultz, unpublished memoir, Sigrid Schultz Papers, Westport Museum, Westport, Connecticut, box 1, folder 10.

CHAPTER 3: ENEMY ALIEN

1. To George Scharschug from Schultz, Nov. 4, 1941, Sigrid Schultz Papers, Wisconsin Historical Society, Madison, box 4, folder 4.

2. Schultz, "Chapter IV. Enemy Aliens in Berlin," Madison, box 34, folder 1.

3. Schultz, "Hitler Pledges Husbands for German Maidens. Nazi Chief Accepts Olive Branch of Hohenzollerns," *Chicago Tribune*, Apr. 5, 1932.

4. Quoted in "Introduction," *Women in the Metropolis: Gender and Modernity in Weimar Culture*, ed. Katharina von Ankum (Berkeley: University of California Press, 1997), 4.

5. Schultz, unpublished memoir, Westport, box 3, folder 7.

6. Alan Green interview, Madison, box 2, folder 5.

7. Green interview, Madison, box 2, folder 5.

8. After the war, Chadirchi held a number of important positions in the newly created state of Iraq, serving at various times as the finance minister, the Iraqi ambassador to London, and legal advisor to the Iraq Petroleum Company. As was the case with many of her friends, well-connected and otherwise, Schultz remained in contact with him for many years.

9. Tribune Oral History Project, Madison, box 2, folder 9.

CHAPTER 4: "HOW TO MEET A REVOLUTION"

1. Sigrid Schultz, "How to Meet a Revolution," Sigrid Schultz Papers, Wisconsin Historical Society, Madison, box 2, folder 11.

2. Schultz, *Germany Will Try It Again* (New York: Reynal & Hitchcock, 1944), 38.

3. Hedwig Schultz, "The Days of the Revolution in Berlin," Sigrid Schultz Papers, Westport Museum, Westport, Connecticut, box 3, folder 7.

4. Hedwig Schultz, "The Days of the Revolution in Berlin," Westport, box 3, folder 7.

5. Malcolm Cowley, *Exile's Return: A Literary Odyssey of the 1920s* (New York: Penguin Books, 1994), 7–8.

6. Historian Nancy F. Cott estimates between a quarter and a third of Americans then in their twenties who would go on to be "notable"—enough to earn an entry in *American National Biography*—lived abroad for more than a year between the wars. Cott, *Fighting Words: The Bold American Journalists Who Brought the World Home Between the Wars* (New York: Basic Books, 2020), 335.

7. Schultz, unpublished autobiographical sketch, 1954, Robert R. McCormick and Chicago Tribune Collection, Northwestern University, XI-127, box 54.

CHAPTER 5: FINDING HER OWN PEOPLE

1. Schultz, unpublished memoir, Sigrid Schultz Papers, Westport Museum, Westport, Connecticut, box 3, folder 7.

2. Letter to E. S. Beck from Robert McCormick, Sept. 19, 1917. Quoted in Richard Norton Smith, *The Colonel: The Life and Times of Robert R. McCormick, 1880–1955* (Boston: Houghton Mifflin, 1997), 194.

3. Schultz, unpublished memoir, 1971, Sigrid Schultz Papers, Wisconsin Historical Society, Madison, box 33, folder 4.

4. This was perhaps a common event in the lean years of World War I and the revolutionary days that followed it. In her memoir, *Silent Muse*, Danish silent-film star Asta Nielson described a similar scene when she saw a skeletal horse collapse on the street soon after she arrived in Berlin in the "hungry winter" of 1916.

5. Schultz, unpublished memoir, 1971, Madison, box 33, folder 4.

CHAPTER 6: THE TRAINING OF A FOREIGN CORRESPONDENT

1. Schultz, unpublished autobiographical sketch, 1954, Robert R. McCormick and Chicago Tribune Collection, Northwestern University, XI-127, box 54.

2. Display ad, "A Thousand Dollars a Day for Foreign News," *Chicago Tribune*, Mar. 24, 1919.

3. Schultz, unpublished memoir, 1971, Sigrid Schultz Papers, Wisconsin Historical Society, Madison, box 33, folder 4; Tribune Oral History Project, Madison, box 2, folder 9.

4. Alan Green interview, Madison, box 2, folder 7.

5. Lilian Mowrer, *Journalist's Wife* (New York: William Morrow & Co., 1937), 221.

6. Schultz, unpublished memoir, 1971, Madison, box 33, folder 4.

7. Schultz, *Germany Will Try It Again* (New York: Reynal & Hitchcock, 1944), viii–ix.

8. Ben Hecht, *A Child of the Century* (New York: Simon & Schuster, 1954), 286–87.

9. The Allied powers did not reopen their embassies until the Treaty of Versailles was signed on June 28, 1919.

CHAPTER 7: MUSICAL CHAIRS

1. Robert R. McCormick and Chicago Tribune Collection, Northwestern University, I-62, box 12, folder 4.

2. Northwestern, I-62, box 6, folder 20.

3. Schultz, undated memoir fragment, Sigrid Schultz Papers, Wisconsin Historical Society, Madison, box 34, folder 3.

4. To Robert McCormick from George Seldes, Aug. 9, 1920, Northwestern, I-62, box 8, folder 13.

5. To Floyd Gibbons from Schultz, Oct. 6, 1922, Madison, box 9, folder 10.

6. To Robert McCormick from Joseph Pierson, Nov. 6, 1922. Northwestern, I-62, box 6, folder 20.

7. Otto Friederich, *Before the Deluge: A Portrait of Berlin in the 1920s* (New York: Harper & Row, 1972), 122, 141.

8. John Clayton, "Sharp Fighting Ends Royalist Coup in Munich. Ludendorff Jailed; Called Traitor," *Chicago Tribune*, Nov. 10, 1923.

9. Schultz, undated memoir fragment, Madison, box 34, folder 3.

10. To Robert Schwinbold, *Chicago Tribune* business department, Mar. 19, 1925, Madison, box 4, folder 1.

11. To George Seldes from Schultz, Aug. 2,1973, Madison, box 4, folder 7.

12. Telegram to Berlin office from Robert McCormick, Nov. 5, 1925, Northwestern, I-62, box 1, folder 19.

13. To Robert McCormick from John Clayton, Nov. 6, 1925, Northwestern, I-62, box 1, folder 19.

14. To John Clayton from Robert McCormick, Nov. 25, 1925, Northwestern, I-62, box 1, folder 19.

15. To Robert McCormick from John Clayton, Dec. 16, 1925, Northwestern, I-62, box 1, folder 19.

16. Schultz, undated memoir fragment, Madison, box 34, folder 3.

CHAPTER 8: FRONT-PAGE GIRLS, STUNT REPORTERS, SOB SISTERS, AND MOB SISTERS

1. Ishbel Ross, *Ladies of the Press: The Story of Women in Journalism by an Insider* (New York: Harper, 1936), 3.

2. Alice Fahs, *Out on Assignment: Newspaper Women and the Making of Modern Public Space* (Chapel Hill: University of North Carolina Press, 2011), 17.

3. Display ad, "The Chicago Tribune Announces an Association with the N.Y. Times for Additional War News Service," *Chicago Tribune*, June 2, 1918.

4. Historian Chris Dubbs estimates several dozen women had credentials as visiting correspondents, but that number may be low. Dubbs, *An Unladylike Profession: American Women War Correspondents in World War I* (Lincoln, NE: Potomac Books, 2020); Caitlin Marie Thérèse Jeffrey reports that the records of the American Expeditionary Force list hundreds of women as visiting correspondents. Jeffrey, "Journey Through Unfamiliar Territory: American Reporters and the First World War," PhD diss., University of California, Irvine, 2006, p. 24.

5. To Robert McCormick from George Seldes, Mar. 11, 1926, Robert R. McCormick and Chicago Tribune Collection, Northwestern University, I-62, box 8, folder 13.

CHAPTER 9: THE "RIGHT MAN" FOR THE JOB

1. To Schultz from Frederick Kuhl, Jan. 20, 1926, Sigrid Schultz Papers, Wisconsin Historical Society, Madison, box 4, folder 2.

2. To Schultz from Charles Stephenson Smith, Feb. 23, 1926, Madison, box 4, folder 2.

3. Display ad, "Watchdogs of Truth on the Frontiers of the News," *Chicago Tribune*, Apr. 26, 1928.

4. Julia Edwards, *Women of the World: The Great Foreign Correspondents* (Boston: Houghton Mifflin, 1988), 63–64.

5. Linda Lumsden, "'You're a Tough Guy, Mary—And a First-Rate Newspaperman': Gender and Women Journalists in the 1920s and 1930s," *Journalism & Mass Communication Quarterly* 72, no. 4 (Winter 1995): 914; Carolyn G. Heilbrun, *Writing a Woman's Life* (New York: W. W. Norton, 1988), 13–15.

6. Gregor Ziemer, "Sigrid Schultz," in *LGJ Pays Tribute to the Literary Women of the Twenties, Lost Generation Journal* IV, no. 1 (Winter 1976): 3.

7. George Seldes, *Witness to a Century: Encounters with the Noted, the Notorious, and the Three SOBs* (New York: Ballantine Books, 1987), 120.

8. To D. M. Deininger from Schultz, Apr. 2, 1926, Madison, box 4, folder 2.

CHAPTER 10: ON THE JOB

1. Gregor Ziemer, "Sigrid Schultz," *Lost Generation Journal* IV, no. 1 (Winter 1976), 4.

2. Robert R. McCormick and Chicago Tribune Collection, Northwestern University, XI-127, box 12, foreign news coverage and staff (general).

3. "Sigrid Schultz Shuns Leisure; Works on Book, Garden in Westport, Conn., Home," *The Trib*, July 1957.

4. Ziemer, "Sigrid Schultz," 4.

5. Ziemer, Sigrid Schultz," 4.

6. To Schultz from Thomas Ybarra, Dec. 2, 1925, Sigrid Schultz Papers, Wisconsin Historical Society, Madison, box 10, folder 19.

7. Schultz, unpublished memoir fragment, Madison, box 34, folder 2.

8. Julia Edwards, *Women of the World: The Great Foreign Correspondents* (Boston: Houghton Mifflin, 1988), 63.

9. Frazier Hunt, *One American and His Attempt at Education* (New York: Simon & Schuster, 1938), 283.

10. "People in the News," transcript, *Pall Mall Broadcasts,* Mar. 8, 1938, Dorothy Thompson Papers, Special Collections Research Center, Syracuse University Libraries, box 111: Pall Mall broadcast 1937–1938.

11. Appendix V, William L. Shirer interview, October 22, 1984. In Cynthia C. Chapman, "Psychobiographical Study of the Life of Sigrid Schultz," PhD diss., State University of New York, 1991, 175.

12. Like Julia Child, Hedwig didn't know anything about cooking until she landed in Paris, where she took cooking classes, perhaps out of boredom during Hermann's wanderings, perhaps out of domestic self-defense given the fluctuating nature of the household's finances.

13. Alan Green interview, Madison, box 2, folder 7.

14. Schultz, unpublished memoir, Sigrid Schultz Papers, Westport Museum, Westport, Connecticut.

CHAPTER 11: LOVE AND LONELINESS

1. To Carl Dennewitz from Schultz, Dec. 15, 1928, Sigrid Schultz Papers, Wisconsin Historical Society, Madison, box 9, folder 3.

2. Gregor Ziemer, "Sigrid Schultz," *Lost Generation Journal* IV, no. 1 (Winter 1976), 3.

3. Schultz, unpublished memoir, Sigrid Schultz Papers, Westport Museum, Westport, Connecticut.

4. To Schultz from Carl Dennewitz, Dec. 23, 1926, Madison, box 9, folder 3.

5. To Carl Dennewitz from Schultz, December 15, 1928, Madison, box 9, folder 3.

6. To Carl Dennewitz from Schultz, June 13, 1928, Madison, box 9, folder 3.

7. To Robert McCormick from Schultz, Nov. 14, 1927, Madison, box 4, folder 8.

8. To Lillian Kohlhammer from Schultz, July 1928, Madison, box 10, folder 1.

9. Letter from Robert Schwinbold, Jan. 5, 1928, Madison, box 4, folder 2.

10. Undated letter to John Steele from Schultz, Madison, box 10, folder 15.

11. To Lillian Kohlhammer from Schultz, July 1928, Madison, box 10, folder 1.

12. To Carl Dennewitz from Schultz, June 13, 1928, Madison, box 9, folder 3.

13. To Carl Dennewitz from Schultz, June 13, 1928, Madison, box 9, folder 3.

14. Undated letter to Carl Dennewitz from Schultz, Madison, box 9, folder 3.

15. Schultz, "Germany, New and Old, Bows to Hindenburg. Cheered on Birthday by Vast Throngs," *Chicago Tribune*, Oct. 3, 1927.

16. To Robert McCormick from Schultz, Nov. 5, 1917, Madison, box 4, folder 8.

17. To Carl Dennewitz, from Schultz Dec. 15, 1928, Madison, box 9, folder 3.

18. To Schultz from Carl Dennewitz, Apr. 17, 1933, Madison, box 9, folder 3.

19. Undated letter from Schultz to Carl Dennewitz, Madison, box 9, folder 3.

20. To Hedwig Schultz from Sigrid Schultz, undated letter, Madison, box 43, folder 5.

21. To Schultz from Carl Dennewitz, Dec. 1933, Madison, box 9, folder 3.

CHAPTER 12: "THE FASCISTI ARE VERY RESTLESS"

1. Schultz, "Germany Seeks 'Man of Iron' to Rescue Nation. And Would-Be Dictators Arise by the Score," *Chicago Tribune*, Feb. 24, 1929.

2. Schultz, "Hitler Angered by Uniform Ban; 'Lays Down Law,' Demands Government to Lift Restrictions," *Chicago Tribune*, June 22, 1932.

3. Schultz, "Germany Seeks 'Man of Iron' to Rescue Nation, and Would-Be Dictators Arise by the Score," *Chicago Tribune*, Feb. 24, 1929.

4. Philipp Blom, *Fracture: Life & Culture in the West, 1918–1938* (New York: Basic Books, 2015), 253, 264; Eric D. Weitz, *Weimar Germany: Promise and Tragedy* (Princeton, NJ: Princeton University Press, 2007), 161, 350.

5. Blom, *Fracture*, 264.

6. Schultz, "Berlin Voters Dodge Bullets on Election Eve, Political Foes Clash in Day of Rioting," *Chicago Tribune*, Nov. 17, 1929.

7. To Robert McCormick from Schultz, Mar. 28, 1930, Sigrid Schultz Papers, Wisconsin Historical Society, Madison, box 4, folder 8, and Robert R. McCormick and Chicago Tribune Collection, Northwestern University, I-62, box 8, folder 7.

8. Schultz, "Many Parties Ask Support of German Voters, Fate of Republic Rests in Balance, *Chicago Tribune*, Aug. 31, 1930.

9. Alan Green interview, Madison, box 2, folder 9.

10. Schultz, unpublished memoir, Sigrid Schultz Papers, Westport Museum, Westport, Connecticut.

11. To Robert McCormick from Schultz, Feb. 20, 1933, Northwestern, I-62, box 8, folder 8.

12. Schultz, "Berlin Police Battle Ends with Gunfire, Strikers Start Night Riot in Workers District," *Chicago Tribune*, Oct. 17, 1930.

13. Schultz, "2494 Prussian Political Riots Recorded in Year and No Relief is Seen by Police in Future," *Chicago Tribune*, Mar. 7, 1931.

14. To Schultz from George Scharschug, Dec. 10, 1920, Madison, box 4, folder 3.

15. To George Scharschug from Schultz, Dec. 22, 1930, Madison, box 4, folder 3.

16. To George Scharschug from Schultz, Aug. 24, 1931, Madison, box 3, folder 4.

17. To George Scharschug from Schultz, Aug. 26, 1931, Madison, box 3, folder 4.

18. Undated letter to George Scharschug from Schultz, Madison, box 4, folder 3.

19. Tribune Oral History Project, Madison, box 2, folders 9 and 11 and Northwestern, XXI-2 box 33, pt. III, p. 2; Schultz-Reid interview, 1980, appendix VII, Chapman, p. 194.

20. Schultz, "Hitler Pledges to Pay Berlin's Debts to World, Nazi Chief Predicts He'll Be in Power Soon," *Chicago Tribune*, Dec. 5, 1931.

21. Schultz, "Hitler Pictures Self as Knight Defending World, Asks Germany Follow Him Through Hell,'" *Chicago Tribune*, Dec. 31, 1931.

22. To George Scharschug from Schultz, Sept. 4, 1934, Northwestern, I-62, box 8, folder 9.

23. Dorothy Thompson, "I Saw Hitler!" *Cosmopolitan*, Mar. 1932.

24. Schultz, "Socialists Back Von Hindenburg for President, Party Reverses Stand in Former Election," *Chicago Tribune*, Feb. 25, 1932.

25. Larry Eugene Jones, *Hitler Versus Hindenburg: The 1932 Presidential Elections and the End of the Weimar Republic* (Cambridge: Cambridge University Press, 2015), 274.

26. To Robert McCormick, Nov. 23, 1932, Madison, box 4, folder 8, and Northwestern, I-62, box 8, folder 8.

27. Schultz, "Berlin Throngs Cheer Hitler as Chancellor; Nazis and War Vets Pay Their Homage," *Chicago Tribune*, Jan. 31, 1933.

CHAPTER 13: WHEN PUTSCH COMES TO SHOVE

1. Robert R. McCormick and Chicago Tribune Collection, Northwestern University, XI-127, box 54, Sigrid Schultz.

2. George Scharschug to Sigrid Schultz, July 18,1934, Sigrid Schultz Papers, Wisconsin Historical Society, Madison, box 4, folder 3.

3. Quoted in Neal Bascomb, "The Cavalry of the Future," *MHQ: The Quarterly Journal of Military History* (Summer 2020): 16.

4. Schultz, "Rule of Hitler Is Opened with Riots; 4 Slain, Many Wounded at Fascist Fetes," *Chicago Tribune*, Feb. 1, 1933.

5. To Robert McCormick from Schultz, Feb. 20, 1933, Northwestern, I-62, box 8, folder 8.

6. Schultz, "Fire Rages in Reichstag; Nab Red for Arson," *Chicago Tribune*, Feb. 28, 1933.

7. Tribune Oral History Project, Madison, box 2, folder 7.

8. Schultz, "Hitler Demands Reichstag Make Him a Dictator: Nazis Raid Country Home of Einstein for Arms," *Chicago Tribune*, Mar. 21, 1933.

9. To Robert McCormick from Schultz, June 16, 1933, Northwestern, I-62, box 8, folder 8.

10. To Robert McCormick from Schultz, June 24, 1933, Northwestern, I-62, box 8, folder 8.

11. Gregor Ziemer, "Sigrid Schultz," *Lost Generation Journal* IV, no. 1 (Winter 1976), 2.

12. Howard K. Smith, *Last Train from Berlin: An Eye-Witness Account of Germany at War* (New York: Knopf, 1942), 47–49, 61.

13. Ziemer, "Sigrid Schultz," 3.

14. Louis Lochner, *Always the Unexpected: A Book of Reminiscences* (New York: Macmillan, 1956), 121.

15. To Robert McCormick from Schultz, Dec. 1, 1933, Northwestern, I-62, box 8, folder 8.

16. "Sigrid Schultz Shuns Leisure; Works on Book, Garden in Westport, Conn., Home," *The Trib*, July 1957.

17. To "Dear Friends" from Schultz, June 16, 1936, Madison, box 11, folder 3.

18. "June 18, 1935," William L. Shirer, *Berlin Diary* (New York: Knopf, 1941), 41–42.

19. The Deuels became two of Schultz's closest friends in Berlin and remained dear friends for the rest of her life. Later, writing to William Shirer about their shared days in Berlin, Schultz remembered, "Though Wallie [Deuel] and I were rivals in the far-away days in Berlin, he and Mary, their children, my Mother and I formed what Goethe used to call a 'Wahlverwanderschaft,' a very harmonious substitute for a real family." Letter to William Shirer from Schultz, Aug. 25, 1971, Madison, box 10, folder 13.

20. "June 18, 1935," Shirer, *Berlin Diary*, 41–42.

21. To "Dear Friends" from Schultz, June 16, 1936, Madison, box 11, folder 3.

22. Christopher Isherwood, "Goodbye to Berlin," *Berlin Stories* (New York: New Directions, 2008), 204.

23. Lilian Mowrer, *Journalist's Wife* (New York: William Morrow & Co., 1937), 287.

24. Schultz, "Prussian Chief Exposes 'Terror Plan' of Hitler, Claims Nazis Propose to Drive Out Jews," *Chicago Tribune*, Nov. 26, 1931.

25. Alan Green interview, Madison, box 2, folder 7; Kline interview in Chapman, p. 293.

26. To "Dear Friends" from Schultz, June 4, 1945, Madison, box 12, folder 1.

27. Schultz, statement "to whom it may concern" regarding her knowledge of Hans Rosenwald, June 4, 1954, Madison, box 13, folder 1.

28. Quentin Reynolds. *By Quentin Reynolds* (New York: McGraw Hill, 1963), 105–9.

29. To George Scharschug from Schultz, Jan. 19, 1939, Madison, box 4, folder 4.

30. To Robert McCormick from Schultz, Mar. 7, 1934, Northwestern, I-62, box 8, folder 9.

31. To George Scharschug from Schultz, Feb. 27, 1934, Northwestern, I-62, box 8, folder 9.

32. To George Scharschug from Schultz, Aug. 13, 1934, Northwestern, I-62, box 8 folder 9.

33. To George Scharschug from Schultz, Aug. 13, 1934, Northwestern, I-62, box 8, folder 9.

34. To Robert McCormick from Schultz, Oct. 31, 1933, Northwestern, I-62, box 8, folder 8.

35. To Robert McCormick from Schultz, July 22, 1935, Madison, box 4, folder 8 and Northwestern, I-62, box 8, folder 9.

36. To George Scharschug from Schultz, Oct. 1, 1936, Madison, box 4, folder 4.

37. Schultz, "Hitler Crushes Out Revolt; Firing Squads of Nazis Shoot Down Ten Leaders, Ex-Premier Slain; No Quarter Give to Plotters," *Chicago Tribune*, July 1, 1934.

38. Schultz, "Scrap German 'Rule by Law': Special Court to Punish Foes of Nazis Set Up. Göring Bares New 'Justice' Policy," *Chicago Tribune*, July 13, 1934.

39. Schultz, "Hitler Defends Nazi Slayings; Flays Press, Charges 'Malicious' Drive on Party," *Chicago Tribune*, July 11, 1934; Associated Press, "Correspondents Are Angered," *Tribune*, July 11, 1934.

40. Schultz, "Sinclair Lewis' Wife Banished from Germany, Expulsion Based on Hitler Interview," *Chicago Tribune*, Aug. 26, 1934.

41. George Seldes, *Tell the Truth and Run* (New York: Greenberg, 1953), 126.

42. William Shirer, *The Nightmare Years: 1930–1940* (Boston: Little, Brown, 1984), 138–39.

43. To George Seldes from Schultz, July 20, 1935, Madison, box 4, folder 4.

CHAPTER 14: LET THE GAMES BEGIN

1. Gregor Ziemer, "Sigrid Schultz," *Lost Generation Journal* IV, no. 1 (Winter 1976): 2.

2. Schultz, "New Goose Steps for 65 Million Germans," *Chicago Tribune*, Mar. 10, 1935.

3. Schultz, "German Colonies Lost in War Must Be Returned: Goebbels," *Chicago Tribune*, Jan. 18, 1936.

4. To Robert McCormick from Schultz, July 22, 1935, Sigrid Schultz Papers, Wisconsin Historical Society, Madison, box 4, folder 8; also, McCormick-Tribune archives, I-62, box 8, folder 9.

5. To Robert McCormick from Schultz, Feb. 11, 1936, McCormick-Tribune archives, I-62, box 8, folder 9.

6. Schultz, "Sound Last Call for Olympics on Radio Today," *Chicago Tribune*, July 5, 1936.

7. To Schultz from William B. Campbell (European manager, Press Wireless), July 31, 1936, Madison, box 4, folder 4.

8. To "Dear Friends" from Schultz, June 16, 1936, Madison, box 11, folder 3.

9. Tribune Oral History Project interview, McCormick-Tribune archives, XXI-2, box 33, Part II, pp. 8–9; also, Madison, box 2, folder 9.

10. Schultz, "Hitler Opens Olympic Games Before 120,000, U.S. Team Gets Cool Reception," *Chicago Tribune*, Aug. 2, 1936.

11. Schultz, "Nazi Political Olympics Go On Behind the Scenes. World Diplomats Talk with Hitler Agents, *Chicago Tribune*, Aug. 4, 1936.

12. Paul Gallico, *Washington Post*, Feb. 17, 1936. Quoted in Deborah E. Lipstadt, *Beyond Belief: The American Press & the Coming of the Holocaust, 1933–1945* (New York: The Free Press, 1986), 81.

13. To "Dear Friends" from Schultz, June 16, 1936, Madison, box 11, folder 3.

14. Schultz, "Olympic Games End with Dramatic Flag Ceremony," *Chicago Tribune*, Aug. 17, 1936.

CHAPTER 15: AKA JOHN DICKSON

1. To Robert McCormick from Schultz, Oct. 3, 1936, McCormick-Tribune archives, I-62, box 8, folder 9.

2. Schultz, "Hitler Reviews Private Army; Hails Strength, Fuehrer Is Saluted by 107,000 Nazi Troops," *Chicago Tribune*, Sept. 14, 1936.

3. Schultz, "Fight Jewry and Sovietism, Nazi Cry to the World, Goebbels Says Reds Plan Conquest of Europe," *Chicago Tribune*, Sept. 11, 1936.

4. To George Scharschug from Schultz, Oct. 1, 1936, Sigrid Schultz Papers, Wisconsin Historical Society, Madison, box 4, folder 4.

5. To George Scharschug from Schultz.

6. To George Scharschug from Schultz.

7. Harold Hutchins, memo regarding his interview with Schultz, April 12, 1977, McCormick-Tribune archives, XI-127, box 54, Sigrid Schultz.

8. Undated letter to Robert McCormick from Schultz, McCormick-Tribune archive, I-62, box 8, folder 9.

9. To Scharschug from Schultz, Aug. 12, 1934, McCormick-Tribune archives, I-62, box 8, folder 9.

10. John Dickson, "Democracy Surrenders, Dictatorship Crushes Freedom in Germany. People Recall with Terror Hitler's Blood Purge," *Chicago Tribune*, Nov. 1, 1936.

11. John Dickson, "German Troops Vanish; Traced to War in Spain. 6,000 Families Grieve over Fate of Soldiers," *Chicago Tribune*, Jan. 3, 1937.

12. John Dickson, "Nazi Hotheads Urge Hitler to Start a Fight. Army Cries,'No! We Are Not Ready,'" *Chicago Tribune*, May 16, 1937.

13. To Robert McCormick from Schultz, Feb. 3, 1940, McCormick-Tribune archives, I-62, box 8, folder 10.

14. Schultz, "Sterilize 20,000 Unfit Germans Under Nazi Law: Expect Work of Purging Race to Be Speeded," *Chicago Tribune*, Dec. 8, 1936.

15. Walter Simmons, "How Some Tribune Reporters Forecast Hitler's Rise," *Chicago Tribune*, Dec. 23, 1945.

CHAPTER 16: NEVER ENTIRELY AT PEACE

1. To Robert McCormick from Schultz, Aug. 30, 1930, Sigrid Schultz Papers, Wisconsin Historical Society, Madison, box 4, folder 8.

2. Thomas Ybarra to Sigrid Schultz, February 2, 1944, Madison, box 10, folder 19.

3. Hermann Göring, Dec. 17, 1936. Quoted in William Shirer, *The Rise and Fall of the Third Reich: A History of Nazi Germany* (New York: Simon & Schuster, 1960).

4. John Dickson, "Nazi Hotheads Urge Hitler to Start a Fight. Army Cries, "No! We Are Not Ready,'" *Chicago Tribune*, May 16, 1937.

5. Schultz, "Duke of Windsor Hears Austrian Nazis Plan Coup. Warned to Stay Away, His Friends Say," *Chicago Tribune*, Feb. 9, 1938.

6. Schultz, "Czechs Offer Nazi Cabinet Job; Scorn It, Berlin Order," *Chicago Tribune*, Mar. 15, 1938.

7. To Robert McCormick from Schultz, Mar. 29, 1938, Robert R. McCormick and Chicago Tribune Collection, Northwestern University, I-62, box 8, folder 9.

8. To Robert McCormick, from Schultz, May 23, 1938, Northwestern, I-62, box 8, folder 9.

9. John Dickson, "Dateline Paris. Germany to Put 1,500,000 Men into 'War Game,''Trial Mobilization' Thrills Nazis," *Chicago Tribune*, Aug. 7, 1938.

10. Schultz, "German Reserve to Make Debut in Army Maneuver. New Post-War Corps to Learn Modern Tactics," *Chicago Tribune*, Aug. 7, 1938.

11. To McCormick from Schultz, Aug. 9, 1938, Madison, box 4, folder 8, also Northwestern I-62, box 8, folder 9.

12. Schultz, "New Peace Pact," *Chicago Tribune*, Oct. 1, 1938.

CHAPTER 17: ON THE AIR FROM BERLIN

1. News 380828 MBS, Sigrid Schultz, "On Munich," Old Time Radio Catalog.

2. Munich broadcast, Sept. 30, 1938, Sigrid Schultz Papers, Wisconsin Historical Society, Madison, box 38, folder 1.

3. To Fred Weber (Mutual Broadcasting System) from Schultz, Feb. 16, 1940, Madison, box 7, folder 7.

4. To Fred Weber from Schultz, Feb. 16, 1940.

5. To Fred Weber from Schultz, Feb. 16, 1940.

CHAPTER 18: WAR SEEMED INEVITABLE

1. Carey Longmore to Schultz, February 20, 1939, Sigrid Schultz Papers, Wisconsin Historical Society, Madison, box 11, folder 5.

2. Schultz to Robert McCormick, March 8, 1939, Robert R. McCormick and Chicago Tribune Collection, Northwestern University, I-62, box 8, folder 10.

3. Display ad, "What Next in Europe? You Are In a Better Position to Know Than the People Who Live There If You Follow These Tribune Correspondents!" *Chicago Tribune*, May 10, 1939.

4. Undated letter to Hedwig Schultz from Janet Fairbank, Madison, box 9, folder 8.

5. Undated letter to unnamed friends from Schultz, Madison, box 11, folder 4.

6. Schultz, "Hitler Seizes 20,000 Jews. Homes Burned; Stores Looted; Terror Reigns. Mobs Run Wild in German Streets," *Chicago Tribune*, Nov. 11, 1938.

7. To Robert McCormick from Schultz, Nov. 20, 1938, Madison, box 4, folder 8, and Northwestern, I-62, box 8, folder 9.

8. Alan Green interview, 1971, Madison, box 2, folder 7.

9. To George Scharschug from Schultz, Jan. 19, 1938, Madison, box 4, folder 4.

10. To George Scharschug from Schultz, Jan. 19, 1938, Madison, box 4, folder 4.

11. Interview with Sidney Kline, 1982, Chapman, appendix XVII, p. 73.

12. To Hedwig Schultz from Sigrid Schultz, Jan. 30, 1940, Madison, box 44, folder 2.

13. To Robert McCormick from Schultz, Feb. 25, 1939, Madison, box 4, folder 8, and Northwestern, I-62, box 8, folder 10.

14. Robert McCormick to William Allen White, Mar. 6, 1940. Quoted in Richard Norton Smith, *The Colonel: The Life and Legend of Robert R. McCormick, 1880–1955* (Boston: Houghton Mifflin, 1997), 391.

15. Green interview, 1971, Madison, box 2, folder 5.

16. To Robert McCormick from Schultz, July 8, 1939, Northwestern, I-62, box 8, folder 10.

17. To Robert McCormick from Schultz, July 30, 1939, Northwestern, I-62, box 8, folder 10.

18. Schultz, "Hitler Gazes at Stars to Guide His Decisions, Studies Astrology in Bavarian Alps," *Chicago Tribune*, July 14, 1939.

19. Schultz, "Seeks Spain as Ally," *Chicago Tribune*, May 10, 1939.

20. John Dickson, "Nazi Dictator Brands Britain World Foe No. 1," *Chicago Tribune*, July 13, 1939.

21. Schultz, "Hitler and Reds in War Deal. Germany and Russia to Sign Pact of Non-Aggression; May Split Poland. Nazis Will Occupy Danzig Thursday, Berlin Hears," *Chicago Tribune*, Aug. 22, 1939.

22. Schultz, "Nazis and Russia Sign Pact; Hitler Defiant on Poland. Warsaw Must Yield or Fight, Fuehrer Says. Wants All Lands Lost to Poles Returned," *Chicago Tribune*, Aug. 24, 1939; unattributed article, "Tribune Writer Says Red Pact Tickles Berlin," *Chicago Tribune*, Aug. 25, 1939.

23. Schultz, "Poles Reject Terms," *Chicago Tribune*, Sept. 1, 1939.

CHAPTER 19: THE BERLIN BLUES

1. To Schultz from Pat Maloney, Apr. 1, 1940, Sigrid Schultz Papers, Wisconsin Historical Society, Madison, box 4, folder 4.

2. Schultz, "German Troops Cut Off Poles in the Corridor," *Chicago Tribune*, Sept. 3, 1939.

3. Schultz, "Every German Now Must Have 7 Ration Cards. Red One Gets You Bread, Blue One Meat," *Chicago Tribune*, Sept. 25, 1939.

4. To George Scharschug from Schultz, Oct. 25, 1939, Robert R. McCormick and Chicago Tribune Collection, Northwestern University, I-62, box 8, folder 10.

5. Louis Lochner, *Always the Unexpected: A Book of Reminiscences* (New York: Macmillan, 1956), 273–74.

6. To Robert McCormick from Schultz, Dec. 5, 1939, Northwestern, I-62, box 8, folder 10.

7. To Robert McCormick from Schultz, Dec. 5, 1939.

8. Sigrid Schultz, *Germany Will Try It Again* (New York: Reynal & Hitchcock, 1944), 208–9.

9. Pat Maloney to Robert McCormick, Oct. 12, 1939, Northwestern, I-62, box 2, folder 6.

10. Alan Green interview, Madison, box 2, folder 7.

11. To Hedwig Schultz from Sigrid Schultz, Apr. 14, 1940, Madison, box 44, folder 2.

12. Schultz, "Germans Take Brussels; 'Paris in 15 Days,' They Cry. Boast 100 Mile Gun Will Force City to Give Up. Louvain Captured by German Army," *Chicago Tribune*, May 18, 1940.

13. "Reich Terms Reported Offered via Sweden; Alleged Peace Plan an 'Ultimatum' to British," *New York Times*, July 27, 1940.

14. William L. Shirer, *Berlin Diary* (New York: Knopf, 1941), 462.

15. Gregor Ziemer, "Sigrid Schultz," *Lost Generation Journal* IV, no. 1 (Winter 1976): 3.

16. To Pat Maloney from Schultz, Sept. 10, 1940, Northwestern, I-62, box 2, folder 3.

17. Schultz, "Tribune Writer Broadcasts as Berlin Is Raided," *Chicago Tribune*, Aug. 27, 1940.

18. Schultz, "Berliners Rush to See Damage of Bomb Attack. Capital Seeks Better Air Defenses," *Chicago Tribune*, Sept. 8, 1940.

19. Schultz, "British Raiders' Bombs Damage Berlin Subway. Strike at Nazi Capital in Two Attacks," *Chicago Tribune*, Dec. 17, 1940.

20. To Hedwig Schultz from Sigrid Schultz, Aug. 31, 1940, Madison, box 44, folder 2.

21. To Robert McCormick from Schultz, Oct. 8, 1940, Northwestern, I-62, box 8, folder 10.

22. Green interview, 1971, Madison, box 2, folder 5.

23. To Alexander von Schimpff from Schultz, Feb. 6, 1970, Madison, box 10, folder 17.

24. To Robert McCormick from Schultz, Oct. 1940, Northwestern, I-62, box 8, folder 10.

CHAPTER 20: GOING HOME

1. Schultz, autobiographical notes, 1951, Sigrid Schultz Papers, Wisconsin Historical Society, Madison, box 2, folder 11.

2. To Emil Schroeder from Schultz, February 9, 1941, Madison, box 10, folder 12.

3. Schultz, "Europe Hopes, and Fears, on Armistice Eve. Sigrid Schultz Tells of 3,000 Mile Tour," *Chicago Tribune*, Nov. 11, 1940.

4. From Robert McCormick to Schultz, Nov. 12, 1940, Robert R. McCormick and Chicago Tribune Collection, Northwestern University, I-62, box 8, folder 10.

5. To Sue and Harold Hutchings from Schultz, Apr. 26, 1973, Madison, box 4, folder 7.

6. To Peter Ilcus from Schultz, Feb. 3, 1941, Madison, box 9, folder 14, trans. Anke Irmscher.

7. To Schultz from Peter Ilcus, Dec. 20, 1940, Madison, box 9, folder 14, trans. Anke Irmscher.

8. To Peter Ilcus from Schultz, Feb. 11, 1941, Madison, box 9, folder 14, trans. Anke Irmscher.

9. To R. F. Stephen (Tribune Insurance Department) from Schultz, Feb. 23, 1942, Madison, box 4, folder 5.

10. Schultz, "Crossing Europe to Peace! A View by Miss Schultz. Beauty Lies a Stranger amid the Ruins," *Chicago Tribune*, Mar. 2, 1941.

11. To Peter Ilcus from Schultz, Feb. 11, 1941, Madison, box 9, folder 14, trans. Anke Irmscher.

12. To Mssr. Chamier from Schultz, May 6, 1941, box 4, folder 4.

13. William Fulton, "Berlin Betting Ten to One on Victory in May: Sigrid Schultz Home with Some Revelations," *Chicago Tribune*, Feb. 28, 1941.

14. To Robert McCormick from Schultz, Feb. 24, 1941, Madison, box 4, folder 8.

15. Fulton, "Berlin Betting Ten to One on Victory in May."

CHAPTER 21: SICK AND TIRED

1. To Arthur Henning from Schultz, early summer 1941, Sigrid Schultz Papers, Wisconsin Historical Society, Madison, box 4, folder 4.

2. To Emil Schroeder from Schultz, Sept. 29, 1941, Madison, box 10, folder 12.

3. To Hedwig Schultz from Sigrid Schultz, Mar. 1941, Madison, box 11, folder 6.

4. To Colonel Robert McCormick from Noel B. Gerson (WGN), Mar. 4, 1941, Robert R. McCormick and Chicago Tribune Collection, Northwestern University, I-62, box 8, folder 10.

5. To Noel Gerson from Pat Maloney, Feb. 27, 1941, Madison, box 4, folder 4.

6. To R. F. Stephens (Tribune Insurance Department) from Schultz, Feb. 23, 1942, Madison, box 4, folder 5.

7. To Pat Maloney from Schultz, Apr. 8, 1941, Madison, box 4, folder 4.

8. To George Scharschug from Schultz, Apr. 14, 1941, Madison, box 4, folder 4.

9. To Pat Maloney from Schultz, May 3, 1941, Madison, box 2, folder 4.

10. To George Scharschug from Schultz, May 18, 1941, Madison, box 4, folder 4.

11. To George Scharschug from Schultz, ca. June 14, 1941, Madison, box 4, folder 4.

12. To Schultz from Pat Maloney, June 21, 1941, Madison, box 4, folder 4.

13. To Schultz from George Scharschug, June 29, 1941, Madison, box 4, folder 4.

14. To Schultz from John Steele, June 29, 1941, Madison, box 10, folder 15.

15. To George Scharschug from Schultz, July 25, 1941, Madison, box 4, folder 4.

16. To Schultz from Pat Maloney, Aug. 2, 1941, Madison, box 4, folder 4.

17. To Pat Maloney from Schultz, Aug. 4, 1941, Madison, box 4, folder 4.

18. To Peter Ilcus from Schultz, ca. Sept. 7, 1941, Madison, box 9, folder 14, trans. Anke Irmscher.

19. To Peter Ilcus from Schultz, ca. Sept. 7, 1941.

20. To Peter Ilcus from Schultz, ca. Sept. 7, 1941.

21. To George Scharschug from Schultz, Sept. 11, 1941, Madison, box 4, folder 4.

CHAPTER 22: "A MILD LITTLE WAR MONGERING TOUR"

1. To George Scharschug from Schultz, Dec. 3, 1941, Sigrid Schultz Papers, Wisconsin Historical Society, Madison, box 4, folder 4.

2. To Pat Maloney from Schultz, May 7, 1942, Madison, box 4, folder 5.

3. To Astrid in San Pedro from Schultz, late Apr.–early May 1942, Madison, box 11, folder 7.

4. To D. M. Deininger from Schultz, Jan. 28, 1942, Madison, box 4, folder 5.

5. To Schultz from Pat Maloney, Jan. 3, 1942, Madison, box 4, folder 5.

6. To Pat Maloney from Schultz, Jan. 7, 1942, Madison, box 4, folder 5.

7. To Schultz from Douglas Miller, Feb. 26, 1942, Madison, box 7, folder 2.

8. To Pat Maloney from Schultz, Mar. 17, 1942, Madison, box 4, folder 5.

9. To R. F. Stephens (Tribune Insurance Department) from Schultz, Feb. 23, 1942, Madison, box 4, folder 5.

10. To Pat Maloney from Schultz, Feb. 27, 1942, Madison, box 4, folder 5.

11. To Schultz from Pat Maloney, Mar. 6, 1942, Madison, box 4, folder 5.

12. To Pat Maloney from Schultz, Mar. 17, 1942, Madison, box 4, folder 5.

13. To Pat Maloney from Schultz, May 2, 1942, Madison, box 4, folder 5.

14. To Schultz from William Donovan, OSS, Sept. 4, 1942, Sigrid Schultz Papers, Westport Museum, Westport, Connecticut, box 2, folder 7.

15. To John Steele from Schultz, June 29, 1942, Madison, box 4, folder 5.

16. To Schultz from Richard Clarke (*The News*), Feb. 1, 1942, Madison, box 11, folder 7.

17. To George Bye from Schultz, Oct. 1, 1942, Madison, box 7, folder 1.

18. To Robert McCormick from Schultz, Jan. 10, 1943, Robert R. McCormick and Chicago Tribune Collection, Northwestern University, I-62, box 8, folder 10.

19. To Astrid in San Pedro from Sigrid Schultz, Late Apr.–early May 1942, Madison, box 11, folder 7.

20. To Dale Warren, Houghton Mifflin, from Schultz. May 15, 1937. Madison. box 7, folder 1.

21. To Schultz from Maxwell Perkins, July 31, 1941, Madison, box 11, folder 6.

22. To Pat Maloney from Schultz, Aug. 4, 1941, Madison, box 4, folder 4.

23. To Schultz from Pat Maloney, Aug. 16, 1941, Madison, box 4, folder 4.

24. To George Bye from Schultz, May 12, 1942, Madison, box 7, folder 1.

25. To George Bye from Max Perkins, June 12, 1942, Madison, box 7, folder 1.

26. To Schultz from Robert Haas, Random House, Sept. 2, 1942, Madison, box 7, folder 1.

27. Letter to Schultz from Elliot McCrae (E. P. Dutton), Apr. 8, 1943, Madison, box 7, folder 1.

28. To Chace Conley (Ziff Davis Publishing) from Schultz, Aug. 10, 1942, Madison, box 7, folder 1.

29. To Chace Conley from Schultz, Aug. 10, 1942.

30. To "Dear Friends," probably the Scharschugs, from Schultz, Oct. 28, 1943, Madison, box 11, folder 8.

31. To Mary Abbott from Schultz, Jan. 26, 1944, Madison, box 7, folder 5.

32. To Annie Laurie (McIntosh & Otis) from Schultz, July 10, 1944, Madison, box 7, folder 5.

CHAPTER 23: FROM FOREIGN CORRESPONDENT
TO WAR CORRESPONDENT

1. Dorothy Thompson, "Why Not Use Our Women," *Ladies' Home Journal*, March 1944, 6.

2. To Pat Maloney from Schultz, July 5, 1944, Sigrid Schultz Papers, Wisconsin Historical Society, Madison, box 4, folder 6.

3. To Pat Maloney from Schultz, Dec. 20, 1943, Madison, box 4, folder 5.

4. To Schultz from Pat Maloney, Jan. 11, 1944, Madison, box 4, folder 6.

5. To Pat Maloney from Schultz, Jan. 31, 1944, Madison, box 4, folder 6.

6. To Schultz from Pat Maloney, Mar. 25, 1944, Madison, box 4, folder 6.

7. To Pat Maloney from Schultz, Apr. 10, 1944, Madison, box 4, folder 6.

8. Undated memo to Pat Maloney, Madison, box 4, folder 6.

9. To Schultz from Pat Maloney, July 29, 1944, Madison, box 4, folder 6.

10. Telegram to Schultz from Otis L. Wiese, *McCall's*, Sept. 16, 1944, Madison, box 7, folder 6.

11. Much of the information about women's magazines, and *McCall's* in particular, comes from Mary Ellen Zuckerman, *A History of Popular Women's Magazines in the United States, 1792–1995* (Westport, CT: Greenwood Press, 1998).

12. "Women's War," *Business Week*, Mar. 7, 1942, 58.

13. Less well known today than Tarbell, Mary Heaton Vorse was a high-profile journalist in the years between the wars. She traveled across the United States and Europe reporting on social justice issues for a wide range of publications, including *New York Post*, *Harper's Weekly*, *Atlantic Monthly*, *New Republic*, and *McClure's Magazine*, as well as *McCall's*.

14. Edmund Stevens, "War Correspondent: Thrills, Danger and Boredom," *Christian Science Monitor*, June 11, 1943, quoted in Carolyn M. Edy, *The Woman War Correspondent, the U.S. Military, and the Press: 1846–1947* (Lanham, MD: Lexington Books, 2017), 56.

15. Margaret Bourke-White became one of the first women credentialed as a war photographer with the US Army Air Force for *Life* in 1942. Margaret Bourke-White, *Portrait of Myself* (New York: Simon & Schuster, 1963), 202.

16. Carolyn Edy, "Trust but Verify: Myths and Misinformation in the History of Women War Correspondents," *American Journalism* 36, no. 2 (2019): 246.

17. To Ellen Hess from Christine Sadler, Oct. 30, 1944, Madison, box 7, folder 6.

18. To "Dear Friends" from Schultz, Jan. 23, 1945, Madison, box 4, folder 6.

19. To Ellen Hess (*McCall's*) from Schultz, Jan. 11, 1945, Madison, box 3, folder 3.

CHAPTER 24: BEARING WITNESS

1. Notice, *Chicago Tribune*, Apr. 15, 1945.

2. Extract from order awarding Schultz the European-African-Middle Eastern Campaign Ribbon, Nov. 16, 1945, Sigrid Schultz Papers, Wisconsin Historical Society, Madison, box 3, folder 3.

3. Schultz, speech in Chicago, Dec. 3, 1945, Madison, box 38, folder 4.

4. To Hedwig Schultz from Sigrid Schultz, Feb. 16, 1945, Madison, box 44, folder 4.

5. Colonel Barney Oldfield, *Never a Shot in Anger* (New York: Duell, Sloan and Pearce, 1956), 189.

6. To Pat Maloney from Schultz, Apr. 9, 1945, Madison, box 4, folder 6.

7. To Schultz from William R. Laidlaw, Mar. 8, 1969, Madison, box 10, folder 2.

8. Schultz, "Dateline, Frankfurt: Dr. Kiep Hanged by Nazis in Fear of Peace Move," *Chicago Tribune*, Apr. 15, 1945.

9. To William Laidlaw from Schultz, Apr. 17, 1969, Madison, box 10, folder 2, and undated interview, after 1976, Madison, box 2, folder 11.

10. Alan Green interview, Madison, box 2, folder 7.

11. Cable to Schultz from Larry Rue, Apr. 18, 1945, Madison, box 4, folder 6.

12. The opening of the baseball season, the war coming to an end in Europe, a new president following the death of Roosevelt, and two major campaigns in progress in the Pacific all competed with news from the concentration camps for column inches. To make things more difficult, the *Tribune* had acquired fifty thousand new subscribers in recent months—more copies used more paper. It was probably the only time in history that the managing editor of a paper complained about an increase in subscribers.

13. From Pat Maloney to all the war correspondents, April 18, 1945, Madison, box 4, folder 6.

14. Quoted in "Eisenhower Asks Congress and Press to Witness Nazi Horrors," April 19, 1945, United States Holocaust Memorial Museum website, https://newspapers.ushmm.org/events/eisenhower-asks-congress-and-press-to-witness-nazi-horrors.

15. Green interview, Madison, box 2, folder 7.

16. Schultz, "Reign of Terror by Nazi Women Guards Is Told. 110,000 Foreign 'Slaves' Undergo Ordeal," *Chicago Tribune*, Apr. 27, 1945.

17. Schultz, speech in Chicago, Dec. 3, 1945, Madison, box 38, folder 4.

18. Schultz, "City That Saw Naziism Born Watches It Die," *Chicago Tribune*, May 8, 1945.

19. Schultz, "GIs Funneling German Hordes Back to Homes. Yanks Wonder When Their Time Will Come," *Chicago Tribune*, June 3, 1945.

20. Autobiographical notes for personal history statement, 1951, Madison, box 2, folder 11; Schultz, "Germany Won't Start 3d War, Goering Asserts," *Chicago Tribune*, May 12, 1945.

21. Telegram to Schultz from *Chicago Tribune*, May 1945, Madison, box 6, folder 8.

22. To "Dear Boys" from Schultz, June 21, 1945, Madison, box 12, folder 1.

23. To Grace, Otis & McIntosh, from Sigrid Schultz, July 1, 1945, Madison, box 12, folder 1, doc. 47.

24. Schultz, "The Final Hours of Adolf Hitler," *I Can Tell It Now*, ed. David Brown and W. Richard Bruner (New York: E. P. Dutton, 1964), 104.

25. OSS confidential files, Report #204, July 5, 1944. Courtesy of John Suggs.

26. To Schultz from Pat Maloney, July 7, 1945, Madison, box 4, folder 6.

27. Undated letter to Bella Fromm from Schultz, Madison, box 10, folder 18.

CHAPTER 25: WAR CRIMES

1. Schultz, telegram to *Chicago Tribune*, Aug. 8, 1945, Sigrid Schultz Papers, Wisconsin Historical Society, Madison, box 6, folder 8.

2. To Pat Maloney from Schultz, Aug. 19, 1945, Madison, box 4, folder 6.

3. To David Darrah from Schultz, Aug. 25, 1945, Madison, box 4, folder 6.

4. Schultz, "Austrian Must Die for Killing Two U.S. Flyers. War Criminal Tried in Dachau Camp," *Chicago Tribune*, Aug. 25, 1945.

5. To Thomas Ybarra from Schultz, Oct. 14, 1945, Madison, box 10, folder 19.

6. Green interview, Madison, box 2, folder 7.

7. Schultz, "Nazi Belle on Stand; Admits Beating Women. Irma Grese Testifies at Belsen Trial," *Chicago Tribune*, Oct. 17, 1945.

8. Schultz, "Testifies 4,500 Died at Wave of Nazi's Hand. Woman Doctor Picks Out Fifteen at Belsen Trial," *Chicago Tribune*, Sept. 22, 1945.

9. Schultz, "Language Snarl Slows Up War Criminal Trial. Fear Nuernberg [sic] Case Will Be Complicated," *Chicago Tribune*, Sept. 23, 1945.

10. Schultz, "Tell How Nazis Experimented on Nude Women," *Chicago Tribune*, Sept. 26, 1945.

11. To Scharschug from Schultz, Oct. 14, 1945, Madison, box 4, folder 6.

12. Schultz, "Find Germans Favor Nazism Despite Trials. Believe the Defense, Not Prosecution," *Chicago Tribune*, Nov. 12, 1945.

13. Tribune Oral History Project, Madison, box 2, folder 9, and Robert R. McCormick and Chicago Tribune Collection, Northwestern University, XXI-2, box 33, pt. 2.

EPILOGUE

1. Letter to Geoffrey Fraser from Schultz, Apr. 5, 1949, Sigrid Schultz Papers, Wisconsin Historical Society, Madison, box 9, folder 9.

2. To George Scharschug from Schultz, Mar. 12, 1946, Madison, box 4, folder 6.

3. To George Scharschug from Schultz, Sept. 25, 1946, Madison, box 4, folder 6.

4. There is always an exception. Dorothy Fuldheim, a retired schoolteacher, became the news anchor on Cleveland's first commercial television station in 1947 in her fifties. After ten years as a news anchor, she became the host of a popular afternoon interview program, a position she held until the age of ninety-one, when she suffered a stroke.

5. To Schultz from Alfred C. Ames, July 29, 1953, Madison, box 4, folder 7.

6. To Martin Sommers (*Saturday Evening Post*) from Schultz, Apr. 2, 1949, Madison, box 7, folder 6.

7. In-house *Collier's* memo from Joe Alex Morris to Walter Davenport, May 12, 1947, Madison, box 7, folder 6.

8. To Schultz from Milton Burgh (Director of News, Mutual Broadcasting System), Mar. 6, 1952, Madison, box 7, folder 7.

9. To Milton Burgh from Schultz, Mar. 12, 1952, Madison, box 7, folder 7.

10. To Milton Burgh from Schultz, May 12, 1952.

11. Judith Cass, "Fashions and Fancy," *Chicago Tribune*, Feb. 17, 1946.

12. To Alexander von Schimpff from Schultz, Nov. 18, 1965, Madison, box 10, folder 17.

13. To Ernst Preuss from Schultz, Jan. 12, 1963, Madison, box 10, folder 10.

14. "Honor Tribune Writer," *Chicago Tribune*, Nov. 22, 1969.

15. Memo to Mr. Cook from Harold Hutchings, Jan. 5, 1976, Robert R. McCormick and Chicago Tribune Collection, Northwestern University, XI-box 54, Sigrid Schultz.

16. Alan Green interview, Madison, box 2, folder 6.

17. To Pat Maloney from Schultz, Aug. 4, 1941, Madison, box 4, folder 4.

18. To "Dear Friends" from Schultz, undated letter, Madison, box 15, folder 3.

SUGGESTIONS
FOR FURTHER READING

A few good books dealing with women in journalism:

Elizabeth Becker. *You Don't Belong Here: How Three Women Rewrote the Story of War.* New York: Public Affairs, 2021.

Chris Dubbs. *An Unladylike Profession: American Women War Correspondents in World War I.* Lincoln, NE: Potomac Books, 2020.

Carolyn M. Edy. *The Woman War Correspondent, the U.S. Military, and the Press, 1846–1947.* Lanham, MD: Lexington Books, 2017.

Alice Fahs. *Out on Assignment: Newspaper Women and the Making of Modern Public Space.* Chapel Hill: University of North Carolina Press, 2011.

Brooke Kroeger. *Undaunted: How Women Changed American Journalism.* New York: Knopf, 2023.

Nancy Caldwell Sorel. *The Women Who Wrote the War.* New York: Arcade, 1999.

General studies of American foreign correspondents and war correspondents:

John Maxwell Hamilton. *Journalism's Roving Eye: A History of American Foreign Reporting.* Baton Rouge: Louisiana State University Press, 2009.

Morrell Heald. *Transatlantic Vistas: American Journalists in Europe, 1900–1940.* Kent, OH: Kent State University Press, 1988.

David H. Hosley. *As Good as Any: Foreign Correspondence on American Radio, 1930–1940.* Westport, Connecticut: Greenwood Press, 1984.

Phillip Knightley. *The First Casualty: The War Correspondent as Hero and Myth-Maker from the Crimea to Iraq*. Baltimore: Johns Hopkins University Press, 2004.

Frederick S. Voss. *Reporting the War: Journalistic Coverage of World War II*. Washington, DC: Smithsonian Institution Press for the National Portrait Gallery, 1994.

Accounts of Americans reporting on Weimar and Nazi Germany:

Deborah Cohen. *Last Call at the Hotel Imperial: The Reporters Who Took On a World at War*. New York: Random House, 2022.

Nancy F. Cott. *Fighting Words: The Bold American Journalists Who Brought the World Home Between the Wars*. New York: Basic Books, 2020.

Deborah E. Lipstadt. *Beyond Belief: The American Press & the Coming of the Holocaust 1933–1945*. New York: The Free Press, 1986.

Robert Lyman. *Under a Darkening Sky: The American Experience in Nazi Europe, 1939–1941*. New York: Pegasus Books, 2018.

Andrew Nagorski. *Hitlerland: American Eyewitnesses to the Nazi Rise to Power*. New York: Simon & Schuster, 2012.

Ronald Weber. *News of Paris: American Journalists in the City of Light Between the Wars*. Chicago: Ivan R. Dee, 2006.

INDEX